STRESS

TOM COX

Stress Research, Department of Psychology, University of Nottingham

MACMILLAN

First published 1978 by
THE MACMILLAN PRESS LTD
Houndmills, Basingstoke, Hampshire RG21 2XS
and London
Companies and representatives
throughout the world

ISBN 0-333-19403-9

A catalogue record for this book is available
from the British Library.

17   16   15   14   13   12
01   00   99   98

Printed in Hong Kong

Contents

iv

Preface

Stress is a threat to the quality of life, and to physical and psychological well-being: that is the thesis developed in this book. If this is so then every effort must be made to understand its nature, its causes and effects, and the different ways in which it can be dealt with. It is hoped that this book makes a contribution to that understanding.

Much has been written about stress, and from many different points of view. There is still a need, however, for an integrated text which can introduce many of these different points of view and relate one to another. This book treats stress at the level of the individual, discussing it as a personal phenomenon. It treats the individual as a member of a developed industrial society, as for example an Australasian, a European or a North American. It is important to keep this in mind.

The stress experienced by man today must be different from that experienced in the past, and the stress experienced by a member of a developed industrial society different from that experienced by a member of a developing and predominantly rural society. Perhaps in the past men were mainly concerned for their physical survival; they worried about the source of their next meal, about shelter, and about not being killed. Their most pressing wants were basic physical needs. In some societies this changed with development, and today, for some, physical needs are not a day-to-day concern. Industrialised man worries about problems of a more psychosocial nature, problems which are perhaps higher in his hierarchy of need. This is probably not so for those, or at least some of those, living in developing societies.

If today's problems for industrialised man are indeed higher-order problems then an interesting argument can be advanced. The removal of physical threat has allowed this type of man to become concerned with threats which were hitherto perceived as of secondary importance. Is it possible that this type of man is actually experiencing *less* stress than ever before? He now lives longer (for various reasons) and enjoys a relatively high standard of living. His luxuries and comforts would far exceed the imagination of his ancestors. However, living longer does not necessarily mean a healthier life, simply a medicosocial system that is effective in keeping people alive. A high standard of living does not necessarily guarantee that the quality of life is good. A surfeit of luxuries can be as harmful as a shortage of necessities. The laboratory rat is longer living than his wild cousin. He is generally housed in a hygienic plastic and metal cage, and is fed on a carefully balanced diet, given a plentiful water supply and the cage regularly cleaned out. Possibly he is occasionally petted and fed the odd morsel of chocolate or condensed milk. He lives in an environment with controlled and optimum conditions of lighting, noise, temperature and humidity. It never rains on the laboratory rat. Despite all these apparent benefits of laboratory life, it cannot be argued that the laboratory rat is stress-free compared with his wild cousin. His life is unstimulating and unvaried in most if not all of its aspects, from his opportunities for activity through to his diet. His sex life is unnatural. Any relief from these stresses comes through involvement in the eventual 'experiment', and 'excitement' and 'stimulation' bought in this way have an extremely high cost. Industrialised man stands to his ancestors and to non-industrialised man very much as the laboratory rat stands to his wild cousin. Neither way of life is stress-free, neither is better, they are simply different.

Stress is a problem for all types of society. This book presents a review of our knowledge. In chapter 1 the different approaches to the definition and study of stress which have been adopted are discussed. Argument centres on a particular sort of definition and model, which is developed in some detail. The author and his colleagues have termed their approach a 'transactional' one, to emphasise the active role that the person plays in his interaction with his environment, and that the consequences of his actions are important. In chapter 2 the relationship between the concepts of stress and emotion is examined. The experience of stress is put into the context of the general experience of emotion, and the neural mechanisms involved in the control of that experience are outlined. These two aspects of emotion are related through a discussion of three theories of

vi

emotion: those of James, Cannon and Schachter. The response to stress is described in chapter 3. This is divided first into its physiological and psychological components and these are then broken down into their many and varied aspects. The cost of stress in terms of its effects on health are discussed in chapter 4. Three particular physical disorders are considered in some detail: coronary heart disease, bronchial asthma and diabetes mellitus. In chapter 5 the different ways in which the experience and effects of stress can be managed are discussed. This account attempts to bring them together into a general framework, one suggested by the transactional model. One particular aspect of stress management, the use of drugs, is developed in chapter 6, and put in the general context of the relationship between psychopharmacology and stress. Finally, in chapter 7, we examine work as a source of stress, and by so doing are thus involved in a growing interest in occupational safety and health. The very last word, chapter 8, includes conclusions reached through preparing this text, and suggestions for further research into stress.

This book is written for a wide range of readers: for the undergraduate and postgraduate, and for the informed and interested layman. Its contents cross many different disciplines and it is hopefully relevant to the training of many different professions. Perhaps the only qualification required to appreciate the information that it presents is that the reader be concerned with how man perceives and copes with his problems. The book makes reference to ergonomics and human engineering, pharmacology, physiology and biochemistry, psychiatry and psychology, community health and a whole range of other social sciences. Because it is an integrated text it should help bridge the gaps between many of these disciplines in the study of stress.

The book presents what is known about stress in two ways. First, it attempts to ensure that all the commonly quoted statements about stress are discussed and explained. By so doing it should provide a comprehensive and rather detailed introduction to the subject. Secondly, it takes these discussions further by examining certain topics in some detail. Many of these relate to my own work; this is only natural. Thus, in several parts of the book the transactional model is used to provide a link between different areas of concern and very different methodologies. It is applied to the study of occupational stress, and used as a vehicle for relating subjective and behavioural change to physiological change. However, not all the topics chosen directly relate to my own work, and they reflect in their range the wide scope of the book.

There are many people whom I wish to thank for their encouragement, help and support. First and foremost, my wife Sue, and children Sara and Prudence, for successfully coping with the experience of a preoccupied husband and father, and at times an irritable one. Second, I wish to thank my friends and colleagues in Stress Research in the Psychology Department at Nottingham University. In particular I am very grateful for the help that Clare Bradley and Colin Mackay gave me in preparing chapters 4 and 7. I also thank the other members of that research group for helping me in my work on stress, especially Helen Wilson and Grenville Burrows. Last, thanks to Eleanor and Ann, my typists, who helped prepare the typescript, and without whose help all would have been long ago lost.

University of Nottingham   Tom Cox

1

The Nature of Stress

Medical and psychological sciences have long been interested in a wide range of phenomena given the common label of 'stress'; and if the substance of this topic was suddenly removed from the literature relating to the quality of life there would be a most drastic reduction in the volume of that writing. The amount of time and effort expended in the pursuit of this elusive concept bears solemn witness to its importance.

The concept of stress is elusive because it is poorly defined. There is no single agreed definition in existence. It is a concept which is familiar to both layman and professional alike; it is understood by all when used in a general context but by very few when a more precise account is required, and this seems to be the central problem.

The fields of psychology and ergonomics, psychiatry, internal medicine, physiology and pharmacology, sociology and anthropology all devote substantial resources to the study of stress. The types of phenomena which they study vary enormously as do the interests they express in their work. There has been concern for individual and community health, for greater work efficiency and job satisfaction. There has been more fundamental interest in the evolutionary and psychophysiological mechanisms underlying stress. Research methods have varied similarly, reflecting different academic backgrounds and different interests, as a function of the substrate of study and, sadly but necessarily, as a function of available funds. With such diversity it is a difficult task to present a brief but comprehensive and clear account of our knowledge of stress. However, such an account is needed, and whatever its final course it must begin by tackling the central problem, that of the nature and definition of stress. Any solution offered at the present time, however, must be

1

premature and incomplete, and should be treated as of heuristic rather than definitive value, as a point for debate rather than as an article of faith.

1.2   WHAT IS STRESS?

The Concise Oxford Dictionary defines stress in five different ways. Three are of interest here. The first definition offered is that of a constraining or impelling force, and one example used is 'under the *stress* of poverty'. The second definition treats it as an effort or demand on energy, as in 'subjected to great *stress*'. The third definition offered talks of a force exerted on a body. The word is not defined by Drever's *A Dictionary of Psychology* (1952), but receives mention in *The Penguin Medical Encylopaedia* (Wingate, 1972). Wingate sees stress as any influence which disturbs the natural equilibrium of the body, and includes within its reference physical injury, exposure, deprivation, all kinds of disease and emotional disturbance.

The word stress has a long history, and is possibly derived from the Latin *stringere*, to draw tight (p.o. *strictus*). One of the first recorded passages in which this word was used was that written by the early English poet Robert Mannyng (Robert of Brunne or Bourne) about AD 1303 in his work *Handlying Synne*. According to *The Oxford English Dictionary* (Murray *et al.,* 1933), Mannyng wrote: '(T)hat floure ys kalled "aungelys mete" that God (g)ate (th)e folke to ete What (th)ey were yn wylderness Forty wyntyr, yn hard stres'. From the fourteenth century onwards a large number of variant words can be found in English literature: stres, stresse, stresce, strest, and straisse.

Distress and strain are words commonly used in association with the word stress. Indeed it is possible that they share the same root. *The Concise Oxford Dictionary* defines distress as severe pressure of pain, or sorrow, and as anguish, exhaustion or breathlessness. Strain is the exertion required to meet demand, injury or change resulting from such exertion, or the condition of a body subjected to stress. Fatigue, another word commonly used in the same context as stress, is defined as weariness after exertion or long strain. Although studying the origins, meaning and common usage of words rarely solves problems of scientific definition, in this particular instance it does provide a particular starting point for an attempt at that solution. Implicit in these dictionary definitions is a model of stress which treats it as a constraining force acting on a person, who in attempting to cope

2

with this force exerts or strains himself, and perhaps feels fatigued as a result, and distressed. Such a model, illustrated in figure 1.1, is also

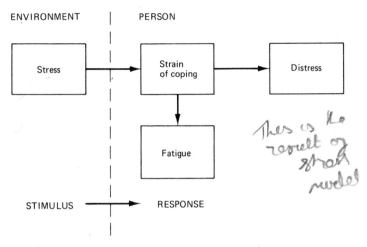

Figure 1.1: Layman's (Dictionary) Model of Stress

a popular scientific formulation and will be discussed later as 'the engineering analogy' (section 3.2).

1.3 SCIENTIFIC APPROACHES TO THE STUDY OF STRESS

A cursory survey of the available scientific literature reveals that studies on stress can be easily placed into one of three groups representing the main approaches to the problem of its definition. These approaches have already been discussed in some detail by several authors such as Lazarus (1966), Appley and Trumbell (1967), Levine and Scotch (1970), McGrath (1970) and Cox (1975a), and the main points raised in those discussions will be developed here. The first approach treats stress as a dependent variable for study, describing it in terms of the person's *response* to disturbing or noxious environments. The second approach describes stress in terms of the *stimulus* characteristics of those disturbing or noxious environments, and thus usually treats it as an independent variable for study. The third, and possibly most adequate, approach views stress as the reflection of a *lack of 'fit'* between the person and his environment. Stress in this form is studied in terms of its antecedent factors and its

3

effects. It is seen as an intervening variable between stimulus and response. There is common ground between these different approaches, and they differ most in where they lay the emphasis in the definitions they propose, and in the methods they adopt.

In all three approaches the word environment is used in the widest sense, and therefore refers to both the person's internal and external environments and both his physical and psychosocial environments.

This is important

1.4 RESPONSE-BASED DEFINITIONS AND MODELS

Approaches to the study of stress which embrace a response-based definition tend to be concerned with the specification of the particular response or pattern of responses which may be taken as

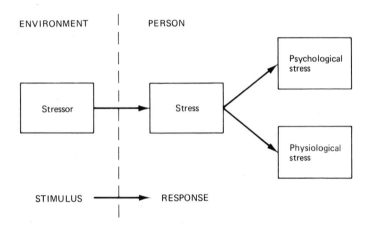

Figure 1.2: Response-based Model of Stress

evidence that the person is, or has been, under pressure from a 'disturbing' environment. That response or pattern of response is either actually treated as the stress or, at least, is treated as its defining parameter. Occurrences of the response syndrome thus are, or represent, the simultaneous occurrence of stress. In studies of this nature, stress is usually treated as the dependent variable, as the response to a stressor agent (see figure 1.2). However, as Frankenhaeuser (1975a) has pointed out, such a response may in turn act as a stimulus for the production of further responses.

4

Another dejenetion of stress

1.4.1 Selye and the General Adaptation Syndrome

This particular view of stress appears to have received its initial impetus from the writings of Hans Selye (see, for example, Selye, 1956). He wrote, 'stress is the nonspecific (physiological) response of the body to any demand made upon it'. Stress he saw quite unequivocably as the person's (or animal's) response to the demands of his environment. Selye's primary concern was for the physiological mechanism and this has led to a close association between response-based and physiological models of stress. *example - caideovascular disease*

Very briefly, there are three basic ideas built into Selye's concept of stress. First, he believed that the physiological stress response did not depend on the nature of the stressor, and not, within reason, on the species in which it was evoked. The response syndrome represented a universal pattern of defence reactions serving to protect the person (or animal) and preserve its integrity. Thus the source of the stress did not matter, and the non-specific defence reaction was essentially the same for all animals. Second, he believed that this defence reaction progresses, with continual or repeated exposure to the stressor, through three identifiable stages. Together these stages represent his General Adaptation Syndrome. During the first phase, the alarm reaction, the body shows the changes characteristic of initial exposure to the stressor, and at the same time its level of resistance is reduced. If the stressor is sufficiently severe, resistance may collapse and death results. The second stage, that of resistance, ensues if continued exposure to the stressor is compatible with adaptation. The bodily changes characteristic of the alarm reaction disappear and are replaced by the changes marking the person's (or animal's) adaptation to the situation. Resistance rises above normal. The final stage, in all senses of the word, is that of exhaustion. Following long-term exposure to the same stressor, and one to which the body has adapted, the necessary energy for adaptation may be exhausted, and the final collapse occurs. The signs of the alarm reaction reappear as the person (or animal) dies. The general adaptation syndrome is shown diagrammatically in figure 1.3.

The third idea is that these very defence responses if severe and prolonged result in disease states, the so-called diseases of adaptation. Illness can be the cost of the defence against exposure to stressor agents. This will occur when defence overextends the

5

resources of the physiological system, or when that defence is excessive.

Selye has placed a critical emphasis on the non-specificity of the stress response. His original observations were made as a medical student when he noted a general malaise associated with being ill, irrespective of the specific nature of the illness. The syndrome was characterised by a loss of appetite and an associated loss of weight

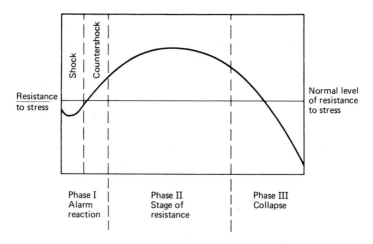

Figure 1.3: Selye's General Adaptation Syndrome

and strength, by a loss of ambition, and by that most recognisable facial expression associated with illness. Further examination of extreme cases and later experimentation on animals revealed enlargement and dark discolouration of the adrenals, intense shrinkage of the thymus, spleen and lymph nodes, and deep bleeding ulcers of the stomach and upper gut. This general syndrome of sickness he believed was superimposed upon all individual diseases, and was a manifestation of the non-specific general adaptation syndrome. This idea of non-specificity became enormously influential, and held sway for many years. However, there is now a growing body of opinion that the position has been overstated. There is evidence, from Mason (1971) for example, that some noxious physical conditions do not produce the general adaptation syndrome. He has noted exercise, fasting and heat. There is also evidence that, if evoked, not all the symptoms of the syndrome appear together. The work of Lacey (1967), for example, argues that one ought not be overly optimistic about the intercorrelation between the different physiological indices of the general adaptation syndrome. Furthermore, there is positive evidence of specificity, particularly in relation to catecholamine excretion. The hypothesis has been developed and debated that situations producing anxiety are associated with adrenaline release, while situations which produce aggression are associated with noradrenaline release. Such a situation makes sense in terms of the slightly different patterns of physiological activity of the analogues. The question of non-specificity is discussed again in chapter 3 (section 3.1.3). The involvement of concepts such as anxiety and aggression focuses attention on the other weakness in Selye's approach. In concentrating his attention on the body's physiological response to stressor agents, he ignored the role of psychological processes. It is now suggested that much of the physiological response is not directly determined by the actual presence of the stressor agent but by its psychological impact on the person. At this point the Selye model begins its development into an interactional model (see section 1.6).

1.4.2   Levi and Kagan: Psychosocial Stimuli and Disorder

Relatively recently Levi and Kagan, at the Laboratory for Clinical Stress Research in Stockholm, have developed Selye's view of stress (Kagan and Levi, 1971; Levi, 1973, 1974), and constructed a theoretical model to describe psychological factors in the mediation of physical disease. Their main hypothesis is that psychosocial stimuli can and do cause such disorders. They focus on the concept of a non-specific aetiology as suggested by Selye, and outline several steps in the development of psychogenic physical disorder. They suggest that most life changes evoke a physiological stress response which prepares the person for the physical activity of coping. This response, at least if prolonged, intense or often repeated, is accompanied by an increase of wear and tear in the person and produces structural as well as functional damage. This leads in the long term to increased morbidity and mortality. Levi and Kagan represent this process diagrammatically in the form of a flow chart. External influences, identified as psychosocial stimuli, interact with genetic factors and with the influence of earlier environments. These personal factors, Levi and Kagan term the 'psychobiological programme'. They define

7

this programme as 'the propensity to react in accordance with a certain pattern'; for example, when solving a problem or adapting to particular environmental conditions. Together the psychosocial stimuli and the psychobiological programme determine the occurrence of the stress response, which in its turn may provoke precursors of disease, and then disease itself. This sequence of events can be promoted or counteracted by intervening variables. These may be intrinsic or extrinsic, mental or physical, and can modify the effects of

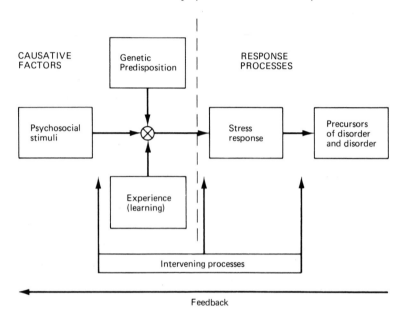

Figure 1.4: Aetiology of Stress-induced Physical Disorder (Levi and Kagan)

the causative factors (the psychosocial stimuli and psychobiological programme) at any subsequent stage in the process. One of the important features of this model is that it is presented not as a one-way process but as constituting part of a cybernetic system with continuous feedback between all its components. Despite this the authors admit that (like all conceptual models) it is probably a gross oversimplification. Oversimplification or not, the model is complex, and this complexity tends to hide the important fact that Levi and Kagan have built it around a straightforward response-based definition of stress. Their model is presented diagrammatically in figure 1.4. Later chapters will discuss aspects of the work of Selye, Levi and Kagan, and more attention will be paid to the concept of non-specificity.

1.4.3   Stress and Performance Degradation

Another response-based definition of stress which has received much attention and use is that in terms of stress reflected in a degradation of performance (see figure 1.5). It has been popular to define stress in these terms in studies of external environmental factors, for example

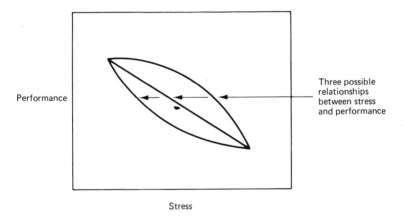

Figure 1.5: Stress as Performance Degradation

those relating to noise and lighting. However, to use such a definition poses immediate problems. Research on conditions which one would intuitively feel were stressful, has led us to the conclusion that such stressors do not always produce performance degradation, especially in the short term. The pattern of effect can in fact be very complex. Noise, for example (see Davies, 1968), can produce no change in the performance of psychological tasks, enhancement or degradation depending on many environmental and individual factors. Noise may even first enhance and then later impair performance simply as a function of increasing length of exposure (see figure 1.6).

Experience has shown that whatever effects are elicited on one occasion with any particular subject they cannot be easily guaranteed to be reproduced on a different occasion with the same or a different person. This difficulty is made more obvious when one recalls that, according to Selye's type of approach, a person is expected to *adapt* to the effects of stressor agents. It is easy to conceive of a situation in which, exposed to an obvious stressor and showing a physiological stress response, the person has adapted behaviourally, and is coping and maintaining his performance at the task under consideration. This would occur during the stage of resistance in the behavioural analogue

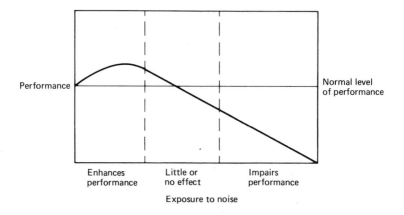

Figure 1.6: Hypothetical Effects of Noise on Performance

to the general adaptation syndrome. Consideration of this example underlines how ill-advised it is to separate out the components of the psychophysiology of stress and rely on one in particular, behavioural, physiological or subjective, for the purpose of definition.

1.4.4   Comments

McGrath (1970), in his suggestions for a conceptual formulation for social and psychological research on stress, has noted several weaknesses generally associated with response-based definitions. He has argued that following this type of definition any stimulus which produces the particular stress response under consideration must be viewed as a stressor. Accordingly, he continues, physical exercise, the various emotions and excitements, fasting and fatigue must be treated as stressors, and this may not meet with general acceptance. While most would agree that all the aforementioned can be related to

10

stress, there must be some question of whether the personal factors, such as emotion and fatigue, are stressors or stress responses. They could, of course, be both (see Frankenhaeuser, 1975a), and this can be most easily accounted for by the sort of cybernetic model proposed by Levi and Kagan. Furthermore, McGrath has argued, the

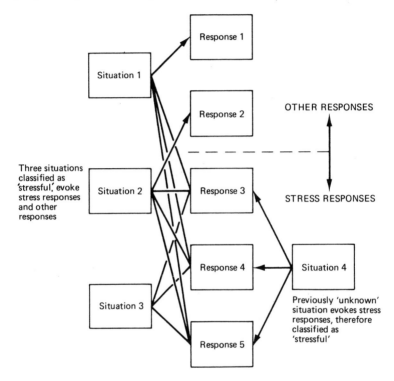

Figure 1.7: Response-based Definition and Classification of Situations as Stressful

same response may be evoked by several different situations, again some of which may not be accepted as stressful. Heart rate, for instance, may increase for many reasons; for example, after the administration of the sympathomimetic drug isoprenaline, with heavy smoking, after exercise, with fear and during pregnancy. The hardline answer to this genre of criticism is that all these conditions are stressful by definition, and the real question is one of the certainty with which the defining stress response is established (see figure 1.7).

As already noted, the enthusiasm for Selye's non-specific (physiological) stress response, and the reliance placed on it by various workers as the defining stress response, is now waning. The lack of a straightforward correlation between the various components of the response across individuals or situations, is now infamous. Indeed, there is good reason to believe that far from there being a unified and unchanging pattern of stress response, there is a more variable, but hopefully no less lawful, relationship both between and within the three main response areas—behavioural, physiological and subjective. It is suggested that one of the advances to be made in stress research will follow on from the acceptance of this point, and involve the development of more appropriate and sophisticated methodologies and models. All future research on the stress response would be well advised to adopt a multivariate approach. An understanding of what patterns of responses are characteristic of stress allows an identification of the stimuli which are associated with (elicit) its occurrence. There is thus a natural overlap between a response-based approach to stress and, what follows in this discussion, a stimulus-based approach.

1.5 STIMULUS-BASED DEFINITIONS AND MODELS

Stimulus-based definitions of stress describe and treat it in terms of the stimulus characteristics of environments which are recognised as disturbing or disruptive in some way. The model used is essentially

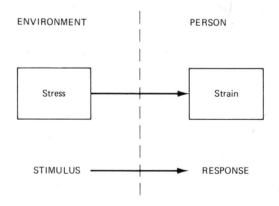

Figure 1.8: Stimulus-based (Engineering) Model of Stress

an engineering one in which external stresses give rise to a stress reaction, or strain, within the individual. This model is not only popular within the realms of engineering, but is also the one constructed by everyday language, and has already been presented diagrammatically (see figure 1.1). It is represented in figure 1.8. Such an approach usually treats stress as an independent variable for study and demands consideration of what stimuli are diagnostic of the stress. This view of stress was expressed very forcefully by Sir Charles Symonds (1947) when discussing psychological disorders in RAF flying personnel. He wrote: 'it should be understood once and for all that (flying) stress is that which happens to the man, not that which happens in him; it is a set of causes, not a set of symptoms'.

1.5.1 The Engineering Analogy

In considering this engineering-type model a parallel has been drawn with Hooke's Law of Elasticity. This law of physical science describes how loads produce deformation in metals. The main factors in Hooke's Law are that of 'stress', the load (or demand) which is placed on the metal, and that of 'strain', the deformation which results. The law states that if the strain produced by a given stress falls within the 'elastic limit' of the material, when the stress is removed the material will simply return to its original condition. If, however, the strain passes beyond the elastic limit then some permanent damage will result. This analogy suggests that just as physical systems have an elastic limit, people have some built-in resistance to stress. Up to a point stress can be tolerated, but when it becomes intolerable permanent damage, physiological and psychological, may result. There appears to be great individual variation in resistance to stress, and levels which one finds easily tolerable may be completely intolerable to the next man. Studies of the Mercury astronauts in the 1960s by Korchin and Ruff (Korchin and Ruff, 1964; Ruff and Korchin, 1964) have thrown some light on the personality characteristics and backgrounds which contribute to a high resistance to stress. Seven astronauts were studied during training and in simulated space flights. Their performance under stress showed little or no impairment and there was little disruption of the positive mood which characterised them much of the time. The astronauts' approach to difficult situations was to stop, appraise the situation, decide on a course of action and then follow it through. The seven were aged between 32 and 37 years, were all married with children, and came from middle-class families. They were all protestant, though not actively religious. They had been brought up in small communities, were educated in state schools, and had graduated in engineering. They were described as ambitious, able, intelligent and successful, free from self-doubts, persevering, highly controlled and accurate in their testing of reality. These sorts of personality factors are referred to again in chapter 3 (section 3.2.6).

The astronaut's backgrounds were perhaps both demanding and stimulating, and this may have contributed to their ability to withstand the effects of stress. Indeed it has been suggested that durability in the face of stress is related to factors of heredity, early experience and later learning.

Levine (1967), for example, has shown that rats subjected to electric shocks and other stresses early in life developed normally, and were able to cope well with later stress. However, animals that had received no such stimulation grew up to be timid and deviant in behaviour by comparison. At the adult stage the two groups of animals differed markedly in their physiological response to stress. The animals that had been stimulated in infancy showed a prompt and effective physiological response; those that had not been stimulated responded slowly and much less effectively. Infantile stimulation, from this and other studies (see Levine, 1975), thus appears to produce more adaptive and variable adult behaviour (and to affect the maturation of neuroendocrine function). It can thus be shown that a person's (or animal's) response to stress is partly dependent on the nature of his early environment.

The engineering analogy in stress research is appealing because of its simplicity, because it allows us to rub shoulders with what is apparently a more clearly formulated discipline, and because it allows us to attempt to measure the stress to which a person is subjected by the same process as we measure that to which a machine is subjected. Proponents of this view might argue that we can even see at what point collapse occurs. They assume that an undemanding situation is not stressful and is a prescription for maximum well-being. However, in this way they are totally erroneous. Men and their organisations are not machines, even if they have machine-like aspects, and the analogy therefore breaks down rather too readily. For example, undemanding (boring) situations are to most persons as stressful as situations in which demand is excessive. Certainly they could not be sensibly prescribed as any sort of general remedy. Furthermore, unless the stress–strain relationship in man functions both unconsciously and automatically, we have to accept some intervening psychological process which does mediate the outcome of that relationship. Stress has to be perceived or recognised by man. A machine, however, does not have to recognise the load or stress placed upon it.

1.5.2 Characteristics of Stressful Situations

The important questions for a stimulus-based definition of stress are, what conditions can be accepted as stressful? and, what are their common characteristics? These questions exactly parallel those one needs to ask of the stress response when working with a response-based definition.

Certain points have arisen through considering the man at work and what situations he might find difficult, uncomfortable or unpleasant. Commonly mentioned are situations which involve extremes of sensory stimulation, and extremes of work load. The first type of situation is immediately recognisable: too noisy, too hot, too cold, too humid, too isolated or too crowded. Perhaps overwork is as obvious. Many, however, tend to ignore underwork and boredom as potent sources of stress. In 1970, Weitz reviewed and attempted to classify the different types of situation which have been treated as stressful in current research. He described eight, which involve speeded information processing, noxious environmental stimuli, perceived threat, disrupted physiological function (perhaps as a result of disease, drugs, sleep loss, and so forth), isolation and confinement, blocking, group pressure and frustration. In addition, Lazarus (1966, 1976) sees perceived threat as the central characteristic of stressful situations and, in particular, threat to a person's most important values and goals, while Frankenhaeuser (1975a and b) would add lack of control over events to Weitz's list. All of these situations can be viewed in terms of the demands made on the person by his environment.

1.5.3 Welford: Performance and Demand

If stress is viewed in terms of demand then the present type of definition has been elaborated on. For example, Welford (1973) has proposed that stress arises whenever there is a departure from optimum conditions of demand which the person is unable or not easily able to correct. Most organisms, including man, appear to have evolved so that they function best under conditions of moderate demand. If a man's performance is less than maximal this may be due to both too high and too low a level of demand. This makes explicit that it is necessary to think in terms of both positive and negative departures from optimum: too hot or too cold, too noisy or too quiet. Welford suggests we accept that an inverted U-shaped function

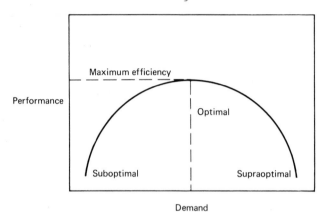

Figure 1.9: Possible Relationship Between Performance and Demand

relates the efficiency of man's performance to the demand placed on him (see figure 1.9).

There is a marked similarity between this formulation and Hebb's (1955), which relates arousal and performance. Although inverted U-shaped relationships are regarded with suspicion by many psychologists, they have some general biological validity. For example, the activity of an enzyme is a most definite inverted U-shaped function of the demand placed on it in terms of both pH and temperature (Conn and Stumpf, 1967). These relationships may be reliably demonstrated, and thus have predictive value. Welford's argument is therefore that submaximal performance is indicative of stress (see section 1.4.3) and that it can exist because of too high or too low a level of demand. A similar type of approach has been offered by Margetts (1975), not in terms of environmental demand but of

16

stimulus input. Living organisms adjust themselves to handle and maintain a reasonable input of stimuli. If the input of stimuli is excessive or insufficient for the individual organism, the excess or insufficiency can be considered as stress. The organism's homeostasis is threatened by stress, and if the organism cannot manage the excessive or insufficient load it goes into a state of disequilibrium or breakdown. This may be temporary, pending readjustment, or may proceed to a more profound disorder, leading to functional or structural pathology.

1.5.4 Comments

Several difficulties are generally associated with stimulus-based definitions of stress. The major one is that of identifying with some surety what is stressful about particular real-life situations. Intuition and consensus seem to be the main agents of decision. It may be immediately obvious as to what is stressful about stoking a blast furnace, but the stressful aspects of a police control-room operator's job or a teacher's job may not be at all obvious. In addition there is a need to be able to quantify the degree of stress present. Measurements of the temperature and noise of the furnace are relatively easy, but what is measured and how in the other two jobs? A further problem arises if a situation appears to be stressful because of its stimulus characteristics and evokes the appropriate response to stress from most *but not all* people. Individual differences perhaps present the greatest difficulty; statements about stressful environments made in this context have by necessity to rely on *normative* data. Possibly the most important question to ask of experiments on stress, which treat it as the independent variable, is, 'does stress exist in the eye of the subject or in the eye of the experimenter?'

1.6 INTERACTIONAL DEFINITIONS AND MODELS

The previous two approaches have been fused to provide a reasonably comprehensive account of the stress system. Such a fusion, however, must still retain the mechanical nature of the two approaches, and view the person as essentially passive in the operation of stress. Furthermore, because of the exclusion of intervening (psychological) processes, the model would find difficulty in dealing with individual differences. In short, it would be inadequate because it would ignore the active role of the person in the occurrence of stress. It would fail to take explicit account of the person in relation to his environment, the essential of ecology. The third approach, the interactional one, expresses the view that stress arises through the existence of a particular relationship between the person and his environment. The problem is to define that relationship.

1.6.1   Cox and Mackay: Man–Environment Transaction

The author and his colleagues suggest that stress can be most adequately described as part of a complex and dynamic system of transaction between the person and his environment. Such a system is shown in figure 1.10. This description of the stress system is eclectic in that it deliberately draws from both response- and stimulus-based definitions, but in so doing it emphasises the ecological and transactional nature of the phenomenon. It underlines that stress is an individual perceptual phenomenon rooted in psychological processes. It also draws specific attention to the feedback components of the system. The existence and importance of these feedback components mean that the system described is cyclical rather than linear.

There are five recognisable stages in the system. The first stage is represented by the sources of demand relating to the person and is part of his environment. Demand is usually regarded as a factor of the person's external environment; however, the present model distinguishes between external and internal demands. A person has psychological and physiological needs, and the fulfilment of these is important in determining his behaviour. These needs constitute internally generated demand. The person's perception of the demand and of his own ability to cope form the second stage. Stress may be said to arise when there is an *imbalance* between the perceived demand and the person's perception of his capability to meet that demand. It is essential to realise that the important balance or imbalance is not between demand and actual capability, but between perceived demand and perceived capability. What is important for man is his *cognitive appraisal* of the potentially stressful situation and of his ability to cope. If a situation demands too much of a man, but he has not realised his limitations, he will work on without being stressed until it becomes obvious to him that he cannot cope. He must then recognise his limitations and the imbalance between demand and capability. He then experiences stress. The presence of this perceptual factor

18

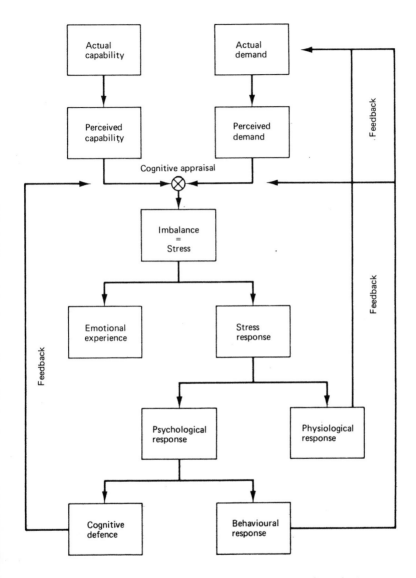

Figure 1.10: Transactional Model of Stress (Cox and Mackay)

allows for the operation of a wide variety of organismic variables, such as personality, which contribute to the existence of interindividual differences. The critical imbalance is accompanied by the subjective (emotional) experience of stress. This is in turn accompanied by changes in physiological state, and by cognitive and behavioural attempts to reduce the stressful nature of the demand. Such activity is usually expressed in a change in the normal pattern of behaviour. These psychophysiological changes can be regarded as the third stage of this model and represent the response to stress. The responses to stress are sometimes thought of as the end point of the stress process but, as already implied, should be regarded as methods of *coping* available to the person; and the fourth stage, a most important one which is frequently ignored, is concerned with the consequences of the coping responses. The actual as well as the perceived consequences are important. It has been suggested that stress may only occur when the organism's failure to meet demand is important (Sells, 1970), or through the anticipation of adverse consequences arising from the failure to meet demand (*feedforward*). The fifth and last stage is one of *feedback*, which occurs at all other stages in the stress system, and which is effective in shaping the outcome at each of those stages. For example, feedback occurs when a physiological response, such as the release of adrenaline, influences the organism's perception of the stressful situation, or when a behavioural response alters the actual nature of the demand. Perhaps one of the most important examples of feedback concerns the effectiveness of the stress response in coping. Inappropriate and ineffective response strategies will invariably prolong or even increase the experience of stress. Abnormal coping often occurs at this point, and this may accelerate the development of damage. It is suggested that functional and structural damage can occur as a result of a prolonged or severe experience of stress. This will result from the effects that the psychophysiological response to stress have on the psychophysiological mechanism itself. Here is another example of feedback. Severe burns may produce abnormally high blood-glucose levels, and this may be easily viewed as a response to the experience of stress. The maintenance of such levels for any length of time tends to damage the regulatory mechanism for blood glucose. As a result the victim of severe burning may become diabetic (Evans and Butterfield, 1951).

The author believes that these stages comprise a system which adequately describes the operation of stress. It treats stress as an intervening variable, the reflection of a transaction between the person and his environment and, like the model offered by Levi and Kagan, it is part of a dynamic cybernetic system.

Howarth (1978) has suggested that four theoretical views of stress exist: the biological, the developmental, the social and the phenomenological. His classification may be thought to provide an alternative to that discussed here, but it is more appropriate to treat it as a further development of the transactional approach. The imbalance between the perceived demand and perceived capability may come about for a variety of reasons. In biological terms stress may arise if the person's life style differs too much from the kind of life to which primitive man became evolutionarily adapted. In developmental terms, it may arise if the person is not prepared by his upbringing and education for the demands imposed on him by his style of life. In social terms, the person may experience stress if exposed to conflicting social pressures, or forced to play inconsistent roles. In phenomenological terms, stress may arise if the person's life style fails to match his aspirations or ideals. Inclusion of Howarth's theoretical overview adds greater breadth to the transactional model. It also relates this approach to stress to a hierarchical view of biological science.

A very similar working definition to that proposed here has been developed by McGrath (1976). He has suggested that there is a potential for experiencing stress when a situation is perceived as presenting a demand which threatens to exceed the person's capabilities and resources for meeting it, and when it is important that the person meets that demand. He goes on to say that it is tempting to treat the amount of stress experienced (S) as a simple function of the degree to which perceived demand (D) exceeds perceived capability (C), and the importance of coping (Co). Such a proposition is expressed by

$$S = Co(|D - C|)$$

This formulation implies, among other things, that a small discrepancy between perceived demand and perceived capability will not be experienced as very stressful, unless coping is absolutely vital. However, Lowe and McGrath (1971) carried out an exhaustive study of little league (junior) baseball players, following all 60 players of all four teams throughout all 36 games of the 1969 season. Measures of experienced stress (pulse rate), batting performance, favourableness of outcome, and situational demand were taken. Lowe and McGrath badly confused arousal and stress in their paper, but nevertheless McGrath (1976) has argued, on the basis of their results, that the closer perceived demand is to perceived capability, and given an imbalance, then the greater is the stress experienced. This proposition is expressed as

$$S = (Co)(K - |D - A|)$$

where K is a constant. There is much sense in their argument that small imbalances between perceived demand and capability may be more stressful than larger imbalances. The outcome of the former type of situation is more uncertain than that of the latter, more obvious situation. This uncertainty must increase the demand perceived by the person or exaggerate his response to it. However, it is difficult to maintain that overwhelming (disastrous) situations are less stressful than more moderate ones. What is more possible is that experienced stress is an inverted U-shaped function of the imbalance between perceived demand and perceived capability. This proposition is expressed by

$$S = (Co)[(I(K - I)]$$

where

$$I = |D - C|, \text{ and } K \text{ is a constant.}$$

It must be borne in mind that it is easier to speculate in this manner than it is to test out the speculations. There is probably no acceptable way of quantifying the various factors in the above equations, and thus there will be no experiments to provide a clear solution to the question of which is more adequate.

1.6.2 Lazarus: Demand and Adjustment

Lazarus (1976) has presented what is essentially an *interactional* definition of stress; he suggests that 'stress occurs when there are demands on the person which tax or exceed his adjustive resources'. He has developed this brief statement and emphasised, like the previous authors, that 'stress is not simply out there in the environment', that it depends not only on external conditions but also on the constitutional vulnerability of the person and the adequacy of his cognitive defence mechanisms. In developing this view of stress Lazarus draws particular attention to the person's appraisal of his or her situation, and to the role of frustration and conflict, and of threat, in producing that stress. Frustration he sees as a form of danger or harm which has already occurred to the person; it is the thwarting or delaying of some important on-going activity or the attainment of some important goal. Conflict is the simultaneous presence of two (or possibly more) incompatible action tendencies or goals. It must lead to frustration as activity designed to attain one goal will necessarily frustrate the attainment of the other. There can be no satisfactory resolution of conflict as long as the person remains committed to both courses of action or to both goals. Threat may also arise from conflict. Unlike frustration, which is harm that has occurred, threat is the anticipation of harm occurring. Lazarus points out that when talking of harm he is referring to physical, psychological or social damage. The intensity of the threat depends on how well the person feels he can deal with the danger or harm which may occur. If a person feels capable of dealing with the danger or preventing the harm, then threat is minimal. However, if the person feels helpless and completely unable to master the situation then threat will be very severe.

1.6.3   Demand

The concept of demand is important for both the author's and Lazarus' (1976) view of stress. A demand in its present usage means a request or requirement for physical or mental action, and implies some time constraint. It is probable that the important feature of time in this context is perceived time. The perception of time can be shown to alter with the experience of stress, and this may be an important factor in deciding the balance between perceived demand and perceived capability.

1.6.4   Comments

It may be argued that the interactional approach does not offer much more by way of definition than the other two approaches discussed. Most workers in this area would not argue with the assertion that stress is to do with the person in relation to his environment and, that in considering that relationship, individual perceptual factors are important. The interactional model is a psychologically based approach and explicitly deals with these factors, in a way in which the other approaches do not and cannot satisfactorily deal. Because of this, and because it is eclectic, it perhaps accounts for more of the available data on stress than either of the other two approaches. Furthermore, it does provide clear guidelines for the study and alleviation of stress (see chapter 5).

Perhaps it does not account for situations where action (perhaps coping) places such a severe demand on the body that physiological fatigue or damage are caused directly without the immediate involvement of other more psychological processes. Such a situation which is more 'mechanical' in nature may be best dealt with by one or other of the previous two approaches.

1.7 GENERAL POINTS

Several general points emerge from the present discussion which warrant reiteration. First, as is made explicit in the transactional approach and recognised to some extent by the other approaches, stress develops from a particular sort of relationship between the person and his environment. Stress has been viewed as an individual phenomenon. As a result, situations cannot simply be labelled as 'stressful' or 'not stressful': they may be potentially stressful or may be stressful for such-and-such a proportion of the population. To determine the existence of stress one must thus consider the status of the individual person in relation to his or her environment. This is most often ignored by those working in the industrial situation when there may be some financial premium on the intuitive categorisation of situations as stressful or not stressful. Perhaps what is needed, particularly in this sphere, is a stress-experience analogue of population stereotype. Not only is there great individual variation in the experience of stress, but also in the response to stress, and this compounds the difficulty in making generalisations.

Second, the social background for the stress experience is a crucial factor and one which is so often forgotten in laboratory studies. Differences in social context make generalisation from such studies to real-life situations very difficult. One of the other problems with laboratory experiments on stress, and this is the third point, is that most assure their subjects final control over the duration and intensity of their stress experience. This obviously does not happen in most real-life situations. It means that laboratory stress experiences are moderate compared with real-life experiences. Considering both points it is obvious that laboratory experiments on stress have to be carefully planned to be meaningful and useful.

Fourth, there is a glut of interrelated and synonymous terminology in existence covering the area of stress research. The reason for this is simple. Cofer and Appley (1964) have noted that the term 'stress' all but pre-empted a field of research previously shared by a number of other concepts: anxiety, conflict, frustration and so forth. It is as though when the word stress came into vogue many researchers working with closely related concepts substituted the word stress for them. Unfortunately the varied influx of workers into stress research has resulted in a grand alliance and confusion of terminologies.

It is a sobering experience to bear these points in mind when working through the available literature on stress.

1.8   A WORKING DEFINITION AND MODEL

The discussion which follows in the ensuing chapters of this book will adopt Cox and Mackay's transactional view of stress. It is thought to be the most adequate and the most useful in helping us organise our existing knowledge. This chapter, therefore, concludes with a summary of that model proposed in section 1.5.

> Stress, it is argued, can only be sensibly defined as a perceptual phenomenon arising from a comparison between the demand on the person and his ability to cope. An imbalance in this mechanism, when coping is important, gives rise to the experience of stress, and to stress response. The latter represent attempts at coping with the source of stress. Coping is both psychological (involving cognitive and behavioural strategies) and physiological. If normal coping is ineffective, stress is prolonged and abnormal responses may occur. The occurrence of these, and prolonged exposure to stress *per se*, may give rise to functional and structural damage. The progress of these events is subject to great individual variation.

2

Emotion and the Experience of Stress

It is the experience of stress which represents a central and personal element of the transactional model. For the individual it is one of the most obvious aspects of the occurrence of stress; it is what they *feel*.

2.1   STATUS AND STUDY OF THE EXPERIENCE OF STRESS

It is the experience of stress which 'troubles' the individual but which by its very nature can only be shared indirectly. It is a private event. Along with all other experiences it is an intimate and protected phenomenon. Only we as individuals can experience stress, and its existence in others has to be inferred from their verbal or written report, or from their appearance or behaviour. It is something un-available to direct public scrutiny, and only available to the person through its spontaneous occurrence and by deliberate introspection. Not surprisingly introspection linked to a verbal or written report has become one of the most popular methods of obtaining informa-tion on the experience of stress. It has, however, an inbuilt error, the recognition of which must caution the investigator. Because of the private nature of experiences it is impossible to standardise the lear-ning of their language labels. The mother has only her own experience to guide her in identifying her childrens' experience from their appearance, behaviour and report. Misidentification and hence misnaming must frequently occur. The mother is trying to name a feeling which she is not herself experiencing. This variation in the association of names and experiences will make learning difficult for the individual child, and will mean that across a group of children each name will come to mean something slightly different for each child. Compounding this, the mothers involved will each also have developed a slightly different conception of what each name means.

There must therefore be a normal variation in the personal meanings of the names used to label experiences, not sufficient to prevent a rough consensus being reached, but sufficient to make individual verbal or written reports of experience difficult to generalise. Despite this, attempts to produce structured interview schedules, question-naires, and adjective checklists to measure experience are common. Such attempts, and the more general study of emotion are con-strained in two ways, by the use and structure of common language and recently by the existence of a common language philosophy. First, the lexicon of the language can restrict description, especially if personal experience is richer than the language, and particularly if the person is using a restricted rather than an elaborated code. Second, common language philosophy insists that buried beneath ordinary language explanations and descriptions, and within com-mon sense, lie the kernels of understanding experience. Myths, folk tales and religions have been invented to explain and describe the evidence of the senses, but they also have the tendency to reshape it. Common language does not deal so much with reality but creates its own version of it, a version which is both explainable and under-standable. Thus, common language and its philosophy in many ways appear to pre-empt a more scientific study of experience.

The extent to which these two problems affect the description and measurement of the experience of stress is a matter for debate. But their very existence means that such information must be treated with caution, and that its analysis should not be too refined.

2.2   STRESS AND EMOTION

The experience of stress is not usually or simply reported in terms of 'being stressed', but is more often described in ways associated with emotions such as anger, anxiety, depression, fear, grief, guilt, jealousy and shame. The experience of stress is indeed an emotional one.

A distinction is made by most psychologists between two types of emotional experience: the pleasant or positively toned emotions, and the unpleasant or negatively toned emotions. This is discussed again in the next section. Lazarus (1976) has termed the negatively toned emotions the 'stress emotions', and sees them solely as products of the occurrence of stress. However, such a direct relationship between the negatively toned emotions and stress is but one possibility; it is most likely that the aetiology of these emotions is multifactorial, and that stress is but one factor, albeit an important one.

Each specific negatively toned emotion possibly reflects a particular transaction between the person and his environment and a particular antecedent context. These factors would be accounted for in the person's cognitive appraisal of the situation, and it is this process of cognition which shapes basic feelings into a specific emotion (Kagan, 1975).

Much has been written about emotion, most of which is applicable to understanding the experience of stress. The work of interest centres on three areas: the nature of emotional experience, the different theories of emotion, and the description of the relevant central neurophysiology. All three topics are discussed in this chapter.

2.3 THE NATURE OF EMOTIONAL EXPERIENCE

One of the earliest psychological writers to be concerned with the topics of emotion and emotional experience was Shand who, in his major work *The Foundations of Character* (1914), formulated no less than 144 'principles' to describe their functioning. One of the important distinctions that Shand made in this book was between emotional experience and sentiment. In emotion, he asserted, the person is always aware of the object of his emotion, and the circumstances provoking that emotion. Among others, he used anger and fear as examples. Sentiment, on the other hand, he saw as more of an habitual response to an object. Shand described it as a disposition to respond, which persisted even when the person was no longer thinking about the object. Love and hate were used as examples. A clearer and more elaborate statement was made by Shand in 1922: sentiment is a system of emotional dispositions having different conative tendencies, connected with a common object and subordinated to a common end. Sentiment, he saw as a way of organising emotional experience and expression. Other more recent authors have supported this later view of sentiment. McKellar (1968) believes it to be a system of dispositions, rather than a single one, which can give rise to a number of different emotional reactions to an object, while earlier Heider (1958) talked of sentiment being a 'connecting link' between situations, feelings, and actions. Kagan (1975) has, most recently, presented a slightly different view of the relationship between emotional experience and sentiment. Basic emotional experience he sees as pleasant or unpleasant sensation shorn of intellectual symbolisation, but sentiment, he argues, is more than this and can be defined as mood plus intellectual content.

Kagan's (1975) treatment of emotional experience in terms of pleasantness or unpleasantness is interesting. It finds current support in the writings of MacLean (1975), who places emotions on an agreeable–disagreeable continuum; and both Kagan's and MacLean's definitions are consistent with Brady's (1975) notion of appetitive (pleasant) and aversive (unpleasant) stimuli evoking emotional responses. Similar views can be found in Shand's work, although described within a more elaborate system, and not as bluntly. Shand believed there were two groups of sentiments, the positive or pro sentiments, and the negative or con sentiments. The former were associated with sympathetic emotions towards their object, the latter with antipathetic emotions. For a positive sentiment, the presence of the object brought pleasure, and its absence brought displeasure. For a negative sentiment, the situation was reserved. The emotions were implicitly treated in terms of a pleasant–unpleasant dichotomy. Such a classification, it has been pointed out by McKellar (1968), should be revised to include ambivalent sentiments (and emotions): 'in the misfortunes of our dearest friends we find something not entirely displeasing to us' (La Rochefoucald). Such ambivalence is not, however, neutral. In developing his view of emotion as pleasant or unpleasant, Kagan (1975) suggests that these sensations are tutored or shaped by our cognitive (intellectual) processes, and we report not those general amorphous feelings but more precise things such as affection, anger, desire, fear or joy. Similarly, as pointed out earlier in this chapter, we tend not to report a general feeling of being stressed, but more particular emotions, those experienced and reported being appropriate to the context in which they exist. According to Kagan it is cognition (intellect) which modifies the pattern of response.

Thus the experience of emotion can be thought of as developing from two basic emotional excitements, pleasure and displeasure. This account has a parallel in the way Bridges (1932) described general emotional development in early infancy. Her observations of infants and young children led her to conclude that specific adult emotions are formed by a differentiation of more generalised reactions. She argues that just after birth the infant shows only general emotional excitement, but from this quickly emerge demonstrations of distress and delight, and then anger, disgust and fear, followed by more positive demonstrations of elation, affection and joy. However, appealing as this scheme is, it is an unlikely explanation of the myriad adult emotions and ambivalent feelings that can frequently occur. A recombination of emotions would appear to be needed to supplement the armoury of experience provided by Bridges' early differentiation. Such a theory of 'emotional mixture' has been proposed by Plutchik (1962). He has assumed that there are eight primary emotional states, including anger, joy, fear and sorrow, from which by mixture the complex emotional experience of the adult is obtained. He has also assumed that each primary emotional state can vary in intensity and thus produce different shades of experience. Thus 'fear' can be experienced from timidity through to panic and terror, and 'joy' from serenity through to ecstasy. Mixing the different basic emotions at different levels of intensity, Plutchik argues, can account for the richness of emotional experience.

Much more has been written on actual emotional experience. However, much of what has been written is not informative from a scientific point of view and, although it can be interesting, detailed accounts of personal emotional experiences are weak evidence when stood alone. James once remarked that he would as soon read through verbal descriptions of the shapes of the rocks on a New Hampshire farm as toil through the literature on emotion (available at that time).

In placing the experience of emotion in its proper context, information about its relationship with the other aspects of emotion, the behavioural and physiological, is required. This information is summarised in three particular theories of emotion.

2.4   THEORIES OF EMOTION

Among the earliest accounts of emotion was that of Aristotle (c. 4 BC). He discussed a distinction between experiences that involve body and soul concurrently and those that only involve the soul. The former included the appetites, passions (emotions) and sensations, while the latter represented thinking. This view was confirmed and more explicitly stated many centuries later by St Thomas Aquinas (thirteenth century AD). It is the description of this relationship between body and soul in emotion which has commanded the attention of many writers since then.

Descartes, in the seventeenth century, produced an elaborate and sophisticated model of emotion (passion) in which can be seen the origins of both James' and Cannon's theories. Descartes introduced a particularly important idea with his model. He believed that emotion had an 'environmental' causation, that it was elicited as much as emitted. The event which triggered the emotion affected, by way of

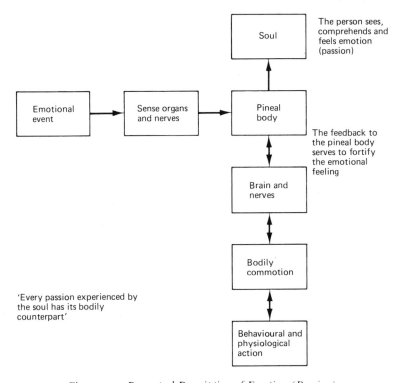

Figure 2.1: Descartes' Description of Emotion (Passion)

the sense organs and nerves, the all-important pineal body. Activity in this organ was communicated to the soul, allowing the person to see, comprehend, and feel passion, and was transmitted through the brain and nerves to the body, causing a physical commotion resulting in behavioural and physiological action. The activity in the brain and nerves, the 'animal spirits', acted back on the pineal body to fortify the feeling of passion. A version of Descartes' model is shown in figure 2.1. It is the feedback from the bodily reaction which serves to fortify the feeling of emotion (passion) that forms a link with James' much later theory, and it is the simultaneous arousing of the 'soul' and that bodily reaction by the pineal that provides the link with Cannon's theory.

2.4.1 James' Theory of Emotion

The first systematic attempts to relate emotional experience and its concomitant bodily reactions were made by James in 1884, and then quite independently by Lange in 1885. Of the two, James produced the more definite account. The view he argued for was later put by Sherrington (1906) in the form of a question:

> does the stimulus which is the exciting cause of the emotion act first on the nervous centres ruling the viscera, and their reaction generate visceral sensations, and do these latter, laden with affective quality as we know they will be, induce the emotion of the mind?

James proposed that emotional experience is produced by, and is secondary to, the more-or-less automatic bodily reaction to emotion-producing stimuli. In *The Principles of Psychology* (1890), James stated:

> My theory . . . is that the bodily changes follow directly from the perception of the exciting fact, and that our feeling of the same changes as they occur *is* the emotion.

He included motor responses along with autonomic discharge as the bodily determinants of emotional feeling. He argued, for example, that 'we are insulted, strike out, and because of that are angry'. Both natural common sense and the then prevailing philosophical thought held such sequence of events to be incorrect. 'We are insulted, become angry and strike out.' We consciously experience an emotion, and the bodily changes follow from that.

The Jamesian theory is illustrated in figure 2.2; it places psychic processes secondary to bodily processes. He argued that the emotion-eliciting events excite bodily changes by a pre-organised reflex mechanism. Those bodily changes are felt the moment they occur. The complex of each emotion James viewed as a sum of elements, each caused by the reflex arousal of a bodily change.

Because these elements can vary indefinitely he saw no limit to the number of possible different emotions.

James argued the case for his view of emotion most cogently from what information he had available, introspection and a little evidence of a more scientific nature. Perhaps, however, he never meant that view to be taken as a formal theory, but more as a current speculation. Despite this his view was taken as a formal theory and came to

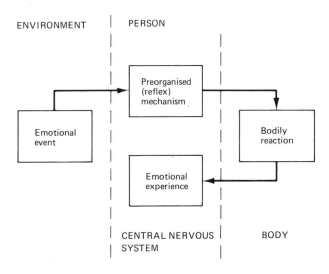

Figure 2.2: James' Theory of Emotion

dominate this area of study. By 1922, Dunlap could write that the theory

> ... has not only become so strongly entrenched in scientific thought that it is practically assumed today as the basis for the study of the emotional life, but now also led to the development of the hypothesis of reaction or response as the basis of all mental life.

However, the theory was incompatible with developing neurophysiological knowledge, and a formal rebuttal was made by Cannon in 1927. Cannon argued that, first, total separation of the viscera from the central nervous system does not alter emotional behaviour; according to James it should. Second, the same visceral changes occur in very different emotional states, and also in states which are not emotional. James had, by necessity, maintained that the different emotions would be characterised by specific patterns of bodily change. Cannon's observations, on the other hand, supported a theory of non-specificity, such as that later put forward by Selye (1950). Third, the viscera are relatively insensitive structures, and are too slow to respond to be a source of emotional experience. Emotional experience may, of course, be immediate on the perception of the appropriate stimuli. Fourth, and last, artificial induction of the visceral changes associated with intense emotional experience does not reproduce that experience.

Cannon's objections held sway, although possibly many were invalid (Lader and Tryer, 1975), perhaps partly because he offered an alternative theory, which was more acceptable in terms of the current physiological knowledge.

2.4.2   The Cannon–Bard Theory of Emotion

The James theory has been described as a 'peripheral' theory, because of the emphasis it laid on feedback from peripheral bodily reactions as the source of emotional experience. Cannon's theory has, using the same rationale, been described as a 'central' theory. He argued that visceral reactions were too diffuse to produce the numerous distinctive patterns required by James in the production of emotional experience; his own work had led him to describe but two broad patterns (see section 3.1.1). It had also led him to reject the idea that feedback from visceral reactions played any part in emotional experience. That belief now appears to be too extreme (see section 2.4.3). Instead, Cannon regarded the thalamus as the critical part of the mechanism of emotion, which, when released for action by sensory input or cortical impulses, led to both bodily reactions and the experience of emotion (see figure 2.3), the latter being an epiphenomenon of central nervous system activity.

Cannon's (1927) exposition of the theory was developed in the following year by Bard (1928), who added further evidence that diencephalic and associated structures were essential for the expression of emotional behaviour. He showed that sham rage induced in cats by decortication was abolished by extirpation of the thalamus. The theory became known as the Cannon–Bard theory.

Cannon (1929, 1931) also pointed out that the bodily changes

34

which occurred in emotion were largely the result of activity in the sympathetic nervous system. This will be discussed in greater detail in the next chapter (section 3.1.1).

Later work showed that Cannon and Bard were mistaken in assigning the chief role in the control of emotion to the thalamus. In 1937, Papez emphasised the possibility that some anatomical circuit involving limbic structures might underlie the experience and expression of emotion. He suggested a circuit that consisted of the

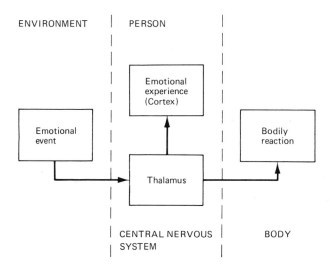

Figure 2.3: Cannon's Theory of Emotion

hippocampus–fornix, mammillary bodies, mammillothalamic tract, anterior thalamic nuclei, thalamocortical radiations, and gyrus cinguli. Like that of James, his hypothesis was not founded on strong experimental evidence, just a few clinical observations, but nevertheless it was supported by subsequent work. The Papez circuit is now widely accepted as one of the key structures in the control of emotion, and the replacement of the thalamus by the limbic system and associated structures is a necessary modification of the Cannon–Bard theory. With this modification the theory has come to provide the basis for most recent psychophysiological theories of brain function. Schachter's theory is an exception, and is discussed below.

2.4.3 Schachter's Theory of Emotion

Schachter (1964) has relatively recently formulated what he calls a 'cognitive–physiological' theory of emotion. He has suggested that when an appropriate stimulus arouses emotional excitement in a person, that person needs to 'label' his bodily reactions. To do so he or she is motivated to obtain information about what is happening to them. The person's cognitions, on past and presently available information, 'steer' him in labelling his emotions, and the label given determines how the person will behave. Emotional experience Schachter sees as a collation of the sensory feedback and the cognitions generated by the stimulus situation. His theory is a development of that of James. There are two important differences, however. First, James believed that our feelings of our bodily reactions as they occur are the emotion. Schachter does not; instead he talks of the person's cognitions 'steering' the labelling of their feelings. Second, Schachter sees emotional arousal as producing heightened motivation to obtain relevant information.

The theory is supported by Schachter's own experiments, in which he studied the interaction between sensory feedback from visceral reactions and cognitions provided by the test situation. The former were manipulated by adrenaline injections, and the latter by instructions and sociosituational arrangements. He has shown that a subject's way of labelling his emotions is markedly influenced by the information he is given. The labels, in turn, determine whether he or she acts in an elated, aggressive or frightened manner. The same visceral reactions, produced by adrenaline, could facilitate the emergence of anger or euphoria depending on the instructions given to the subjects or the social arrangements prevailing. He also found that adrenaline by itself (devoid of emotional cognition) was not likely to produce any emotional experience although it produced the usual visceral reaction. Maranon, as early as 1924, had shown that most of his patients who had been injected with adrenaline in a neutral setting, felt 'as if' they were experiencing emotion (cold emotion). However, in anxiety-suggesting situations, subjects showed evidence of 'real' anxiety and some even panic.

There are two particular points to note about the theory. First, it does account for how people tend to react to ambiguous stressful events. Janis (1962) has discussed how a single informative announcement to the residents of a city threatened by flooding can make the difference between a mass panic and subsequent flight in terror, and a calm stoical effort to maintain normal routine. The theory can also account for the effects of prior experiences (learning) on emotional experience in the face of stress. The second point is more negative, and concerns the extent to which information can change the nature of emotional experience. Can, say, anxiety or fear be transformed into joy simply by inducing emotionally aroused people to change the labels they use? Can the skilful counsellor or friend dramatically change one's mood with an appropriate word?

2.4.4   Comments

Together the James, Cannon–Bard and Schachter theories serve to place emotional experience in the sequence of environmental, neural and behavioural events which add up to the scenario of emotion. The former theories ascribe to it the role of epiphenomenon, a secondary feature possessing no faculty for controlling other events. It is an end point in their systems. Such a belief must appear extreme to the layman and must conflict with common sense. Both would hold that emotional experience is a powerful determinant of man's behaviour. However, to deny this is not to deny the importance of studying this experience, for by its very nature it offers a window onto, and a correlate of, the other aspects of emotion. (The built-in difficulties of such study have already been discussed, and need only to be mentioned again as a necessary caution.)

James emphasised the role of the autonomic (visceral) nervous system and of motor events in the aetiology of emotional experience. Cannon and Bard drew attention to the central nervous system mechanisms involved, and Schachter has emphasised the interaction between central (cognitive) and peripheral events. All three have been proved correct in their identification of important mechanisms underlying emotional experience, and these will be discussed later in this chapter and in the next.

2.5   THE NEURAL CONTROL OF EMOTION

Much has been learnt in the past few decades about the neural mechanisms involved in the control of emotion. In accord with present knowledge, it is suggested that the main brain areas concerned with this function are within the forebrain, or closely associated with it. Most often mentioned in this context are the cerebral cortex, the limbic system and the hypothalamus, and the reticular formation. These structures interact in their function, and like all of the brain's component structures show some flexibility in the way they process information and determine the flow of behaviour. As a consequence it is difficult to specify with precision which structures are most important for which behaviours. Indeed it can be forcibly argued that the total condition of the brain is important in the generation of all behaviour. This neoholistic position is gaining ground, and it may soon be unfashionable to talk of specific control systems in the brain. Despite this each of the four structures mentioned above will be discussed in the context of the neural control of emotion.

2.5.1 The Forebrain

The forebrain in man is dominated by the massive cerebral hemispheres (figure 2.4). The outer grey matter of these hemispheres forms the cerebral cortex. The cortex is, in evolutionary terms, the most recently developed of brain structures. It has long been assumed that it is the seat of 'intelligent' behaviour, being the structure in which most of the information processing necessary for the control of man's complex behaviour takes place. The forebrain is not entirely composed of the cerebral hemispheres and cortex, however, but is also made up of older structures such as the thalamus and hypothalamus, basal ganglia, and the limbic system. Each of these has a role to play in the control of emotion but, as already stated, of these older structures the limbic system and hypothalamus are of particular interest.

MacLean (1975) has described man's forebrain as a 'triune' brain (figure 2.5). It has developed and expanded through three types of brain which can be characterised as reptilian (centre core, including basal ganglia), palaeomammalian (intermediate layer, including limbic system), and neomammalian (outer layer, including neocortex and its associated brainstem structures). Despite the great differences in their structure and in their chemistry, all three 'brains' must intermesh and function effectively together. The reptilian brain is man's oldest heritage, followed by the palaeomammalian cortex, and then the neomammalian cortex. In MacLean's (1970) words, these latter structures 'might be regarded as Nature's attempt to provide

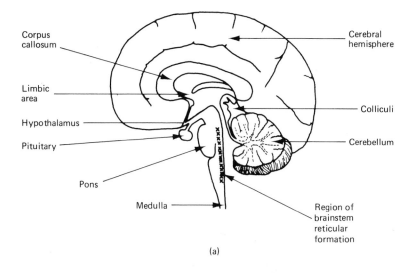

(a)

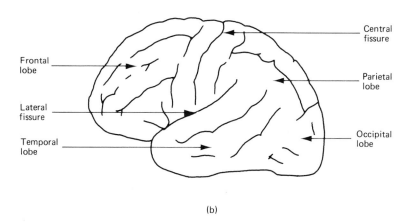

(b)

Figure 2.4: The Brain: A General Schema (a) and the Cerebral Cortex (b)

the reptilian brain with a "thinking cap" and emancipate it from stereotyped behaviour'. Because of the differences in their evolutionary status, greater similarities might be seen across species

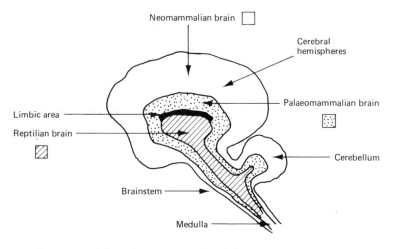

Figure 2.5: Schematic Representation of the Primate (Triune) Brain

in the functions of the older areas than in the functions of the neomammalian cortex.

2.5.2   The Cerebral Cortex

The assumption that the essential function of the cerebral cortex lies in the information processing necessary for complex behaviour is by-and-large supported by the available evidence. The cognitive processes important in the occurrence of stress (and emotion), the evaluation of the significance of events, the anticipation of future events, and the choosing between various coping strategies, are all thus functions of the cortex. Fundamental to these secondary psychological processes are the primary ones of perception and memory. There is perhaps nothing special in the way the perceptual and memory processes operate with respect to emotionally significant events, other than that their emotional significance may feed back to affect these processes. For example, Freud has described how the expression of, among other things, the memory of events which involve some form of threat, may be 'repressed'. Repression makes access to these 'emotional' memories more difficult.

The *temporal lobes* appear to provide a functional link between the rest of the cerebral cortex and the subcortical structures, and there is strong evidence of their involvement in the experience, interpretation, and expression of emotion. Much of the information that we have on the functions of the temporal lobes has come from Penfield and his colleagues. They have conducted many studies on temporal lobe epilepsy and have examined the effects of stimulating the cortex in conscious patients.

During operations epileptics have frequently reported feelings of fear when areas of the temporal lobe are stimulated. These reported feelings appear to be genuine and not simply due to a general fear of the operation itself. Stimulation of certain temporal areas produced fear, while stimulation of other areas did not. Fear could be evoked from stimulation of the anterior and inferior surfaces of the temporal lobe (Penfield and Jasper, 1954; Penfield, 1958; Roberts, 1961). Furthermore, in psychomotor epilepsy resulting from seizure discharges in the mediotemporal region, feelings of fear may occur at the start of an attack (Macrae, 1954; Weil, 1956; Williams, 1956). Rage has rarely been reported as a result of stimulation of the temporal cortex or as part of an epileptic aura. However, once an attack is under way, aggressive behaviour often occurs. Gloor (1960) has shown that patients with psychomotor epilepsy often exhibit personality changes, including a tendency to explode into violent anger. In all, the changes which do occur seem to be a reverse of the Kluver–Bucy syndrome (see later), and may result from a continuous, irritative process originating with the lesion. However, many unilateral ablations of the anterior temporal lobe have been carried out in man for the relief of epileptic seizures with no subsequent changes in emotional state being observed. Bilateral lesions have been produced in patients with severe psychomotor epilepsy and in some a decrease in aggressiveness has been obtained (Green *et al.*, 1951; Pool, 1954; Terzian and Ore, 1955). The results are, however, very variable.

The superior and lateral portions of the temporal lobes appear to be concerned with the interpretation of sensory input (Smythies, 1970) and stimulation here leads to 'interpretative illusions'. For example, sounds seem louder or fainter, clearer or less distinct, visual objects look larger or smaller, nearer or further, experiences become endowed with familiarity (déjà vu) or a lack of familiarity, a strangeness.

The two functions of the temporal lobes referred to above could sensibly be related, and both make natural sense in terms of the involvement of the temporal lobes in limbic system function.

2.5.3 Information Processing and Arousal

The information about the environment that the senses make available is largely processed at the level of the cerebral cortex. Its input appears to be through the classical sensory pathways, and through the reticular formation. The term 'reticular formation' refers to a number of subcortical structures. These structures have been divided into two main groups, which to some extent subserve separate functions. The first group has been called the brainstem reticular formation (this is discussed here), and the second group is the thalamic reticular formation.

According to Hebb (1955) the classical sensory pathways serve a 'cue' or 'informational' function and the reticular formation serves an 'arousal' function. All sensory modalities, with the exception of the olfactory system, project to specific areas of the cerebral cortex through specific nuclei of the thalamus. The lateral geniculate nucleus, for example, receives inputs from the optic tract, and sends projections to the visual areas of the occipital lobe, while the medial geniculate nucleus receives an auditory system input and sends projections to the auditory areas of the temporal lobe. Both nuclei form part of the thalamus. Collaterals (branches) from the ascending sensory tracts connect with the diffuse polysynaptic network of the reticular formation. This, in turn, projects to more-or-less the whole cortex through the non-specific thalamic nuclei. The input to the reticular formation appears to be pooled, regardless of its source, and its output to the cerebral cortex appears to reflect this overall pooled level of activity.

In 1952, Lindsley showed that lesions in cats made in the reticular formation, with the classical sensory pathways intact, left the animal permanently asleep. Severing the classical pathways but leaving the reticular formation undamaged did not prevent the animal from moving around. The electrical activity of the cortex in the first case was characteristic of sleep, and in the second was that of being awake and alert. Corroborating evidence that the reticular formation is involved in arousal comes from experiments involving stimulation of this area. Moruzzi and Magoun (1949), for example, found that stimulation of the reticular formation led to the cessation of cortical electrical activity characteristic of drowsiness and sleep, and a switch to electrical activity associated with wakefulness. This ascending activating function of the reticular formation is only one of its several functions.

Much research has been concerned with the relationship between the level of arousal mediated by reticular formation activity, and the efficiency of information processing. One popular, but often

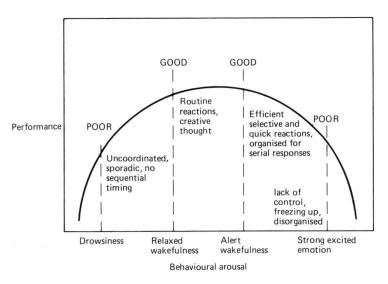

Figure 2.6: Behavioural Arousal and Performance

criticised, description of this relationship is in terms of an inverted U-shaped function; both low and high levels of arousal are associated with poor processing, while a moderate level of arousal is optimal for this function. Such a description was offered by Hebb (1955) and by Lindsley (1952) (see figure 2.6).

Levi (1972) has extended this description to the relation between stress and arousal: high and low levels of arousal, he argues, are experienced as stressful (see figure 2.7). Combining these functions produces a linear relationship between stress and performance. Increasing stress produces a progressive degradation of performance.

There is evidence to suggest, however, that the experience of stress is not directly related to the level of arousal (Burrows *et al.*, 1977); and it has been suggested that these 'factors' are independent (Mackay, Cox, Burrows and Lazzarini, 1978). The author and his colleagues have recently developed a checklist of mood adjectives which appear to measure stress and arousal. Two separate, factor analytical studies using British undergraduates in different situations have

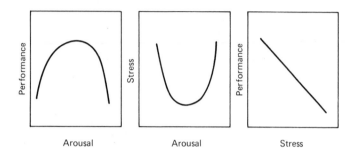

Figure 2.7: Arousal, Stress and Performance

produced nearly identical factor structures: two independent bipolar factors have been clearly identified. The way the mood adjectives load on the factors suggests that one is a stress factor and the other an arousal factor. The mood adjectives used in this stress–arousal checklist were derived from a similar checklist developed by Thayer (1967) using an American undergraduate population. High arousal may therefore be associated with high or low stress, and similarly for low arousal. Such a situation is represented in figure 2.8. Performance can still be treated as an inverted U-shaped function of arousal, and as a monotonic function of stress.

The information which is used in processing is not only drawn from the person's environment and from present events, but also concerns past events drawn from memory. An important part of information processing is thus the integration of current input with the existing schema of past experience. This process is an essential part of establishing the person's perception of the world and of planning his activities in it. This planning can be viewed in terms of a decision-making process necessarily divided into problem identification, clarification and solution, and then response coordination and execution. These subprocesses, it is assumed, all originate in or at least involve cortical function. The response if cognitive must also reside in this structure, but if behavioural or physiological must be transmitted through the lower centres to the relevant effector organs. The behavioural response is mediated through the mechanism of the pyramidal system, the somatic nervous system of the periphery, and skeletal muscle. This mechanism is affected by activity in the extrapyramidal system, and governed by activity in the motor cortices. It has been variously suggested that the prime function of the

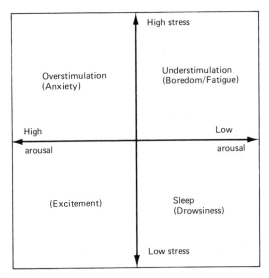

Figure 2.8: Arousal and Stress: Orthogonal Model

cortex is to decide the 'directional' properties of the different types of response, including the quality of the emotional experience. The intensity of the response may, according to this thesis, be determined elsewhere, in lower brain centres such as the limbic system. However, as will be discussed later, it has also been argued that the limbic system retains some executive (directive) functions.

2.5.4 The Limbic System

The structures of the limbic system (figure 2.9) have been said to include the amygdala, the cingulate gyrus, the hippocampus, the septum and their interconnecting pathways. This loose network of cortical and subcortical areas was originally and simply regarded as part of the olfactory mechanism. It was known as the rhinencephalon, or 'smell' brain. Doubt arose as to the validity of this view as it became obvious that there was scant correlation between the development of this area and the development of, and dependence on, a sense of smell. An important and dramatic departure from this view was reached in 1937, when Papez formulated a theory which ascribed to the limbic system and associated

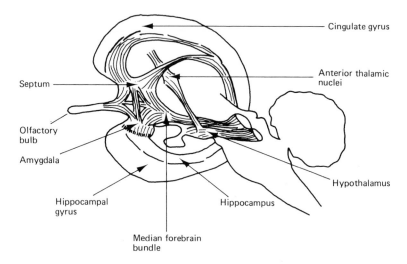

Figure 2.9: The Limbic System

structures an important role in the experience and expression of emotion. He wrote:

> Is emotion a magic product, or is it a physiological process, which depends on an anatomical mechanism? . . . It is proposed that the hypothalamus, the anterior thalamic nuclei, the gyrus cingulae, the hippocampus, and their interconnections constitute a harmonious mechanism which may elaborate the functions of central emotion as well as participate in emotional expression.

Papez's theory was extremely speculative and put together on very weak evidence, but it formed a conceptual framework which immediately became a focus for further work. About the same time

46

Klüver and Bucy (1939) reported a, now classic, series of experiments on wild Rhesus monkeys. In their experiments, they ablated various brain areas and observed the effects on the animals' behaviour. Following bilateral ablation of the temporal lobes with the amygdala and anterior hippocampus, the hitherto wild monkeys became more placid and more manageable. The experimental operation had 'tamed' them. Other effects were also observed, including hypersexuality and what has been termed psychic blindness. The monkeys lost their appreciation of the meaning and significance of other animals and objects. The occurrence of the so-called Klüver–Bucy syndrome was taken as confirmation of the existence and function of the Papez circuit. The currently available evidence suggests that, of the structures ablated by Klüver and Bucy, the amygdala was the most important in the production of the emotional changes observed. Following on from their work it has been shown in many different species that increased tameness can follow amygdaloid ablation (Anand and Brobeck, 1952; Schreiner and Kling, 1953, 1956; Rosvold et al., 1954; Weiskrantz, 1956). Perhaps the most interesting demonstration of this was that of Schreiner and Kling in 1956. They 'tamed' a mountain lion by removal of its amygdala, and following the operation the lion behaved like a domesticated cat and could be safely left to roam freely about the laboratory. Somewhat paradoxically, however, stimulation of the amygdala has also been reported to produce a calming effect, making the experimental animals involved more friendly and less aggressive (Anand and Dua, 1956; Fonberg and Delgado, 1961; Egger and Flynn, 1963). Amygdaloid placements producing this paradoxical type of response were in the lateral nucleus and in the basal nucleus. More usually manifestations of fear and rage are elicited by stimulation of these and other amygdaloid nuclei. Kaada, Anderson and Jansen, in a paper published in 1954, described such responses following stimulation of the lateral nucleus and of the lateral part of the basal nucleus, while Ursin and Kaada (1960) reported fear and rage, and attentional responses as a result of stimulating not only the lateral and basal nuclei but also an area extending medially through the area of the central nucleus and into the internal capsule. Emotional responses have also been obtained from the central, medial and mediobasal nuclei (Magnus and Lammers, 1956; Shealy and Peele, 1957; Wood, 1958; De Molina and Hunsperger, 1959).

The basolateral amygdala has a characteristic rhythm of about 40 to 45 cps (see Smythies, 1970). This is evoked by meaningful and noxious stimuli. It may represent an alerting alarm call to amygdala to operate quickly in situations where its function is to react to such stimuli and in turn alert the pituitary–adrenal axis. It is also reported that low-voltage stimulation of the basolateral division of the amygdala evokes a 'searching' response, while stimulation at a higher voltage produces panic. Stimulation of the medial division, in contrast, produces aggression. The amygdala may therefore represent a

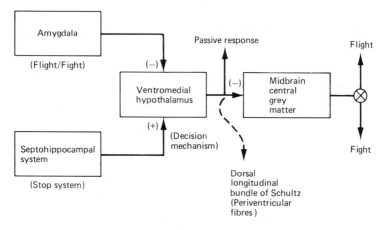

Figure 2.10: Gray's Model of Limbic Function

subcortical decision-making mechanism affecting a choice between exploration or flight on one hand, and fight (aggression) on the other.

Gray (1971) makes a somewhat similar suggestion, believing the amygdala to have an executive role in the control of defensive rather than predatory attack, and of escape behaviour (flight). He sees the amygdala associated in this respect with ventromedial hypothalamus, to which he assigns a key decision-making role. The ventromedial nucleus of the hypothalamus exercises a tonic inhibition over the midbrain central grey, and this area is the ultimate executive area for flight or fight. The inhibitory influence of the ventromedial hypothalamus is itself inhibited by the amygdala and enhanced by the septohippocampal system, Gray's 'stop' system. This model is shown in figure 2.10. The outcome of the effects of the amygdala and septohippocampal systems is decided by which of the inputs to the

48

ventromedial hypothalamus is the stronger in any particular circumstances. Inhibition of the ventromedial hypothalamus produces an active (fight/flight) response, while stimulation produces a passive response.

Kling and Hutt (1958) showed that lesions in the amygdala made cats docile, and that further lesions in the ventromedial hypothalamus could make them ferocious. However, cats made ferocious by ventromedial hypothalamic lesions could not be calmed by subsequent amygdalectomy. Other studies have shown that damage to the septal area (part of Gray's septohippocampal system) produces a syndrome known as septal hyperirritability. Animals demonstrating this syndrome show increased startle response, exaggerated aggression, increased defaecation, and increased resistance to capture. This syndrome can be prevented by prior lesions to the amygdala (King and Meyer, 1958).

Gray's model of limbic function is in many ways consistent with that of MacLean (1970). MacLean has suggested three main subdivisions of the limbic system. The first, the lower part of the system (including the amygdala and hippocampus), appears to be concerned with feelings, emotions and behaviours which ensure survival and self-preservation. It is concerned with the selfish demands of feeding, fighting and defence. The second, the upper part of the limbic system (including the cingulate gyrus), appears to be involved in the feelings and expressions related to sociability, sexuality, and species preservation. The third subdivision involves the fibres which branch down from the hypothalamus, by-pass the olfactory mechanism, lead to the anterior and medial hypothalamus, and on to the cingulate gyrus. This pathway is virtually nonexistent in reptiles, and becomes progressively larger in the evolution of the primates. It is biggest in man. There is some evidence that it reflects a shifting of emphasis from olfactory to visual influences in sociosexual behaviour.

There is thus a general agreement that the limbic system and associated areas are important in the neural control of emotion, feeling and expression. Many clinical observations support this thesis. Zeman and King (1958), for example, have noted that a syndrome of hyperemotionality, including outbursts of violence and constant crying, may be associated with tumours of the anterior midline structures, especially the septum and fornix. However, despite the wealth of evidence, both clinical and experimental, which demonstrates the importance of the limbic system in emotion, there

49

remains an interesting case reported by Nathan and Smith in 1950. Despite gross anatomical defects in his limbic system their 'subject' appeared normal in both behaviour and intellect. The man in question died of cancer, and before his death was studied intensively as part of a research programme concerned with operations for the relief of pain. He appeared intelligent, sociable and popular, normal both intellectually and emotionally. Post-mortem examination of his brain showed that in place of the corpus callosum and cingulate gyrus there was an irregular mass of white matter covered by overlying grey matter. The fimbria, fornix and septum were absent, the hippocampus was small and abnormal and the amygdala was grossly abnormal. For this one person, at least, a large number of limbic structures did not appear essential for normal function. Perhaps this case bears dramatic witness to the brain's inherent flexibility.

2.5.5 The Hypothalamus

Whatever coping action the other executive areas of the brain decide on, the body must be prepared for the appropriate level of physical exertion. Organising this process of preparation is largely the function of the hypothalamus. Notwithstanding this, many hypothalamic areas have already been discussed in relation to the executive functions of the limbic system. Some distinction may therefore be made between its higher and its vegetative functions.

It is at the level of the hypothalamus that the most obvious link can be seen between central and peripheral processes, and between the different peripheral processes. The hypothalamus appears to have some control over both the pituitary–endocrine system and the autonomic nervous system. Indeed it has sometimes been referred to as the 'head ganglion' of the latter system. The classical experiments of Hess (1957) demonstrated that electrical stimulation of the hypothalamus could bring about physiological and behavioural changes characteristic of emotional states. Hess believed that he could identify two areas which performed distinct and separate functions. The middle and posterior hypothalamic areas appeared to be concerned with general excitation and the facilitation of bodily work. This region he termed the ergotrophic zone. In contrast, the rostral and lateral hypothalamic areas appeared to be responsible for protective, restitutional and recuperative changes. This region he termed the trophotrophic zone. Generally speaking, the ergotrophic zone appears to regulate sympathetic nervous system activity, while the trophotrophic zone appears to regulate parasympathetic nervous system activity. More recently Gellhorn and Loofbourrow (1963) have developed this idea, and suggested that the general emotional state is

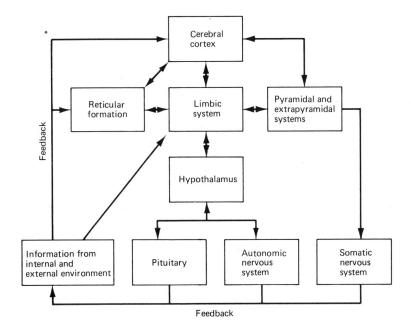

* Other pathways exist, but for the sake of clarity only those considered particularly important for emotion are shown

Figure 2.11: Neural Control of Emotion

associated with specific activity in one of these hypothalamic zones. This phenomenon has been referred to as 'hypothalamic tuning'. It could be predicted on this basis that a state of ergotrophic tuning would be associated with increased activity in the sympathetic nervous system, and behavioural excitement, and the release and utilisation of energy. Chronic fear and anxiety might result from prolonged ergotrophic tuning, while depression or helplessness could arise from prolonged trophotrophic tuning.

51

While there is much evidence to support the notion that the cerebral cortex, limbic system, hypothalamus and reticular system are very important in the control of emotion, the exact relationships between the components of this control system are far from obvious. Perhaps it will suffice for present purposes to summarise our knowledge as in figure 2.11. The limbic system has been placed in the centre of this control system not only for graphical convenience, but because it does appear to play a central role. The real executive function and the experiential aspect of emotion must reside in the interaction between the cerebral cortex and limbic system, or, in MacLean's (1975) terminology, between the palaeo- and the neomammalian forebrain. Perhaps it is only those animals possessing highly developed neomammalian structures which can be thought to process 'emotion' in any way similar to that processed by man. Truly emotional behaviour may only be demonstrated by the higher primates, and research into 'emotion' which has used animals lower down the phylogenetic scale may on these grounds be badly misguided.

The control system outlined here decides emotional experience of man, and his cogntive, behavioural and physiological responses to the events producing that experience. The following chapter deals in some detail with those responses.

3

The Response to Stress

The previous chapters have discussed when and how stress may occur and how it is experienced. That experience is accompanied by an organised set of responses, the aim of which is to reduce or remove the stress. These responses may be conveniently thought of as either physiological or psychological in nature, and the latter may be subdivided into the cognitive and the behavioural. The psychological responses have often been described as coping mechanisms, and the function of the physiological responses has been seen as the facilitation of coping.

Viewed in this way the physiological response to stress is itself a form of coping mechanism. The physiological response is dominated by the major psychoendocrine systems, the sympathetic–adrenomedullary and pituitary–adrenocortical systems. Both are influenced by hypothalamic and higher-brain activity. It is worth speculating at this point whether this psychoendocrine domination of the physiological stress response makes biochemical rather than electrophysiological measurements the more appropriate. If so, it is unfortunate that until recently electrophysiology has dominated stress psychophysiology, especially that of an applied orientation.

Apart from the description of what is known about the different types of stress response, the major task in this area is to offer a solution to the problem of their interrelation. It seems an article of faith for many that they are meaningfully related, but as yet there has been no final convincing demonstration of this offered.

3.1 THE PHYSIOLOGICAL RESPONSE TO STRESS

In considering the physiological response to stress, it is useful to start with the work of Cannon, who initiated the description of the animal's

53

immediate responses to stressful stimuli, and of Selye, whose general adaptation syndrome includes, besides Cannon's immediate 'emergency reaction' the long-term adjustments elicited by prolonged stress. Both writers figure prominently among the originators of stress research, and together they have provided a physiological framework, albeit controversial, on which our observations on stress can be arranged.

3.1.1 Cannon and the Structure and Functions of the Autonomic Nervous System

In 1898, Langley wrote: 'I propose the term "autonomic nervous system" for the sympathetic system, and the allied nervous system of the cranial and sacral nerves, and for the local nervous system of the gut.' This term did not gain immediate acceptance, but the passage of time favoured Langley, and today the autonomic nerves are generally regarded as the 'motor' nerves of the sympathetic and parasympathetic systems. It is probably important to note at the outset that the concept of a parasympathetic 'system' is more anatomical than functional, as activity in the parasympathetic nerves is not necessarily integrated and certainly not general.

The autonomic nervous system governs the activities of cardiac and smooth muscle, of the digestive and sweat glands, and of certain endocrine organs such as the α and β pancreatic cells and the adrenal medulla. It is concerned with those processes which are normally not under voluntary control, and for the most part beneath consciousness. Control of autonomic function is, however, partly central, the hypothalamus being regarded as its immediate regulator and in many respects its 'head ganglion'.

Through its various activities the autonomic nervous system appears to exercise the function of maintaining the constancy of the fluid environment of the body's cells (the internal environment: *milieu intérieur*). The stability of this environment has been regarded, since the early work of Bernard, as characteristic of health. Its maintenance was referred to by Cannon as 'homeostasis', although it is important to note that by homeostasis he did not mean to imply a static condition. Perhaps the term 'homeokinesis' would be more appropriate to describe this dynamic process. Cannon referred to the autonomic nerves as the 'interofective' system, and spoke of the cen-

54

tral nervous system as the 'exterofective' system, since through its exteroceptors and effectors a direct relationship is established with the external environment. A person could survive without an autonomic nervous system, but to make up for the lack of internal compensation due to homeostasis he would require a very constant and favourable external environment, free from threat.

The great majority of effector organs of the autonomic nervous system are innervated by both sympathetic and parasympathetic divisions, and generally the effects exerted by the two types of nerve are antagonistic. For example, the heart is supplied by the vagus nerve (cranial nerve X: parasympathetic) and by medial nerves of the sympathetic system from the cervical and thoracic ganglia. If the vagus is stimulated the heart beats more slowly (with a latency of less than a second), the diastolic interval is prolonged, and the blood pressure falls considerably. If stimulation is increased the heart may be brought to a stop in diastole. If stimulation is then stopped the heart will beat again. Furthermore, if stimulation is continued the ventricles, but not the atria, will resume contracting. This is termed vagus escape, and indicates that when deprived of impulses from the atria the ventricles can beat independently at their own rhythm. It also indicates that the vagus has little direct effect on ventricular activity. Stimulation of the sympathetic nerves causes an increase in heart rate after a latent period of six to ten seconds. This is at the expense of a shortening of the diastolic interval.

Impulses continually passing down the vagus nerves exert a retarding action on the heart, and it is chiefly by variations in this vagal tone that alterations in heart rate are produced. In athletes the heart rate is often quite slow (about 40 beats per minute), and it may be that the tonic effect of the vagus is more marked in them than in non-athletes. If, in man, an injection of atropine is given to inhibit vagal activity, the heart rate increases. The sympathetic nerves also appear to exert a tonic influence on the heart because their section is followed by a slight slowing.

Some autonomic effector organs are innervated by only sympathetic nerves. Of particular interest are the blood vessels of the skin and of the muscles, the sweat glands, and the adrenal medulla. Sympathetic activity tends to cause constriction of the cutaneous blood vessels, dilatation of the muscle blood vessels, the secretion of sweat and of the catecholamines from the adrenal medulla. A few effector organs receive nerves from both divisions of the autonomic nervous system, whose influences act synergistically. For instance, the salivary glands receive sympathetic nerves from the superior cervical ganglia, and are also innervated by branches of the facial and glossopharyngeal nerves (parasympathetic supply). All the salivary glands seem to receive their main secretory innervation from the parasympathetic system. Stimulation of these nerves causes an increase in salivary flow, and the rate of this increase matches the rate of stimulation. Stimulation of the sympathetic nerves also causes an increased rate of secretion but the response is more variable and usually much smaller than that obtained by parasympathetic stimulation. A common finding is that the flow of saliva, whether rapid or slow, is shortlasting. It diminishes quickly and often ceases wholly in spite of continued sympathetic stimulation. As a result of observations such as this, it has been suggested that the effect of sympathetic stimulation is to expel saliva already present in the ducts of the salivary glands. Very early experiments by Bradford and Langley in 1888 had shown that the salivary response to sympathetic stimulation could be increased by previous stimulation of the parasympathetic nerves. This would be predicted from the hypothesis outlined above.

Taken together the actions of the sympathetic nervous system seem to be directed towards strengthening the body's defences against the various dangers which might beset it. Cannon described the function of this system in terms of it preparing the animal for the behavioural activity involved in 'flight or fight'. Increased sympathetic activity mobilises the body's resources for immediate action. In this respect the sympathetic nervous system acts in conjunction with the catecholamine secretions of the adrenal medulla. The former brings about the rapid change in cardiovascular function which permits immediate exertion, while the latter supports this exertion through alterations in the metabolic processes. Taken as a whole these changes are what Gray (1971), among others, has called the 'emergency reaction'. There is an increase in the rate, strength and regularity of the heart beat, contraction of the spleen, the release of glucose stored as glycogen in the liver, the redirection of the blood supply from the skin and the viscera to the muscles and the brain, deepening of respiration and dilation of the bronchi, dilation of the pupils, an enhancement of the blood coagulation process and of the supply of blood lymphocytes. These changes can be seen to be adaptive for the emergency mobilisation of bodily resources. Blood is pumped round the body more rapidly and directed to the more essential structures, the brain and muscles, more energy-producing substances are available to it and its oxygen-carrying capacity is increased. The body's ability to seal wounds, repair tissue and combat infection is also increased. Changes in pupillary status may increase visual efficiency. Other less obviously adaptive changes also occur, sweating increases, while salivation decreases (dry mouth) and gut activity decreases. All these changes take place relatively rapidly, within seconds or, at the outside, several minutes.

Parasympathetic activity appears to dominate in situations characterised by relaxation or recuperation. In these situations heart rate slows, respiration becomes shallow and noisy, the lacrymal and salivary glands become more active (tears and saliva), the sweat glands become less active, pupillary constriction occurs, blood glucose levels fall, blood is directed to the gut and skin (flushing), and gut activity increases. A picture of post-prandial drowsiness is suggested. Parasympathetic activity also appears to dominate during periods of sleep.

3.1.2 Comments

Several general points arise from the decription of autonomic structure and function. First, and perhaps most important, the work of Cannon and his successors has demonstrated that the sympathetic–adrenomedullary system is responsive to environmental stimuli, both physical and psychological (see sections 3.1.4. and 3.1.5), and that its function should be discussed in relation to the animal's behaviour. This point should not now stimulate much debate. The second point concerns the totality and non-specificity of the sympathetic–adrenomedullary response. As mentioned in chapter 1, it had been assumed that the complete emergency reaction occurs irrespective of the exact nature of the eliciting emergency. This assumption can, and has been, challenged. Third, and closely related to the previous point, it has been assumed that an important functional balance exists between the two branches of the autonomic nervous system, and which regulates the 'tone' of the person's behaviour. Such a balance or interaction could be the mechanism by which any apparent patterning or specificity in the sympathetic–adrenomedullary response might occur. The fourth and last point concerns the role and status of the parasympathetic nervous system. It has often been assumed that this branch of the autonomic nervous system is somehow the more quiescent, the sleeping partner to the more dynamic sympathetic branch, that it is the provider of the background against which the emergency reaction is manifested. Such a view is outdated by current research and a more vital role has to be assigned to at least the vagal component of the parasympathetic nervous system. Several of these points will be picked up in greater detail later in this chapter.

3.1.3 Selye and the General Adaptation Syndrome

A general description of Selye's work and an account of his formulation of the general adaptation syndrome has already been given (see chapter 1). There are, according to Selye, three stages to the general adaptation syndrome: the first, the alarm or emergency reaction, the second, the period of resistance, and the third and final stage, the point of exhaustion and collapse. The occurrence of this stress syndrome can be pathogenic and cause diseases of adaptation, affecting one or other of the organ systems involved in its function.

Several questions have arisen about the operation of the syndrome. The most important is the question of its non-specificity. This has already been discussed in chapter 1 (section 1.4.1). Consideration of the currently available information must lead to the conclusion that while many stress-producing situations produce similar patterns of physiological response, this is not true of all. Furthermore, any particular situation may on one occasion produce the prescribed pattern of change but may not do so on others. Understanding why this is so has led to the recognition that important psychological processes intervene between stimulus and response. Having accepted that on some occasions and for some stress-producing situations the response syndrome produced is more or less that described by Selye, there arise two further questions. These concern the variability in response that has just been accepted. Qualitatively different stressors, but of the same potency, do not elicit exactly the same syndrome, and the same degree of stress induced by the same stressor may have different pathological effects in different individuals. Selye (1975) has provided answers to these problems. First, different stressors may only differ in their specific effects and not in their non-specific (stress) effects. For example, cold produces shivering and heat produces sweating. These are specific effects. They both produce increases in adrenocortical activity, which is a non-specific (stress) effect. It has to be accepted that in some instances the specific effects may modify the non-specific effects. Individual differences in the pathogenic effects of the stress response Selye (1975) ascribes to 'conditioning' factors, both endogenous (genetic predisposition, age, sex, personality, etc.) and exogenous (learning, drug and other physical treatments, diet, etc). Such conditioning factors can selectively enhance or inhibit different aspects of the stress response. The two concepts introduced

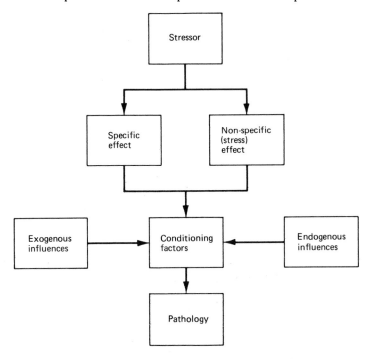

Figure 3.1: Conditioning Factors and the Stress Response

here, specific effects and conditioning factors, are related and summarised in figure 3.1. This figure describes a mechanism within a mechanism; the context for it is the general adaptation syndrome. According to many writers, the initial alarm reaction or emergency stage of the syndrome involves increases in sympathetic–adrenomedullary activity, while the stage of resistance is characterised by increased adrenocortical activity. Selye, in his earlier writings, concentrated on the latter. Having made this distinction between the alarm reaction and stage of resistance, it should be added that it is now necessary to recognise that changes in adrenocortical activity occur during the alarm reaction, and are of importance.

The adrenal glands are usually situated on the apices of the kidneys and within the peritoneal membrane. They consist of two more-or-less functionally separate areas, the inner medulla and outer cortex. The activity of the medulla is regulated by the splanchnic nerve, which is a (preganglionic) sympathetic nerve. The release of acetylcholine by the nerve stimulates the release of both adrenaline and noradrenaline from the chromaffin cells of the medulla. In man the ratio of the catecholamines released is very heavily in the favour of adrenaline. This sympathetic–adrenomedullary system is regulated at the level of the peripheral sympathetic reflex arc, and by activity in the posterior areas of the hypothalamus. This system appears to dominate during the emergency or alarm reaction of the general adaptation syndrome.

The activity of the adrenal cortex appears to be regulated to a large extent by the level of adrenocorticotropic hormone (ACTH) in the blood. ACTH is released by the anterior pituitary, its output being controlled by the secretion of corticotropin-releasing factor (CRF) into the pituitary portal blood vessels by the hypothalamus. Overall, the anterior pituitary releases two hormones which act in their own right, growth hormone and prolactin, and four tropic hormones, including ACTH, which act by controlling the behaviour of other glands. All have been related to the response to stress, and might appear to be involved in the stage of resistance. However, it is the anterior pituitary–adrenocortical system which appears to dominate, if not in reality, then certainly in terms of the attention paid to it in research.

The adrenal cortex produces three different groups of steroid hormones: the mineralocorticoids, the glucocorticoids and the androgens. The most important of the mineralocorticoids is aldosterone. Collectively the mineralocorticoids are concerned with the mineral content of the body, in particular with the body content of sodium ions. They stimulate the kidney to remove sodium from the urine and so to retain it in the body. The output of the mineralocorticoids is little affected by ACTH, but is sensitive to a renin–angiotensin mechanism which in turn is sensitive to blood sodium levels and to blood pressure. The most important member of the glucocorticoid group is cortisone. The main actions of the glucocorticoids in normal concentrations are the facilitation of water excretion by the kidney, the maintenance of normal blood pressure, and an involvement in the manufacture of red blood cells. In higher concentrations, as the result of stress or clinical intervention, they block the inflammatory response, interfere with the manufacture of proteins, cause the loss of calcium and phosphate from the kidneys, and raise blood sugar levels. The latter action may be necessary to fuel the activity of coping during the stage of resistance, while the other actions may account for part of the cost of this coping. The glucocorticoids are released under the action of ACTH. The adrenal androgens seem to be important in both sexes, despite the fact that their name implies that they act like male sex hormones. Little, however, is known about their exact function, although they stimulate pubic and axillary hair growth at puberty, they stimulate grease production by the skin, facilitate the development of muscle, and appear to contribute to the development of sexual desire.

All three groups of corticosteroids operate in response to stress.

3.1.4 Stress and Catecholamine Excretion

A small fraction of the catecholamines released by the sympathetic–adrenomedullary system is excreted in a free form in urine, and this fraction can be estimated quantitatively by spectrophotofluorimetric methods. Most of the adrenaline excreted in urine is derived from the adrenal medulla, and urinary adrenaline can be taken as a rough estimate of the activity of this gland. Most of the noradrenaline released by the sympathetic nerves is reabsorbed by the nerve endings or bound to various tissues, and does not enter the bloodstream or urine. However, it can be accepted that urinary catecholamines represent estimates of sympathetic–adrenomedullary activity, but integrated over extended time periods, usually 1–3 hours. Using urinary catecholamines as a measure of the stress response, many laboratory experiments and field studies have been carried out in the investigation of the occurrence and effects of stress.

It has been shown that enhanced sympathetic–adrenomedullary activity, albeit of short duration, occurs in subjects exposed to a variety of stresses. A list of such demonstrations has been drawn up by Kagan and Levi (1975): before a boxing match (Elmadjian, 1963), riding in a centrifuge (Silverman and Cohen, 1960; Berman and Pettit, 1961: Frankenhaeuser *et al.*, 1962; Goodall, 1962), acrobatic, supersonic and space flights (Klepping *et al.*, 1963; Colehour and Graybiel, 1964), car driving (Smith and Bennett, 1958; Schmid and Meythaler, 1964), taking university exams (Bogdonoff *et al.*, 1959, 1960), medical examination (Ulvedal *et al.*, 1963), dental treatment (Weiss *et al.*, 1965), hospital admission (Tolson *et al.*, 1965; Nelson *et al.*, 1966), sensory deprivation (Mendelson *et al.*, 1960), and water immersion (Goodall *et al.*, 1964).

Froberg and his colleagues (1971) and Levi (1972) have observed increased sympathetic–adrenomedullary activity in subjects exposed for longer periods in simulations of real-life situations. Simulations of six different situations were considered: repetitive industrial work (sorting ball bearings), office work (proof reading); appearing before an audience, film programmes chosen to induce emotional reaction, psychomotor tasks, and ground combat conditions. In a series of field studies the reactions of various occupational groups were studied in real-life situations. The situations studied included those facing telephone operators, invoicing clerks and others working on salary and on piece-rate bases, office clerks subjected to changes in work environments, supermarket cash-desk girls during rush hour and ordinary conditions, and paper-mill workers working in three shifts, night and day. From these and other studies Levi (1972) concludes that there can be little doubt that psychosocial stimuli can effect changes in sympathetic–adrenomedullary activity and adrenaline excretion. Most importantly for studies of the response to stress, he also concludes that, although intersubject variability is great, within the individual subject catecholamine excretion roughly parallels the degree of reported emotional arousal.

The study of pleasant and tranquil situations has allowed us to extend our knowledge of the control of the sympathetic–adrenomedullary system. Experimental situations evoking the experience of calmness and equanimity lower catecholamine excretion below control levels, while situations evoking amusement or a more general pleasant experience are nearly as potent as the aforementioned unpleasant situations in enhancing catecholamine excretion.

3.1.5 *Frankenhaeuser's Studies on Catecholamine Excretion*

Frankenhaeuser, working in the Experimental Psychology Unit at the University of Stockholm, has conducted a number of well-controlled laboratory studies which have served to identify a variety of factors affecting catecholamine excretion. These studies will be discussed in some detail.

The influence of *situational control* is illustrated in an experiment reported by Frankenhaeuser and Rissler (1970a). This experiment was designed to vary systematically the amount of control the subject was able to exert over his situation. This was accomplished by threatening him with punishment by electric shock, and by manipulating his ability to avoid that shock. In session I, the subject was exposed to unpredictable and uncontrollable shocks. Under these conditions, adrenaline excretion was about three times as high as when the subject was relaxed and not threatened (session IV). In sessions II and III, the subject performed a choice reaction task through which he could avoid some of the shocks. The degree of control possible was greater in session III than in session II. Increasing control in this way reduced adrenaline excretion from its high level under the conditions of session I. Noradrenaline excretion appeared elevated by participation in the shock sessions, but unaffected by variations in situational control.

Overstimulation and *understimulation* also appear to produce increases in catecholamine excretion. This was demonstrated in an experiment by Frankenhaeuser *et al.* (1971). This experiment involved three different levels of stimulation. During understimulation subjects performed a prolonged vigilance task in a sound-proof chamber, thus deprived of normal social and sensory inputs. During medium stimulation they read magazines and listened to the radio. Finally, during overstimulation they performed a very complex and demanding sensorimotor task involving both visual and auditory input. This was a modification of the Kieler test which has been used in the selection of airforce personnel. Both of the extreme conditions produced increased adrenaline and noradrenaline excretion in comparison to the moderate condition. Overstimulation in this experiment produced a greater effect than understimulation. Both situations were experienced as unpleasant.

Anticipation and *uncertainty* also appear to affect catecholamine excretion. In an experiment reported by Frankenhaeuser and Rissler (1970b) measurements of catecholamine excretion were made with subjects in two contrasting conditions of inactivity. One was characterised by anticipation and uncertainty. The subject was isolated in a sound-proof chamber and wired up for the recording of heart rate and for the presentation of electric shock. The subject was told that each change in heart rate would produce a shock. Some shocks were given. The other condition was one of relaxation in which the subject read magazines in a familiar part of the laboratory. The results showed that the more 'difficult' condition produced higher levels of adrenaline excretion, but did not alter noradrenaline output.

Physical activity has an interesting effect on catecholamine excretion as described by Frankenhaeuser and colleagues in 1969. Subjects were required to work on a bicycle ergonometer under conditions of increasing work load. A bicycle ergonometer was chosen as a suitable vehicle for studying the effects of physical activity in a 'psychologically neutral' situation. Excretion rates for both adrenaline and noradrenaline remained close to control levels at low work loads (<400 kg/m min). Higher work loads produced increases in the excretion of both catecholamines. The increased noradrenaline output appeared to be related to the cardiovascular response to muscular work, while, Frankenhaeuser (1975*a* and *b*) suggests, the rise in adrenaline output may be partly associated with the subjective emotional experience of that work.

Together these experiments appear to argue for a specificity in the stress response. Some situations produce changes in adrenaline output, others in both adrenaline and noradrenaline output. The former appear to be those that by their very nature involve a passive mode of response, the latter an active mode of response.

Over and above the effects of the four factors discussed are the large differences which occur in catecholamine excretion between individuals. Such differences can be partly accounted for in terms of differences in adjustment and coping and by sex differences.

Experimental analysis of relations between human performance and catecholamine excretion have revealed interesting results. Within a population of normal and healthy individuals those who have relatively higher catecholamine excretion levels tend to perform better in terms of speed, accuracy and endurance than those who have lower levels. This is demonstrated in two experiments. In the first experiment, (Frankenhaeuser and Rissler, 1970*b*) using a choice reaction time task, low catecholamine excretors had slower reaction times and made more errors than high catecholamine excretors. In the second experiment (Frankenhaeuser and Andersson, 1974), low catecholamine excretors performed more poorly than high catecholamine excretors in learning nonsense syllables by the anticipation method.

Although it has been generally assumed that when catecholamine excretion is expressed in relation to body weight no sex differences can be demonstrated (Kärki, 1956), Frankenhaeuser has provided an important qualification to this assumption. The assumption appears to be based on data collected from conditions of rest and inactivity; and when the sexes are compared under conditions of stress, differences can be seen (Johansson, 1972; Johansson and Post, 1972; Frankenhaeuser, 1975a). The two experiments reported by Frankenhaeuser's colleague Johansson serve to illustrate this difference. In the first experiment, Johansson (1972) investigated excretion in twelve-year-old boys and girls in a passive condition (watching a non-engaging motion picture) and in an active test condition (performing an attention-demanding arithmetical task). In the group of girls, adrenaline excretion was only slightly higher in the active condition than in the passive condition. In the group of boys, however, there was a significant and much more marked increase in excretion in the active compared with passive condition. In her second experiment, Johansson (Johansson and Post, 1972) examined adrenaline excretion in adult males and females during periods of routine activity and during intelligence testing. A similar pattern of results was obtained with the adult subjects as was obtained with twelve year olds. Little increase in adrenaline excretion was observed in females in the test situation compared to routine situations, while a marked increase was observed in males. Overall it is possible to postulate that women may be hypoactive in terms of their sympathetic–adrenomedullary response to stress.

3.1.6 Stress and Corticosteroid Excretion

Increased adrenocortical activity is reflected in increased plasma and urine levels of 17-hydroxycorticosteroids. Such increases have been noted in response to a variety of stresses: hospitalisation (Mason *et al.*, 1965), anticipation of laboratory procedures (Mason, 1959; Persky *et al.*, 1959), anticipation of thoracic surgery (Price *et al.*, 1957), medical exams (Bliss *et al.*, 1956), psychiatric interviews (Hetzel *et al.*, 1955; Persky *et al.*, 1958; Oken *et al.*, 1960), psychological tests (Freeman *et al.*, 1944; Korchin and Herz, 1960), driving (Frost *et al.*, 1951), flying activities (Craven and Smith, 1955; Colehour, 1964;

Hale *et al.*, 1968) and intense combat activity (Elmadjian, 1955; Pace *et al.*, 1956).

3.1.7 The Integration of the Endocrine Response to Stress

Much work in this area has been carried out by Mason at the Walter Reed Army Medical Center in Washington (see Mason, 1975), using male Rhesus monkeys working on a conditioned avoidance schedule. In the avoidance procedure the monkeys had to press a hand lever at a moderate but continuous rate to avoid an unpleasant foot shock. Measurements of response of a number of endocrine systems were taken before, during and after 72 hours of avoidance activity. During this test period urinary 17-hydroxycorticosteroids, adrenaline and noradrenaline levels rose, as did plasma levels of butanol-extractable iodine (indicator or thyroid activity) and growth hormone. However, urinary androgens and oestrogen levels fell, as did plasma insulin levels. The pattern of response suggests, according to Mason (1968), an organisation of neuroendocrine response in which levels of those hormones promoting catabolic mobilisation of energy resources rise during avoidance, whereas levels of those promoting anabolism decline. Investigation of hormone activity following the avoidance period revealed that, while the catabolic hormone levels declined, the levels of the anabolic hormones rose, and this during a period when restorative processes might logically be expected to occur.

Mason has also conducted a series of observations on the pattern of hormonal response in monkeys restrained in a chair. In comparison to the conditioned avoidance situation, restraint offers an unconditioned emotional stimulus, permitting only a passive behavioural response. The pattern of hormonal response observed was almost identical to that elicited by the early phase of the conditioned avoidance situation. The catabolic hormone levels rose and the anabolic hormone levels fell.

From these and other studies Mason (1975) has ventured some general conclusions on the pattern of hormonal response to stress. There can now be little doubt that a broad range of hormones and endocrine systems respond *concurrently* to stress. This supports the point made earlier in this chapter with regard to the involvement of adrenocortical activity in the alarm reaction. The broad range of systems referred to include not only adrenomedullary and adrenocortical systems, but also pituitary–thyroid, pituitary–

gonadal, growth-hormone and insulin systems. The most commonly observed pattern of response is that of an elevation of catabolic hormone levels and suppression of anabolic hormone levels. Within the systems mentioned the adrenocortical, sympathetic–adrenomedullary, and thyroid systems appear the most consistent from subject to subject in producing this pattern of response.

Mason (1975) has also discussed the important issue of the non-specificity of the stress response. To the points already raised, and in some cases answered, he adds one more. He has argued that the early research which appeared to demonstrate a non-specificity in the physiological response to stress-producing situations failed to identify a common component in those situations. It was assumed that there was no single stimulus which all the situations shared. Mason argues from his research that, although physiological systems respond to a variety of stimuli, the degree of non-specificity still remains to be determined. His research indicates that the more aspects of the physiological response that are measured the more distinctive the response pattern appears for each eliciting stimulus. The more stimuli studied the more distinctive the eliciting profile for each component of the physiological response becomes. He concludes that the integrative mechanisms controlling the response appear to be organised to react selectively in producing patterns of multiphysiological change which differ according to the specific stimulus. The theoretical interpretation of the significance of these specific patterns must be approached in terms of their metabolic effects. One aspect of this, changes in glucose metabolism, is dealt with in the next section.

3.1.8 Blood Glucose Levels and Stress

In stress-producing situations glucose is the person's most important source of immediately available energy. Both the central nervous system and the musculature are almost entirely dependent on it for the efficient performance of their functions. Neuromuscular activity plays a critical role in controlling and permitting the person's behavioural response to stress. Furthermore, glucose may also be required as a source of energy for the repair and regeneration of tissues damaged during the execution of those responses, and for heat generation during the period of shock when the body's temperature falls. In contrast to fats and proteins, which are other

67

possible sources of energy, carbohydrates tend not to yield toxic metabolites even if large quantities are suddenly catabolised. The utilisation of glucose by peripheral tissues therefore proceeds without risk to the person even if severe shock disrupts hepatic detoxification and renal elimination of metabolites. In acute emergencies the person is dependent on carbohydrate reserves, and primarily on blood glucose.

Normally the concentration of glucose in the blood is within the range 60–90 mg per 100 ml of plasma. It is kept within this range by a

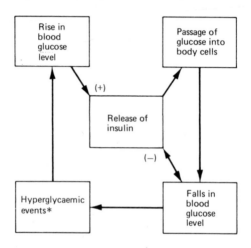

* Meals, action of glucagon or adrenaline, etc.

Figure 3.2: The Role of Insulin in Blood Glucose Regulation

complex set of regulatory mechanisms. The main problem of this regulation results from the average person's tendency to eat infrequently and then to consume relatively large quantities of food. Blood glucose levels rise dramatically immediately after such meals, and the main aim of regulation is to iron out this fluctuation.

The first line of defence is provided within the liver which receives all the portal vein blood from the gut. After a meal this blood is rich in glucose, and much of that glucose is converted to glycogen for subsequent storage. In contrast, between meals, when portal blood has a low glucose concentration, the liver glycogen breaks down to liberate glucose into the bloodstream. The liver mechanism thus tends to smooth out the naturally fluctuating blood glucose level.

The second line of defence is provided by the various endocrine secretions which affect total blood sugar level. Insulin is one of the better known. It is a protein which is released by the β cells of the pancreas, the islets of Langerhans. Insulin is known to be a hypoglycaemic agent—it lowers blood glucose levels. It does this in two ways. It stimulates the liver to convert glucose to glycogen and facilitates the passage of glucose from the blood into the body cells. In the absence of insulin many of these cells are virtually impermeable to glucose. Insulin also stimulates the formation of triglycerides in adipose tissue from the free fatty acids in the blood, and the manufacture of proteins from amino acids. Overall, it increases the availability of glucose and decreases that of fat. The output of insulin is directly controlled by the level of glucose in the blood. When this level rises, after a meal, more insulin is released, and as it falls under the action of the insulin, less of that agent is subsequently released. This mechanism provides a good example of a negative-feedback closed-loop control system (see figure 3.2). Insulin output is also affected by the activity of the vagus nerve. Direct control by blood glucose levels, however, appears to be the most important for moment-to-moment control of those levels.

Although hypoglycaemic activity is dominated by insulin, several hyperglycaemic agents are known. Most texts would until recently have stated that insulin worked in concert with adrenaline in moment-to-moment blood-glucose regulation. However, there is a growing belief that glucagon and not adrenaline fulfils this role. There are many reasons why this must be so. These range from embryological arguments, noting the similarities in the development and structure of the insulin and glucagon mechanisms, and the differences between these and those of adrenaline, to the more functional. The level of circulating adrenaline is too low to alter blood glucose levels significantly. Adrenaline release is mainly sensitive to conditions of stress.

Glucagon is a far more potent, hyperglycaemic agent which is directly affected by blood glucose levels. Adrenaline appears not to be. Glucagon is produced by the α cells of the pancreas (islets of Langerhans), and has precisely the opposite actions to insulin. It is argued here that moment-to-moment blood-glucose regulation is a matter of a push–pull mechanism involving insulin and glucagon (see figure 3.1). The glucocorticoids released by the adrenal cortex also stimulate glucose metabolism by depressing its utilisation by the

69

body cells, by increasing production of glucose from proteins, and by increasing storage of glucose as glycogen. Adrenaline, as has been stated above, is not routinely important in the control of blood glucose. It is, however, of great significance in emergencies, when it can raise levels rapidly. It does this by stimulating the breakdown of glycogen to glucose, and slowing down the rate at which muscle cells take glucose from the blood.

To understand glucose regulation, several points need to be borne in mind. Glucose is stored as glycogen in the liver, and also in muscle. When there is a severe or chronic call on glucose to provide a source of energy, blood glucose will be insufficient and stored glucose will need to be released. Muscle cells, which need glucose and which contain glycogen, face no problem, neither do brain cells which do not require insulin to promote their supply of glucose. For the other body cells there occurs a paradoxical situation in which the hyperglycaemic agents which can bring about increases in blood glucose also tend to inhibit its use by those cells. Hyperglycaemic agents therefore favour muscle and brain cells. This parallels and is obviously linked to the diversion of the blood supply by the sympathetic nervous system from the surface and visceral regions to the brain and to muscle. Brain cells, because they do not store glucose nor require insulin to accept it, are directly and uniquely reliant on circulating blood glucose.

The changes in blood glucose levels which occur in emergencies, in stress, can be accounted for by three models of the stress response, two of which have already been outlined. The first model is that of Selye's general adaptation syndrome, and describes the changes which occur when a person is exposed to chronic stress. The model describes a sequence of changes, starting with the early phases of the alarm reaction through to the final changes of death. According to Selye (1950), immediately upon exposure to stress (during the period of shock) there is an increase in the blood glucose level, the magnitude and persistance of which is determined by the liver glycogen reserves. This initial hyperglycaemic response was thought to be largely brought about by the emergency release of adrenaline. If the stress is sufficiently severe or liver glycogen reserves are low, there may follow a period of hypoglycaemia. If the stress is then prolonged, blood glucose levels return to normal, or just above normal, and remain so while the person appears to be coping effectively. This apparently normal situation, it is argued, may be a result of an increased production *and* utilisation of glucose, and this may reflect changes in glucocorticoid activity. Final exhaustion and collapse are accompanied by a drastic fall in blood glucose levels, and death may result from hypoglycaemia. Selye (1950) offers considerable evidence that, although certain stress situations may have specific effects on glucose metabolism, if these are allowed for it is striking how closely the most diverse of them produce the pattern of blood glucose change just discussed. Such evidence was, and is, part of Selye's argument for the non-specificity of the stress response.

Mason's research, as reviewed in 1968 and in 1975, has shown how blood glucose responds to the presentation and recovery from stress. On the occurrence of stress, blood glucose levels rise as part of an integrated pattern of catabolic response, and on the removal of the stress fall back towards and perhaps below normal, as part of a pattern of anabolic response. The decrease in blood glucose levels is not simply a passive reflection of a release from catabolic influence, but also involves, and this must be emphasised, an active anabolic process.

The third model is that derived from the work of the author and his colleagues at Nottingham. This model takes explicit account of the degree of stress experienced and the context in which it occurs, the two being very closely related. The model also introduces the hitherto unexplored possibility that blood glucose levels may, in some situations, *decrease* in response to stress. This is by no means an original suggestion, but is a possibility which is frequently ignored. Consider noise as a source of stress. The change in blood glucose levels which is brought about by different types of noise has been described in a number of isolated studies (Finkel and Poppen, 1948; Serra *et al.*, 1964; Ashbel, 1965; Fecci *et al.*, 1971), and by the present author and his colleagues as part of a developing line of research (Cox *et al.*, 1973; Simpson *et al.*, 1974*a* and *b*: Bradley *et al.*, 1975). Various patterns of response have been described, involving both increases and decreases. From what has been written earlier in this section, the demonstration of decreases during the presentation of stress is surprising. However, there is now much evidence from the activities of other physiological systems to support the possibility of a decrease. Cox and his colleagues extended their analysis of this 'decrease' and found its degree to be a function of a number of factors. The difficulty or demand involved in the situation appeared to be important. The decrease noted when their subjects were exposed to low levels of noise (after previously being loaded with extra glucose) was exaggerated when the noise level was increased and when a psychomotor task was added into the situation. The decrease response was obvious in their male subjects, but not in their female subjects. The original work used a relatively complex psychomotor task, but the generality of the phenomenon and the non-specificity of the response were established by later investigations of more simple psychomotor tasks, of choice reaction tasks, and of purely cognitive tasks.

Based on a consideration of the differences between these experiments (and others showing similar results) and those which show the classical increase response, it seems to the author and his colleagues that the degree of stress experienced is the key factor. In laboratory experiments the subject has final control over his situation, and most conditions of stress are not extreme. Most laboratory stresses are perceived as annoying, distracting or irritating rather than actually threatening. They can usually be dealt with by attentional strategies. When the subject is engaged on a specific task such stress and its effects can disrupt performance, perhaps by altering the ratio of signal (relevant information) to noise (irrelevant information). Stresses experienced in real situations are different in each respect. The person suffering the stress will probably not have a large degree of control over it. The stress may be very severe, and experienced as a real threat to survival; physical, psychological or social. The response to this stress involves much more than shifts in attention. Stress in the first context we would judge to be moderate, and believe that the response to moderate stress is a decrease in blood sugar levels moderated by activity in the vagal–insulin system. Stress in the second context we suggest is severe, and the response to severe stress is an increase in blood glucose levels brought about by sympathetic–adrenomedullary activity, pituitary–adrenocortical activity, or even vagal–glucagon activity.

To a certain extent this hypothesis was tested by the author and colleagues (Burrows et al., 1977) in an investigation of the response of trainee salesmen to a difficult communications exercise embedded in an induction course. Their responses were compared with those of members of the company's operations research department who were also taking the course. For the trainees, less well-equipped to handle the communications exercise, and who felt they were under assessment, the course was very threatening. However, for the operations research men the course was a release from their routine of work and was without critical payoff. As a result the course was not experienced as threatening or stressful. In the first group, the trainees, blood glucose levels rose dramatically in response to the communications exercise. In the second group, there was little or no blood glucose response. This fits the model.

Together the three models go a long way to describing the effects of stress on blood-glucose regulation in normal people. In chapter 4, this discussion is reopened and extended to embrace the diabetic.

3.2 THE PSYCHOLOGICAL RESPONSE TO STRESS

There has been a considerable volume of research concerned with the psychological response to stress, although much of it has not attracted that particular title. A number of distinct areas of concern can be recognised. In animals lower down the phylogenetic scale, interest has been shown in the behavioural concomitants of emotion (especially negative emotion such as fear), in the behavioural effects of punishment, and in conflict behaviour. In man, interest has centred on clinical, industrial and military situations. In the clinical situation the main concern has been the aetiology of neurotic disorder, and its possible precursors in changes in psychological well-being. In the industrial and military situations interest has also centred on individual well-being, but more particularly on the person's ability to maintain performance when exposed to extreme conditions. The key concept in understanding man's psychological response to stress is that of coping, which has already received mention in this book. As a result of these different foci of research there have been several different models developed to explain the psychological response to stress, each more-or-less adequate within its specific context but only partially adequate as a general model. None at present can provide a full and satisfactory account.

3.2.1 Flight, Fight and Freezing

Cannon's extensive research on cats led him to describe an active pattern of response to the acute stress of emergency situations, which was characterised as flight or fight. The preparation for, and facilitation of, these behaviours he saw as the function of the sympathetic nervous system and adrenal medulla. This has already been discussed earlier in this chapter. Another type of behavioural response often observed in animals exposed to danger is that of freezing. Gray (1971) has described freezing as 'silent, tense immobility'. There is some confusion as to whether freezing is an active or passive type of response. It is passive in that the animal shows no locomotor activity and is immobile. However, it is active in that the immobility is tense and involves considerable skeletal-muscle activity and energy expenditure. The animal's immobility is not a flaccid state, it is *not* a helpless response.

The literature on the behavioural response to punishment (aversive stimulation) presents a similar view of the possible types of response that can be elicited by acute noxious situations.

Miller and Weiss (1969) have suggested that two contrasting patterns of response exist. One, the suppression of behaviour, involves freezing, muteness, piloerection, defaecation and, in the extreme, feigning death (Miller, 1951). The other, the activation of behaviour, involves increased startle responses, vocalisations, and running and leaping. Azrin and his colleagues (1967) have discussed a third pattern of response, aggression, which can occur in response to aversive stimulation. Their view of the aetiology of aggression stands in marked contrast to that presented by Lorenz (1970). Lorenz expresses the belief that aggression is the result of an inherited spontaneous tendency, whose properties are much the same as those of the hunger or thirst drives. Ulrich and Azrin see it as a pattern of response elicited by aversive stimulation or pain. They (1962) report a series of experiments which illustrate their view of aggression. Pairs of normally docile and lethargic Sprague–Dawley rats were placed in a relatively small test chamber. At first they moved about the chamber, sniffing it and each other. They did not attack each other. However, on being shocked, a drastic change occurred in their behaviour. They reared up on to their hind legs, facing each other, and began lunging, striking and biting at the other. Such behaviour has been described by Scott and Frederickson (1951) as fighting, and this it obviously is to any observer. Increasing the intensity and frequency of the shock and reducing the size of the test chamber increases the frequency of the fighting response.

Gray (1971) has attempted to introduce some order into the relationships between the three response patterns. Freezing, he suggests, occurs during the anticipation of danger (or aversive stimulation). Escape (flight) and aggression (fight) occur, by contrast,

74

as a response to the presence of danger, or the presentation of aversive stimulation. It is adaptive, he argues, for an animal to respond to, say, the pain inflicted by a predator by struggling or running away. However, the adaptive response to the impending danger of a predator is to remain still, and thus escape attention. Such a scheme holds true for many species, for example the hare, the pheasant and the partridge, but not for all. The hedgehog will freeze and roll into a protective ball in response to immediate danger, while deer will take flight at the merest sign of danger. The rabbit will freeze when confronted by a stoat. It is obvious from these examples that there appears to be a natural variation between species in the dominant pattern of response to stress. Some demonstrate behavioural activation, others behavioural suppression. Obviously Gray's (1971) scheme is not completely adequate in describing which occurs in any situation. Two factors need to be considered in addition to Gray's. One is the species differences which occur in the relative dominance of the response patterns. The other is the physical (and psychosocial) constraints on the possible responses. For example, Blanchard and Blanchard (1969, 1971) have demonstrated that an approaching cat will elicit escape behaviour in a rat which is not confined, and freezing in one which is.

The description of the behavioural response to acute stress in terms of flight, fight and freezing is relatively well established in research with species other than man. The important question then remains, to what extent does it describe man's behaviour? The answer would appear to be 'only partially', as it relates in Lazarus' (1966, 1976) terms to 'direct action tendencies' only, and by the very nature of its development ignores 'cognitive' response processes. For man these may be at least as important as direct behavioural action, if not more important. Furthermore, it does not account for long-term exposure to stress.

Most discussions on the appropriateness of the flight, fight and freezing model in the description of man's behaviour under stress have an underlying evolutionary theme.

3.2.2 Evolution and the Stress Response

Behavioural and evolutionary processes are intimately related. Behaviour, like other biological parameters, is shaped by evolution, but at the same time it is a powerful force in determining natural selection and survival to reproduce. It can be assumed that patterns of behaviour, like flight, fight and freezing, are adaptive, or at the very least neutral, because they are common to a large number of species. Their independent emergence in these species must provide a good example of convergent evolution. The adaptiveness of these behaviour patterns is a reflection of the species' particular interactions (or transactions) with their environments. If an environment changes radically, previously adaptive behaviours may become maladaptive, and begin to evolve out as a species responds and changes its characteristics, or are lost as the species is lost through extinction. The question for industrial man is that of the adaptiveness of behaviours like flight and fight in the context of his civilised environment. If they are maladaptive, as many writers suggest, that may be at the core of the so-called human dilemma. It is possible that, although such behaviours may be innate responses to stress, they are suppressed in industrial man in favour of cognitive responses which are more appropriate in his present environment. Their potentially maladaptive nature may not find expression. However, this in itself may be the source of another problem—Catch 22. The physiological response to stress according to, say, Cannon, prepares for flight or fight, which are suppressed in man. There results a failure to utilise, in an appropriate manner, the energy mobilisation caused by the physiological changes, and this may increase the rate of wear and tear on the body, giving rise to the pathology of stress. Self-control may take a toll in the long run. This is the cost of 'civilised' behaviour.

One aspect of cost is reflected in physical illness, another in mental illness. The expression of the latter may involve an evolutionary throwback. This has been suggested by Price (1967). The evolution of man as a hunter involved a move from a forest life to life on the savanna, and according to some authorities a shift from relaxed and loosely organised social hierarchies, characteristic of chimpanzees, to more rigid baboon-like hierarchies. The change was necessitated by the need for group hunting. With the change in the nature of social organisation, evolution tended to favour individuals who correctly identified their position and role in the hierarchy and behaved accordingly. Price (1967) believes that mental illness first occurred in these hierarchies and that some current disorders could be viewed in that context. For example, anxiety neurosis and schizophrenia may have been diseases of humility, occurring among subordinate individuals subjected to unusually severe stress. Dominant individuals, in contrast, would be vulnerable in other ways. Perhaps not being subjected to poor shelter, food storage, or to being attacked as their subordinates were, they would suffer diseases of arrogance—megalomania, delusions of grandeur, and psychopathy. Depression might reflect loss of position, and mania reflect movement upwards, in the hierarchy. Current mental illness, in response to stress, may be re-enactments of conflicts in these early evolutionary hierarchies. An interesting point about this view is that it could discourage the establishment of hierarchies in psychiatric institutions, and of competition among patients leading to dominant and submissive behaviours.

3.2.3   The General Adaptation Syndrome and Man's Behaviour

The experience of stress in man has been viewed as producing a disruption of psychological equilibrium which brings into play homeostatic mechanisms to reduce its impact. These mechanisms have been described as coping (see the next section), and are a part of the overall pattern of behaviour. Coping may simply involve a reorganisation of the usual pattern of behaviour, and the reorganised behaviour may still be within the range of normal behaviour. However, if this normal coping is unsuccessful in reducing or removing the experience of stress, then reorganisation may give rise to the disorganisation of behaviour. As the normal pattern of behaviour breaks down, abnormal behaviours may arise. Finally, if this extreme form of coping fails then there may be a total collapse of behaviour. This progression may represent a behavioural analogue to the general adaptation syndrome (see figure 3.3). In the face of the continued experience of stress, the immediate response gives way to a marked reorganisation of behaviour which may continue to the point of disorganisation, and lead to final collapse. During Selye's alarm reaction, the immediate response and the subsequent reorganisation of behaviour are an attempt to effect a level of coping sufficient to meet the level of demand. The reorganisation that occurs may maintain this balance or it may not. This represents Selye's phase of resistance. If it does not, the change in behaviour may become more and more radical in a desperate attempt to achieve and maintain the critical balance. Disorganisation may occur, and lead to total behavioural collapse. The final collapse represents Selye's final phase of exhaustion.

The reorganisation of behaviour may involve several particular changes. First, newly acquired behaviours may be shed with a reversion to older more established ones. Under the experience of stress man tends to 'do what he knows best'. This may, from the evidence of common experience, be accompanied by a switch from behaviour guided by more-or-less logical reasoning to that determined more basically by the emotions. With reorganisation, one particular response may come to dominate and stereotypy occur. This sort of

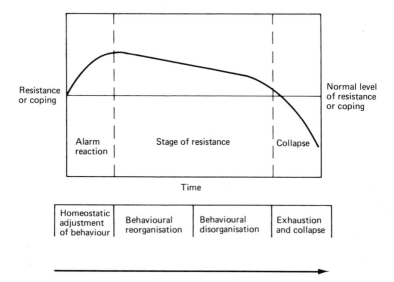

Figure 3.3: The General Adaptation Syndrome: Behavioural Analogue

response fixation or perseveration may result from situations where none of the possible forms of coping represents a solution to the problem of stress. None is thus rewarded, and all are, in this sense, punished. Stereotypy may result from the operation of this particular reinforcement schedule, and may be an accompaniment or alternative to helplessness.

3.2.4   Lazarus: the Concept of Coping

Important for the preceding discussion is the concept of coping. The development of this concept owes much to the writings and thoughts of Lazarus at the University of California at Berkeley. 'Coping', he writes, 'is best considered as a form of problem solving in which the stakes are the person's well-being, and the person is not entirely clear about what to do'. It specifically refers to dealing with demanding situations which are experienced as stressful. Through coping the person attempts to master those situations. According to Lazarus (1966, 1976), coping can involve two processes, one direct action, and the other palliation.

Direct Action. Direct action refers to actual behaviour aimed at changing the person's relationship with his environment, and can take several forms: preparation against harm, aggression and avoidance (and inaction). What Lazarus means by 'avoidance' is removing oneself from the presence of actual danger of threat. Perhaps 'escape' is a more appropriate term: it is the one adopted by the present author.

Preparation against harm is a form of true avoidance behaviour in which the person can take action in anticipation of danger. If his avoidance behaviour is appropriate and effective, then the signs of danger will recede. If not the danger may become manifest. Among the possibilities which exist for this form of direct action are the reduction of the actual danger, and the reduction of its threat value. Both may take the form of strengthening the person's resources to withstand the danger when it occurs.

Students' reactions to their final examinations provide good examples of preparation against harm. Since their examinations usually conform to a well-established pattern, the students have months, if not years, in which to make ready. As the danger (that of failing, with all its implications for career development) approaches, more and more of the students adopt the strategy of intensive study, progressively increasing the hours and depth of their work. As the examinations draw still closer, further increasing effort is possibly no longer productive or feasible, and other coping strategies have to be employed. One common phenomenon is the appearance of rumours and predictions about the actual nature of examination questions, and the severity in marking of different examiners. Despite the obvious inadequacy of the evidence on which these speculations are repeatedly based, they tend to be accepted and taken into account by the students. Should these attempts at coping fail to reduce the anticipated danger more extreme courses may be embarked on. The first is the denial of the importance of the examinations, and thus an immediate reduction in the penalty for failing. This denial may be supported by a reorganisation of the person's social relations, with the student seeking the company of other 'deniers', and avoiding the more realistic of their friends. When all else has failed the students may become physically ill, to an extent that requires hospitalisation. This removes them from the examination, and places the responsibility for this action on the illness or the attending physician. If the students are unable to become ill they may simply opt out, and after walking out of an examination, the public declaration of opting out, leave their university or college for some outside retreat. Two short case studies serve to illustrate some of the points made; both refer to final year university students facing their degree examinations.

L. A month before his examinations this student withdrew from academic contact with his tutor and fellow students. However, he continually assured them that he was working well. Close to the examinations he openly expressed fears that some of the examiners were biased against him, but these fears were allayed. He sat the first of his examination papers, and did reasonably well. He walked out of the second paper and left the university. He explained in a letter to his tutor that he had decided to opt out, and had ensured that he could not be contacted.

D. This student had always worked hard, and was most conscientious. About two months before the examinations she complained that a bad 'cold' was disrupting her work. The 'cold' continued to affect her for several weeks, and during this time she became more and more concerned with anticipating likely questions, and biases in the examiners. Close to the examinations, the student began complaining of an irritant 'rash'. As the 'rash' developed, the 'cold' receded, and the student became more concerned with studying the examiners than her subject. Fortunately, she managed to sit her examinations and achieved an acceptable grade.

Several of these observations on the behaviour of students preparing for critical examinations have also been made by Mechanic (1962) in his studies of American graduate students working towards their doctorate examinations.

Aggression often appears to accompany the experience of stress, but may not always be appropriate and thus effective as a form of coping.

As a form of coping it involves attacking the source of the person's problems, which may be perceived as a particular individual, or as a group of individuals, or as an organisation. Destroying, or at least hurting, the source of the problem may remove the person from danger, or reduce his experience of stress. The critical aspect of aggression in response to stress is the identification of a target. Targets may not always represent the actual source of the person's problems as much as a suitable and acceptable focus for action. This will be discussed again later in terms of displacement. A man may thus attack his wife when the real source of his problem is his immediate superior at work. His wife, however, may be a more vulnerable target with less counter-strike capability. For such a redirected attack to be an effective form of coping the man must come to perceive his wife as a source of demand in his stressful situation. If this is an obvious misperception, then subsequent feelings of guilt may arise and augment his experience of stress. Whatever its mechanism and implications, the fact of such an attack fits with Azrin and Ulrich's description of aggression as a response to aversive stimulation in rats (see section 3.2.1).

If the problems facing human society increase then there will probably be an increase in stress-induced aggression. Possibly this may come to be a dominant theme in future societies, and unless 'managed' may give rise to the next phase of human development, and the final phase of civilisation, a return to barbarianism. In the same vein as this forecast, one can detect in history a recurrent theme of internal national crises being 'solved' by the countries' engagement in external disputes or wars. For example, the internal upheaval of the French Revolution was partly solved by the precipitation of the Franco-Austrian war. The usual explanation offered is that these external adventures divert the people's attention from the country's internal problems and produce unity. An alternative hypothesis, and one which is as feasible in the present context, is that increased aggression becomes the dominant response to crisis and this shapes the country's policy, including foreign policy. A suitable target is chosen for attack, and the aggressive response can be worked through at an international level.

Perhaps it is sensible to classify aggressive behaviour at the individual level in three ways. First, in terms of the target chosen for the aggressive act, then in terms of the nature of the act, and last in terms of whether or not the aggression is accompanied by the emotion of anger. The outline of this classification is laid out in figure 3.4. One example will suffice. Consider first a dispute between neighbours resulting in one verbally abusing the other in an obvious outburst of anger, accompanied and made more dramatic by appropriate posturing and fist waving. The analysis of this event would be: target—particular individual; nature of aggression—verbal with ritualisation; and emotion—with anger. Such behaviour may settle the dispute and remove the source of stress, or increase the

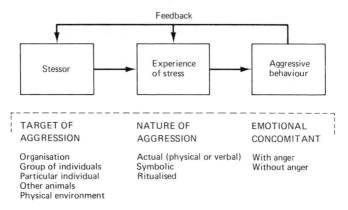

Figure 3.4: *Possible Classification of Aggressive Behaviour*

neighbours' individual self-esteem and reduce their experience of stress.

Escape is the third form of direct-action coping discussed by Lazarus (1966, 1976). Just as anger is often cited as the emotional correlate to aggression, then fear is cited as the same for escape. The soldier who runs from the field of battle, who deserts, may be showing escape with fear.

Aggression and escape have thus been described by Lazarus as responses to stress. Renamed as fight and flight they are already familiar (see section 3.2.1), as is the last of his direct action concepts, inactivity. This has already been discussed in terms of freezing, as an immediate response to the onset of stress. Inactivity may also be discussed as a long-term response to the chronic experience of stress. It may then be related to depression and feelings of hoplessness.

Hopelessness. Depression appears to be a common clinical result of severe (chronic) exposure to stress. In depression, the patient may express feelings of hopelessness, and display what is called psychomotor retardation. This is a form of relative inactivity, obvious in an extremely slow and apathetic response to any kind of stimulation.

Certain situations which produce stress may permit no grounds for hope that that stress may be relieved and actual harm avoided. Perhaps because of the absence of any obvious ways of coping, the person may not develop any desire to cope, and loses the ability to do so. Inaction may result from the apparent hopelessness of the situation (Lazarus, 1976). Such situations in which a person is totally resigned to his fate are possibly rare, and certainly not well understood. They are rare, because people are normally sufficiently imaginative to create grounds for hope, no matter how small or shaky. People do tend to grasp at straws. Furthermore, it is an unresolved debate as to whether hopelessness is lack of coping, as suggested above, or indeed a form of coping; a parallel to freezing and perhaps feigning death.

Relatively recently, Seligman (1975) has promoted the development of this concept. From his research on infra-human species, which was within the framework of operant conditioning, he has argued that life events have their greatest effects when the person is unable to control them. If they cannot by their actions affect their situation then feelings of *helplessness* develop along with the associated behavioural inactivity. This response can become generalised and eventually lead to the development of clinical depression and anxiety.

Both hopelessness (Lazarus, 1976) and helplessness (Seligman, 1975) may result from a perceived or actual ineffectiveness of coping or lack of opportunity to cope, and both may develop into clinical disorder. In accepting them as valid aspects of the response to stress, one immediately places a constraint on the way help is administered. To be effective, help should re-establish the person's control over his situation, if only through suggesting possible ways of coping. Help which does not do this may leave the person still feeling helpless, and seeing *his* situation as hopeless. Although such help may provide immediate relief, if that occurs at all it will be short-lived.

Palliation.   Instead of being expressed in the form of direct action, coping may involve palliation. Palliation is a matter of moderating the distress caused by the experience of stress, and reducing its psychophysiological effects. This may be achieved in several ways.

Lazarus (1976) distinguishes between *symptom-directed* modes and *intrapsychic* modes. The former include the use of alcohol, tranquillisers, and sedatives, training in muscle relaxation and other body-centred techniques. Intrapsychic palliation, on the other hand, has been discussed in terms of cognitive defence mechanisms. The description of these owes much to the development of psychoanalytical thought. Freud (1946) used the term defence mechanism to refer to an unconscious psychological manoeuvre by which means the person may deceive himself about the presence of threatening impulses or external dangers. Implied in 'defence' is that it is the perception of the threat of danger that is reduced and not its reality. Lazarus (1976) discussed intrapsychic palliation in terms of these mechanisms, and has named several as of particular importance: identification, displacement, repression, denial, reaction formation, projection and intellectualisation.

There are two major problems associated with the use of the concept of the defence mechanisms. First, is it necessary to hold that this form of palliation is unconscious? This would seem to be an unnecessary and unwarranted restriction of the concept; in many situations the person may deliberately employ one or other of the named defence mechanisms to convince themselves that their dilemma is not as bad as originally perceived. Second, embedded as it is in the body of psychoanalysis, the concept of defence is difficult to evaluate scientifically, and is thus open to criticism on those grounds. Theories of defence are in the main loose and descriptive, and not predictive. Despite this they have, like most psychoanalytical concepts, had some impact on psychological thought and the practice of psychology.

Of the defence mechanisms mentioned, three will be commented on in more detail: displacement, denial, and intellectualisation. The direct expression of coping may not be possible because of the psychosocial or physical consequences of that coping. Such frustration may be avoided by the *displacement* of coping activity into new and acceptable channels or forms of expression. Displacement most often occurs in the context of aggression and sex. Displaced or redirected aggression often appears inappropriate, and this apparent inappropriateness has been noted in many species other than man. Much of our knowledge of displacement activity has come from the study of conflict situations by contemporary European ethologists.

The displacement of aggression occurs, for example, when a person inhibits the expression of aggressive behaviour toward a more powerful adversary, and displays it toward another less powerful one. This process has already been referred to in the context of choosing a suitable target for aggressive direct action.

In *denial*, the person copes with threat or danger simply by denying that it exists. Denial is usually seen as related to repression, in that repression involves a denial of internal threatening impulses. Denial to be effective may require the construction of elaborate cognitive mechanisms for dealing with information which makes false the denial. For example, the physician who informs the heart-attack victim of the seriousness of his attack, in the face of the victim's denial, may be discredited in the eyes of that victim and his information thus dismissed.

Intellectualisation is a defence through which the person can gain emotional detachment from a threatening situation by treating it analytically, as a subject for study or of curiosity. For example, the physician mentioned above may treat his heart-attack patient as emotionally neutral, an impersonal case, number so-and-so, as a typical cardiac arrest or whatever. The physician may control his own feelings by avoiding identifying too closely with the patient or his suffering. A professional person, the physician, the psychologist or nurse, may for this reason not bring his skills to bear on someone who is emotionally close to him. In such a situation detachment could not be easily maintained.

3.2.5 A Case Study: M

The following case study will serve to underline the comments made on displacement, denial, and intellectualisation.

The person in question, M, is in her late twenties, and married with two children. She-comes from a middle-class professional background, is 'protestant', though not actively religious. She was brought up in a traditionally close community, and educated in fee-paying schools, eventually qualifying in one of the 'helping' professions. Her background is remarkably similar to that described for the American Mercury astronauts (see chapter 1: Korchin and Ruff, 1964; Ruff and Korchin, 1964). They were described by Korchin and Ruff as able and intelligent, free from self-doubts, persevering, highly controlled and accurate in their testing of reality. Such a description would also fit M. One of the differences between M's personality and that of the astronauts lies with M's apparent lack of (career) ambition; the astronauts all were ambitious men.

M's husband was transferred from one part of the country to another as a result of job promotion. Following the announcement of the impending move a very demanding situation arose for M. Difficulties in finding a house near to her husband's new job meant that he had to live away from home for several months. The practical and emotional problems which this gave rise to were compounded by another factor. M did not want to leave the community in which her immediate family was, until then, well established. Furthermore she had a particular dislike for the part of the country and the type of community into which she was to move. The move itself meant a fall in her standard of living, for although it was the result of promotion for her husband, house prices and the general cost of living were significantly higher in the area of his new job. The finding of a new house would signal M's actual move and was thus perceived as threatening. It would, however, reunite her family. A period arose for M in which she was thus subjected to a number of pressures: first, the practical and emotional difficulties of maintaining a 'separated' family, a second the threat of the unwanted relocation, and third, a near classical approach–avoidance over the purchase of a new house.

Viney and Bazeley (1977) have carried out a comprehensive study of the impact of community relocation, of the sort described here, on the affective state of Australian housewives. Their data, albeit collected after relocation, confirm that it can have a considerable emotional effect on housewives. They noted two particular sources of anxiety in their affective responses, one involving feelings of loneliness and loss (separation anxiety), and the other, feelings of inadequacy and embarrassment. Following on from this and their other observations, they suggest that 'women who are at risk for one of several reasons may, on relocation, develop depression and loneliness, and with the high cost of every attempt at coping this could characterise 'suburban neurosis'.

As M's situations developed she demonstrated various forms of cognitive defence. *Denial and repression* were perhaps the most obvious, and for quite a long time her pattern of life continued with complete and deliberate ignorance of the impending move. Her increased feelings of aggression were, at first, *displaced* from her husband, the actual but innocent source of her problems, towards her neighbours and their children. However, both these mechanisms became less effective as time passed. Denial in the face of the progression of events became no longer feasible and gave way to *intellectualisation*. M began to admit to her situation and the move but approached them dispassionately, planning and behaving as if for someone else. It is easy in this instance to see the element of denial and repression in her intellectualisation, and why one developed into the other. Her aggression now became directed towards her husband.

Up until the failure of intellectualisation and displacement M had remained in apparent and effective control over herself and events which pertained to her. However, just before the move, following completion on her new house and a farewell party, cognitive defence broke down. Her aggression gave way to depression. She experienced classical feelings of loneliness and hopelessness, along with apathy, and she became obviously inactive.

At the crisis point, help was forthcoming and was aimed at re-establishing the effectiveness of her cognitive defences, and thus allowing her to regain control over her situation. This was partially effective, and the physical relocation was accomplished without further emotional crises. After relocation, M became depressed for a short time, and as the depression lifted she developed a very active involvement with her new church.

This particular case illustrates a number of phenomena already discussed in this and other chapters. It shows the development of different coping strategies in the face of continued stress, and it shows the point at which 'normal' coping becomes, in a sense, 'abnormal'. It provides an example of three types of cognitive defence mechanism, and the aetiology and syndrome of depression. It is worth noting that the present brief case description does not do justice to the severity of the demands faced by M. Her ability to cope was remarkable, and only briefly interrupted by her experience of depression. The similarities between her background and personality and those of the Mercury astronauts were noted earlier because the latter were presented as examples of people with high resistance to stress.

Resistance to stress and the ability to adjust to cope with it are sorely tested by extreme life experiences such as heart attacks, severe burning, bereavement, community catastrophes, prison camps and war, attempted muder and rape. All can question the person's very physical and psychological survival. Of these, rape will be considered in more detail.

3.2.6 Rape: the Coping Behaviour of the Victim

Rape is a crisis situation which unexpectedly breaks the balance between the victim and her world; it is an interaction between an extreme environmental situation and the adaptive capacity of the victim. It is an overwhelmingly frightening experience in which the victim fears for her life, and is forced to pay for the chance of survival in a sexual act. Rape is a crisis of self preservation.

In a relatively recent series of papers, Burgess and Holstrom (1974, 1976) have described the responses of a diverse group of women to forcible rape. Their studies are interesting, not only because they have concentrated on rape victims rather than offenders, but because the authors have analysed in some detail the coping behaviour of those victims.

The sample that they studied consisted of 92 adult women who entered the emergency ward of Boston City Hospital during a one-year period with the complaint of being forcibly raped. From the results of their study, Burgess and Holstrom have described the victims' response to the threat of attack, their response during the attack, and their long-term response. The word attack is used here deliberately because Burgess and Holstrom (1974) appear to emphasise that it was not the rape that many victims felt so upsetting but the feeling that they would be killed as a result of the assault.

The *threat of attack* occurs when the victim realises that there is a definite danger to her life through sexual assault. Coping at this stage generally took the form of an attempt to 'avoid' the situation, and two definite types of strategy were observed. The majority of victims used one or more of a variety of *verbal strategies*, such as stalling for time, reasoning, pleading, joking or threatening. Some victims attempted to defend themselves by *physical action*, by attacking their assailant or by fleeing. One-third of the victims, however, reported being unable to do anything in response to the threat of attack. Some said they felt physically paralysed, others blanked out, others were simply overpowered before they could act. Multiple attempts at coping were common.

At the moment of the actual rape assault it is obvious to the victim that forced sexual attack was inescapable. Coping then became a matter of survival. Victims coped at this point in a variety of ways. *Cognitive strategies* played a most important part in survival. Victims said that they often attempted to concentrate on some specific thought or mental activity to prevent the reality of the situation from having its full impact. Denial of and dissociation from the events of the rape were common. Victims reported trying to keep calm not to provoke further violence and to be compliant to 'get it over with'. They also reported praying for help, and trying to memorise details about their assailant. *Verbal strategies* were again common. They either took the form of screaming and yelling to relieve tension, to defer the assailant and to attract attention, or of talking to avoid further violence or demands. Occasionally sarcasm and threat were used. Some victims struggled although this was usually what the assailant wanted. Several reported uncontrolled physiological responses (including screaming) such as choking, nausea and vomiting, hyperventilation, and loss of consciousness.

The *long-term responses* could be divided into an acute phase of disorganisation, followed by a long-term reorganisation. In the immediate hours following the rape, the victims experienced an extremely wide range of effects. Generally, however, these are consistent with one of two emotional styles: the expressed style, and the controlled style. The first type was manifest in crying and sobbing, restlessness and tenseness, the second type was one in which feelings were masked or hidden, and a calm, composed or subdued effect was seen. A fairly equal number of women were observed to show each style.

During the first several weeks following a rape many acute somatic reactions became apparent. These seemed to relate either to the physical effects of the attack or to its psychological effects. Tension headaches, fatigue and sleep disturbances were common reactions, as were loss of appetite and nausea.

Victims expressed a wide gamut of feelings as they began to deal with the after-effects of the rape. These feelings ranged from fear, humiliation and embarrassment to anger, revenge and self-blame. Fears of physical violence and death were the primary feelings reported. All the victims studied by Burgess and Holmstrom experienced disorganisation of their life style following the rape. The rebuilding of their lives, the long-term reorganisation, began at different times for the different victims. The different types of reorganisation had several common components. Many victims moved house or took long trips. Most changed their telephone numbers, taking unlisted (ex-directory) ones. The victims tended to relate more closely to family members and friends. More than three-quarters had some social network support to which they turned. Neurosis developed in many. Nightmares were common. Two types seemed to occur, both related to assault. In the first the victim wished to act against the assault but awoke before they could. In the second, which usually followed on from the first as time passed, the victim managed to master the situation, perhaps extracting revenge. Strong fears were also common, of further assault or trauma, of sex, of crowds and of people in general—'Inside I feel every man is the rapist'.

The sociobehavioural readjustment, the psychological and physical damage represent only part of the cost of rape. Society has tended to make victims of victims, not always treating them with understanding and compassion, and supporting and counselling them, but often blaming them, rejecting them and exposing them.

The work of Burgess and Holmstrom has detailed the way in which a group of women reacted to an extremely stressful situation. It has also provided a real example of much of what has been written in the latter half of this chapter. Most important of all it has helped in the development and improvement of the way in which rape victims are helped.

4

Stress and Health

Clare Bradley and Tom Cox

The World Health Organization defines 'health' as the presence of physical and emotional (psychological) well-being. The cost of stress is expressed in terms of its effect on that well-being. Perhaps the disorders which have attracted most attention in this respect are the neuroses, coronary heart disease, and alimentary conditions such as dyspepsia and ulcers. With a wealth of available evidence there can be little doubt that the experience of stress is important in these disorders, in contributing to their aetiology, and in producing an unfavourable prognosis. However, stress is possibly important for a large number of other conditions, including diabetes mellitus and bronchial asthma. In 1973, Ferguson reported a study on the health of Australian telegraphists; this study is also discussed in chapter 7. The telegraphists work was held to be highly stressful, the causes of stress being identified as monotony, machine pacing, and highly skilled but repetitive work carried out in noisy conditions. The evidence collected by Ferguson showed that neurosis among this group was high. Twenty-one per cent of all telegraphists, for example, had been absent from work for reasons attributable to neurosis, whereas of engineers and clerks only three and eight per cent, respectively, had been absent for this reason. Among the disorders found to be more prevalent for telegraphists were asthma, tremor (fingers) and chronic nasal disorders due to smoking. Moreover, those telegraphists diagnosed as neurotic exhibited higher incidences of peptic ulcers, dyspepsia, occupational cramp, and chronic eczema. Table 4.1 lists some of the many behavioural, physiological and 'health' effects which have been variously suggested to be linked to the experience of stress.

Table 4.1   The Effects and Cost of Stress

1. Subjective Effects	2. Behavioural Effects
Anxiety, aggression, apathy, boredom, depression, fatigue, frustration, guilt and shame, irritability and bad temper, moodiness, low self-esteem, threat and tension, nervousness, and loneliness.	Accident proneness, drug taking, emotional outbursts, excessive eating or loss of appetite, excessive drinking and smoking, excitability, impulsive behaviour, impaired speech, nervous laughter, restlessness, and trembling.
3. Cognitive Effects	4. Physiological Effects
Inability to make decisions and concentrate, frequent forgetfulness, hypersensitivity to criticism, and mental blocks.	Increased blood and urine catecholamines and corticosteroids, increased blood glucose levels, increased heart rate and blood pressure, dryness of mouth, sweating, dilation of pupils, difficulty breathing, hot and cold spells, 'a lump in the throat', numbness and tingling in parts of the limbs.
5. Health Effects	6. Organisational Effects
Asthma, amenorrhoea, chest and back pains, coronary heart disease, diarrhoea, faintness and dizziness, dyspepsia, frequent urination, headaches and migraine, neuroses, nightmares, insomnia, psychoses, psychosomatic disorder, diabetes mellitus, skin rash, ulcers, loss of sexual interest and weakness.	Absenteeism, poor industrial relations, and poor productivity, high accident and labour turnover rates, poor organisational climate, antagonism at work and job dissatisfaction.

The present chapter considers three particular disorders: coronary heart disease, bronchial asthma and diabetes mellitus. An account of the neuroses in relation to stress and drugs is presented in chapter 6. The three rather different physical disorders have been deliberately chosen for study to make the point that stress is not only important in psychological disorders, or in a narrow group of 'special' physical disorders. Taking an extreme position one may even argue that the very nature of stress as defined in chapter 1 means that it cannot fail to be implicated in some way in every illness and disease. Research should not therefore be concerned with which disorders are affected or caused by stress, but with how each disorder is affected.

4.1 DISEASES OF ADAPTATION

It has been argued in chapter 1, and the argument is developed in chapter 3, that excessive or inappropriate stress responses can produce structural or functional damage in the person. This is Selye's thesis, and it is mainly concerned with the ability of the physiological stress response to produce physical disease. Such diseases Selye termed diseases of adaptation; they are the outcome of an essentially useful defence mechanism. He argues that this group of diseases includes, among other disorders, all the psychosomatic diseases, allergies, and other immunological responses, as well as excessive inflammatory reactions. Thus peptic ulcer may be caused by a burn, or a cardiac accident may follow a violent marital dispute.

Diseases of adaptation follow from the non-specific stress response. Their apparent specificity is produced by the action of conditioning factors; these were discussed in chapter 3. They determine which pathways and organ systems will be most sensitive and affected in any stress situation. Some individuals may respond to stress by developing coronary heart disease, others by suffering alimentary disorder or diabetes mellitus, and so on.

Most of the conditions named by Selye as diseases of adaptation have been shown to have some psychological factors important in their aetiology and progress. However, where theories exist as to the mechanism by which these factors have their impact, they are not always completely consistent with Selye's general theory. It has become obvious that the concept of diseases of adaptation is one which is applicable but only superficially.

4.2 STRESS AND CORONARY HEART DISEASE

It is a very popular belief that coronary heart disease is related to the experience of stress, and this belief is by no means new. Corvisart, 150 or so years ago, attributed all heart disease to two principle causes: 'from the action of the organ and from the passions of man'. He believed that the heart could be injured by crying in infancy, by wrestling, by fencing, by playing wind instruments, by laughing and weeping, by reading and declamation, and by 'every kind of effort', as well as by 'anger, madness, fear, jealousy, love, despair, joy, avarice, cupidity, ambition, (and) revenge'. Thus exposed it is a wonder that man has survived the century and a half since Corvisart.

4.2.1   Stress in the Aetiology of Coronary Heart Disease

In 1958, Russek and Zohman reported a study of 100 young coronary patients between 25 and 40 years of age. Of these, 89 had confirmed myocardial infarctions, while 11 suffered from typical angina pectoris without infarction. Evaluations and interviews were conducted during the late convalescent period following acute myocardial infarction or in the succeeding months following the attack. The patients with angina pectoris without myocardial infarction were studied in a similar manner while under treatment for their disorder. Information was gathered concerning, *inter alia*, habits, diet, sources of tension and life events preceding the onset of clinical symptoms. For comparison, a control group of 100 healthy subjects of similar age, occupation and ethnic origin was studied. The most striking differences between the two groups are due to the experience of stress. Prolonged stress, largely associated with job responsibility preceded the attack in 91 per cent of the coronary group, but was experienced by only 20 per cent of the controls. In the coronary group, 25 per cent were coping with two jobs, and an additional 46 per cent had worked 60 hours or more per week for some time prior to the onset of symptoms. In another 20 per cent, there were reports of unusual fear, insecurity, discontent, frustration, restlessness or inadequacy in relation to their work. The authors concluded that stress associated with job responsibility appears far more significant in the aetiology of coronary disease in young adults than hereditary conditions or a prodigiously high fat diet. They also added that more-or-less without exception the young coronary patient was aggressive and ambitious, and had lived beyond his normal capacity and tempo (see section 4.2.4).

In 1962, Russek reported a study on American physicians which largely supported his earlier conclusions. Four professional groups were investigated: two prejudged by independent assessors to be in 'high stress areas of medical practice (general practitioners and anaesthetists) and two in low stress area (pathologists and dermatologists). Questionnaires were sent out to 1000 physicians in each group. From an analysis of the return (64.7 per cent), it was im-

94

mediately and clearly obvious that the high stress groups were more prone to coronary heart disease than the low stress groups. The prevalence of coronary disease was least among dermatologists, 40 to 69 years, and highest among general practitioners of the same age; 3.2 per cent compared with 11.9 per cent.

There is wide support for both sets of findings in the literature. For example, in relation to the cause of coronary heart disease mentioned in the first study, Buell and Breslow (1960) have also shown that hours of work is an important factor. In a study of the registered mortality rate of men in California, they observed that workers under the age of 45 in light industry, who are on their job more than 48 hours per week, had twice the risk of death as other 'light' workers of a similar age. More recent evidence is provided in a study reported by Wolf in 1971. Sixty-five patients who had undergone a well-documented myocardial infarction were studied over a subsequent period of seven years. These findings were compared with those from an equal number of healthy control subjects matched for age, sex, race, height and weight, education and occupation. Many different psychological and physiological measurements were taken during a period of study. Evidence of dejection and dissatisfaction with achievements was encountered in two-thirds of the patient population, but in only 10 of the 65 controls. Moreover, these depressive manifestations were found to be associated with marked fluctuations in the patients' physiological state. For example, in terms of diastolic and systolic blood pressure, the patient group showed a greater variability in blood pressure from time-to-time than did the control group. The patients that died of coronary heart disease showed even greater variability. A study by Bruhn and his colleagues (1970) confirms this suggested relationship between emotional state, physiological condition and coronary heart disease. Forty-eight patients suffering myocardial infarctions, who were admitted to a four-bed coronary care unit over a period of 90 consecutive days, were studied. Of particular interest were their reactions to cardiac emergencies, sudden arrests or death, which involved other patients in the unit. Of 17 patients who were exposed to such an emergency, 13 reacted with anxiety or depression, reporting premonitions of death and morbid dreams. Also noted in all 13 were one or more abnormal physiological events, including ventricular tachycardia, elevation of blood pressure, angina, their own cardiac arrest and death.

There can be little doubt that the weight of the available evidence underlines the importance of the experience of stress in coronary heart disease. However, because most studies have been retrospective it is not always possible to say that the reported high experience of stress was a cause or an effect of the disease. In addition there have been few studies which have questioned the importance of stress for this type of disease. Despite the limitations of the available data it is now widely accepted that psychological factors are of significance in the aetiology and prognosis of heart disease. If this belief is justified then a number of more detailed questions may be posed, three of which will be dealt with here. First, what is the mechanism by which stress affects the heart? Second, how does stress relate to other coronary risk factors? Third, is there a particular personality which is high risk for coronary heart disease?

4.2.2 Stress-induced Coronary Heart Disease: Carruthers and Raab

In 1969, Carruthers proposed that emotion (stress) acting through the intermediary of enhanced sympathetic activity resulted in the increased mobilisation of free fatty acids (FFA) from fatty tissues. In the absence of metabolic demand these were converted to triglycerides and were then available to be incorporated into atheroma. There is evidence available to support each of the steps in Carruther's hypothesis. The studies of Frankenhaeuser and her colleagues, reviewed in chapter 3, have repeatedly demonstrated increased catecholamine excretion in response to stressful situations. Both adrenaline and noradrenaline increase circulating FFAs by stimulating lipolysis of triglycerides. Noradrenaline is particularly potent in this respect, and the elevation of FFAs which it causes is more prolonged. In the absence of immediate metabolic requirements, the circulating FFAs are converted to triglycerides by the liver, and hypertriglyceridaemia is correlated with an increased tendency to develop clinically overt coronary heart disease (Lewis *et al.*, 1974). Taggart and Carruthers (1971) reported a study of racing-car driving which demonstrates several of the hypothetical links simultaneously. In this study rises in plasma catecholamines and FFAs were observed which were positively correlated and which roughly coincided in time. Rises in plasma triglycerides also occurred but were delayed, supporting the suggestion of an interconversion from FFA to triglyceride. There was a negative correlation between

FFA levels and triglyceride levels.

An alternative hypothesis has been offered by Raab (1971). He has suggested that three different factors operate on the myocardial electrolyte balance, producing a major derangement which in turn causes potentially fatal cell destruction. The first factor is a vascular one: coronary vascular insufficiency, which reduces the oxygen supply to the heart muscle. One cause of insufficiency is atherosclerosis. The second factor is a stress factor: sympathetic–adrenomedullary activity, which increases oxygen demand. These factors acting together produce a myocardial hypoxia. The third factor is another stress factor: adrenocortical activity, which produces a change in the myocardial electrolyte balance. This is enhanced by the hypoxia. Potassium and magnesium are lost, and sodium retained. The normal myocardial potassium:sodium ratio in man is 2:2.5; if this is reduced by more than 35 per cent life-preserving cardiac contractility is lost. There is much evidence to support this hypothesis. For example, Lund (1964) has reported that, in a series of sudden deaths, the post-mortem plasma catecholamine concentrations were found to be higher than during phaeochromocytoma-induced paroxysms and as high as in fatal adrenaline poisoning. Rabb (1943, 1944) has reported two cases of cardiac death in which no atherosclerosis of the coronary arteries was observed, but where excessively high accumulations of catecholamines were found in the myocardium. In both cases, emotional factors were usually involved in the patient's demise. Furthermore, congestive heart failure is regularly associated with low potassium and magnesium and high sodium concentrations in the ventricles (Raab and Kimura, 1971).

The two hypotheses are not necessarily alternatives, and it is probable that both describe important and interrelated processes in the development of coronary heart disease. Both give prominence to the sympathetic–adrenomedullary response to stress. Carruther's model involves that response in the production of hyper-triglyceridaemia, and Raab's model invokes myocardial hypoxia. However, whatever the actual mechanism is by which stress affects the heart it is undoubtedly sensitive to the action of other risk factors such as diet, and in particular dietary fat.

4.2.3 Stress and Dietary Fat

There is much evidence to suggest that the apparent lethality of a high fat diet in Western society is interdependent on the effects of stress; one acts as a predisposing or catalytic factor for the other. An early study by Snapper (1941) reported that, in the Chinese population suffering the severe experiences of Japanese invasion, stress had little or no effect when their diet was poor in animal fat. Groen and his colleagues (1959) reported a study of Benedictine and Trappist monks. Both groups live pastoral lives, free from most of the problems that the urban family man faces. The Benedictines have a normal European diet, the Trappists do not. Their's is free of fish, meat, eggs and butter. Blood cholesterol levels were obviously much higher in the Benedictine group, but there was no difference in the prevalence of coronary heart disease between the two groups; both showed a far smaller incidence than the general population. Furthermore, there are several accounts of groups living on high animal fat diets with low incidence of coronary heart disease, possibly accreditable to the simplicity and non-competitiveness of their life styles (Lapiccirella et al., 1962; Stout et al., 1964; Mann et al., 1965). All these studies demonstrate that a high fat diet alone does not produce the disease, while the first study suggests that, alone, neither does stress. Given the high fat diet and common experience of stress in Western society, the final question is, who is particularly at risk?

4.2.4 The Individual at Risk

A long-term study of the prevalence of coronary heart disease in Evans County, Georgia, by Hames (1975), has shed important light on the determinants of individual susceptibility. The coronary prone were found to be involved in roles that were changing and in so doing were requiring the ability for new adaptation. They were less physically active and smoked more. They had recently acquired many status symbols relating to education, ownership and property. The physiological response to stress was exaggerated; for example, they produced twice as much adrenaline in twenty-four hours as did the less prone. From Hames' findings it would seem that achievement and success are costly in individuals who physiologically overreact to stress.

The results of the Hames study are consistent with the work of Friedman and Rosenman (1959, 1974) in describing a coronary-prone 'personality' type (type A). They initially interviewed by questionnaire a large number of business executives and physicians on their views of the causes of coronary heart disease. About 70 per cent of each group believed that the major causal factor was 'a particular and rather specific type of emotional activity' that was concerned with excessive drive, competition, meeting deadlines, and economic frustration. This work was developed, and Friedman (1974) has described the 'personality' characteristics of the typical coronary-prone individual: they have

(1) an intense sustained drive to achieve self-selected but usually poorly defined goals,
(2) a profound inclination and eagerness to compete,
(3) a persistent desire for recognition and advancement,
(4) a continuous involvement in multiple and diverse functions constantly subject to time restrictions,
(5) an habitual propensity to accelerate the rate of execution of many physical and mental functions, and
(6) an extraordinary mental and physical alertness.

The coronary-immune type, type B, was held to be the opposite of the type A individual. The original typing of individuals was carried out on a subjective basis, although later questionnaires to identify and measure type A characteristics have been developed. Several studies have been carried out using this typology, but as with many studies in this area they have tended to be retrospective. However, a personality study by Ostfeld and his colleagues (1964) was *prospective*. These authors interestingly enough report no differences in precoronary personality between individuals who subsequently suffered myocardial infarction and those who did not. Personality was measured using the Minnesota Multiphasic Personality Inventory. It might therefore seem that the personality differences uncovered in *retrospective* studies are due to the impact of coronary heart disease on the individual and not part of the cause of it. However, this may not be so for the Friedman typology. In a prospective study of over 3500 men in the Western Collaborative Group Study (1970) it has shown that type A individuals had higher serum lipids and daytime catecholamine excretion than type B individuals. Furthermore, of the 25 deaths from coronary heart disease during a five-year period, 22 were of type A. Finally, regardless of the cause of death, post-mortem assessment showed that coronary atherosclerosis was six times more prevalent in type A than in type B individuals. A study by Jenkins and

99

his colleagues (1971) also serves to confirm the validity of the Fried-man typology. Within the Western Collaborative Group Study, men who sustained *recurrent* myocardial infarction were more extreme on type A than the population mean, and those that had had two attacks tended to be more extreme than those that had had one.

4.2.5 Comments

Not all the available evidence on stress and coronary heart disease has been mentioned here. Despite this it is obvious that there is sufficient evidence to argue that stress cannot be ignored as a potent aetiological factor in this type of disease. Furthermore, there are credible hypotheses of how it contributes to that aetiology. Enough is known to be able to suggest some simple preventive measures, such as low-fat diets, relaxation, and blocking different aspects of the physiological response to stress. Such measures are dealt with in more detail in chapter 5.

4.3 STRESS AND THE OCCURRENCE OF BRONCHIAL ASTHMA

Bronchial asthma is a form of dyspnoea of unknown origin, which is characterised by wheezing, audible at a distance, and mainly oc-curring during expiration. It occurs in attacks or periods, and is commonly associated with an increased susceptibility of the upper and lower air passages to acute and chronic infections. The aetiology of bronchial asthma and the causes of attacks are largely unknown. Several theories have been put forward, but there is not yet enough evidence to choose between them.

Very early in the investigation of bronchial asthma, Talma (1898) made two very important observations. First, he noted that during an attack the expiratory wheeze is identical when heard from a distance and through the stethoscope at different places over the thorax and trachea. This indicates that it must be caused by a centrally situated narrowing of the trachea or large bronchii. The sound must then be conducted both upwards and downwards. Talma's second observa-tion was that typical wheezes could be produced on request both by asthmatics and some healthy individuals. Thus the changes in the respiratory passages which cause the wheeze can be produced volun-tarily, indicating the involvement of central nervous system mechanisms. This has been confirmed experimentally by Groen and his colleagues (Dekker and Groen, 1956, 1957; Dekker and Ledeboer, 1961). A considerable narrowing of the lumen of the main bronchi and the trachea was observed during voluntarily induced wheezing in both asthmatic and healthy subjects and during spontaneous wheezing in the former.

Groen (1971) has described a psychosomatic theory for bronchial asthma which takes account of Talma's early observations. He suggests that the changes in respiratory physiology which produce the wheezing attack are centrally mediated and are a response to emotional or stressful psychosocial influences. He believes that, for certain individuals with a predisposing personality, interpersonal conflict situations, which produce frustration through forced adaptation of submission, also produce changes in the pattern of breathing. The disturbance of the normal pattern is through the use of the voluntary (striated) respiratory muscles. Breathing is characterised by a forceful active contraction of the abdominal and thoracic respiratory muscle during expiration. This produces such a high pressure in the thorax that the trachea and major bronchi are compressed and wheezing is produced.

The other major theory, and one which tends to be treated as more orthodox, is the allergy theory. The disease, it is held, is due to a hypersensitivity of the mucosa, especially of the smaller air passages, to substances which are present in the air in such small amounts that they are innocuous to non-allergic individuals. The wheezing attacks occur because on contact with these substances the mucous membrane swells and reacts with excessive secretion of mucous and the smooth muscles of the small bronchi contract. It can be seen that the two theories are quite different, and it has been suggested that asthmatics can either be psychogenic or allergic.

In 1956, Dekker and Groen reported a study in which wheezing attacks were precipitated in asthmatics by exposure to emotionally significant situations. For the study series of patients were asked about the life situations in which they experienced attacks. These situations were then reproduced in the laboratory, as far as it was possible. These situations were clearly shown to be as capable of eliciting an attack as were allergens. The psychogenic and allergic attacks could sometimes be elicited in the same patient. All the attacks, irrespective of cause, responded similarly to isoprenaline.

Despite the argument which suggests that stress can be an important factor in bronchial asthma, the proposition is not widely accepted by the medical profession. Certainly more resistance is encountered in discussing this disorder than in discussing coronary heart disease.

4.4 DIABETES MELLITUS AND STRESS

There is much evidence, both observational and experimental, which suggests that stress is intimately linked with both the onset and the course of diabetes mellitus.

Diabetes mellitus is a disorder of carbohydrate metabolism, characterised by hyperglycaemia and glycosuria, which affects a significant proportion of the population. Figures published in 1976 by the British Diabetic Association estimated that 3 per cent of adults in this country suffer from some form of this disorder.

4.4.1 The Pathophysiology of Diabetes Mellitus

Diabetes is the result of a deficiency of insulin function. There may either be insufficient insulin produced by the pancreas, or the insulin produced may not be effectively used so that the person requires more insulin than the pancreas is secreting. This relative insufficiency of insulin may be due to hypersecretion or hyperactivity of insulin antagonists such as the pituitary, adrenomedullary or thyroid hormones. It may also be due to the action of the glucagon produced by the a cells of the pancreas itself. Antibodies which combine with and neutralise insulin may also be the cause of the diabetes.

Insulin is produced by the β cells of the pancreas, and promotes the uptake of glucose from the blood by the body cells. Without insulin glucose may neither be consumed as a fuel nor adequately stored. It simply accumulates in the blood. When it reaches a sufficiently high level (and passes the renal threshold), it 'spills over' into the urine and is excreted. When this occurs, an increased volume of urine is required to carry away the excess glucose, and the body may become dehydrated. Thus severe thirst may be a symptom of untreated diabetes. When glucose is not available as a fuel, fat is used instead. However, complete combustion of fats requires the presence of substances produced during combustion of glucose. In the absence of glucose metabolism, fat combustion is incomplete, resulting in the production and accumulation of toxic ketone bodies in the blood. If they collect in sufficient amounts they cause acidosis and eventually coma, which may be fatal.

The occurrence of coma is an interesting and frightening aspect of diabetes, especially as it can be associated with both hyperglycaemia and hypoglycaemia. The treatment for the first may be fatal for the second. To understand the mechanisms involved one has to consider the implications of changes in blood glucose level for the body and brain cells independently. Brain cells, unlike body cells, do not require insulin to avail themselves of blood glucose. In hyperglycaemia, although the blood is rich in glucose, the body cells are starved, and the breakdown of fat produces ketone bodies. These may be responsible for coma. Hypoglycaemia in diabetics tends to follow insulin overdosing or inadequate carbohydrate intake. The glucose from the blood is largely taken up by the body cells, and this makes it unavailable to brain cells. Their glucose starvation may then be responsible for coma. Hyperglycaemic coma is treated by insulin administration, but this aggravates hypoglycaemic coma. One of the indicators of the appropriate course of action is whether or not ketone bodies can be smelt on the breath of the comatose person. Typical symptoms of hypoglycaemia include tremor, sweating, visual disturbances and increased appetite. Euphoria, slurring of speech and unsteady movements may be mistaken for drunkenness. The person rapidly recovers, however, if glucose is given orally or intravenously. The risk of coma is slight in well-controlled diabetes, but greater with the more severe forms of the disease.

There are at least two very distinct forms of the disease, namely juvenile and maturity-onset diabetes, although they do present some similar symptoms. Further subdivisions of each of these forms can be described in aetiological terms. Juvenile or growth-onset diabetes is invariably an insulin-requiring form of the disease, while maturity-onset diabetes is generally a milder form of the disorder. Juvenile diabetics tend to be underweight because of large losses of glucose, whereas maturity-onset diabetics tend more often to be overweight. With overweight patients it is often possible to reduce carbohydrate intake to within the range with which the endogenous insulin can cope. In cases of underweight maturity-onset diabetics there is insufficient utilisation of carbohydrates, and hypoglycaemic drugs such as tolbutamide or chlorpropamide can be used to stimulate the pancreatic cells to secrete more insulin or to increase the effectiveness of the insulin that is already being produced.

Diabetes has for a long time been described as an inherited metabolic disease but the mode of inheritance is still largely unknown. One reason for this may have been that the characteristic symptoms of glycosuria and hyperglycaemia have, in the past, been thought to be indicative of a single disease entity. More recently, however, it has been accepted that diabetes is a range of disorders of differing aetiology.

It is clear that if there is a hereditary component to the disease it is only partially responsible for its manifestation or alternatively is the cause of only one form of diabetes. When one of a pair of identical twins is diabetic the other twin will not necessarily develop the disease. Froesch (1971) estimates the chances at 70 per cent, with the possibility of a child of diabetic parents under the age of 40 years developing diabetes being approximately 50 per cent. Blóom (1976) reports that only one in ten diabetic children have immediate relatives with diabetes. Factors other than hereditary factors therefore also predispose a person to diabetes or play a part in precipitating the disease. Danowski (1963) cited some of these other factors which have been implicated, including obesity, injury to the pancreas, repeated pregnancies and the ageing process.

Over the past four decades, attention has focused on the role of stress in the aetiology of diabetes. In non-diabetic patients many forms of stress such as those experienced in starvation, infection or emotional trauma, lead to a delay in the disposal of carbohydrates in the body and this delay results in an undue elevation of blood glucose level. Hinkle and his colleagues (1950) observed that ketosis, characteristic of unregulated diabetes, can appear in non-diabetic individuals who have been subjected to stress. Evans and Butterfield (1951) have described how severe burning may precipitate diabetes (this has already been mentioned in chapter 1). During a period of stress, previously non-diabetic individuals may manifest diabetic-like glucose-tolerance curves in response to a carbohydrate load and increases in blood and urine ketones, similar to those of individuals with untreated diabetes. However, unlike the diabetic individual the non-diabetic's blood glucose and ketone levels generally return to normal following the removal of the stress. The small proportion of patients whose blood glucose levels fail to revert to normal are often referred to as prediabetic, the assumption being that some predisposition towards diabetes was already present and that stress had merely precipitated the condition, making the symptoms apparent. In the prediabetic individual the reaction to stress may lead to exhaustion of already vulnerable pancreatic cells and hence to a permanent insulin deficiency and diabetes. Thus stress is often treated as a factor precipitating symptoms of an already dormant condition rather than as a direct causal factor. In populations of people subjected to sources of stress such as war or starvation, only a minority develop diabetes. If stress alone were a causal factor, a significantly greater number of people could be expected to develop diabetes.

4.4.3   Diabetes and the Response to Stress

Because there are at least two distinct groups of diabetics, juvenile-onset and maturity-onset, it is possible that there are at least two patterns of stress response present in the diabetic population. Such a variation in diabetic response and the differences between diabetic and non-diabetic responses may be partly due to perceptual differences among the people concerned, and partly to their different problems of blood glucose regulation. The extent of the differences may also depend on the severity of the disorder.

In juvenile-based diabetes, where there is little or no endogenous insulin, the fragile homeostasis maintained by insulin administration may easily be disrupted by the occurrence of stress. In such situations the action of the insulin antagonists, in particular adrenaline and glucagon, may be unchecked, leading to marked elevation of blood glucose levels. In maturity-onset diabetes, however, homeostasis in the face of stress may be maintained to the same extent as in the non-diabetic. This may be particularly so if the disorder is being effectively treated by diet alone, or if insulin function is being enhanced by the use of oral hypoglycaemic drugs.

In the light of these differences it would seem obvious to study the response to stress separately for the different populations of diabetics. However, much research has failed to do this. The unproven assumption has been made that the differences which might or actually do exist are merely quantitative.

In addition to the differences in response to stress within the diabetic population due to the nature of the disorder, there are clearly marked individual differences similar to those found in the non-diabetic population. Personality differences are one source of this individual variation. They make themselves most obvious in the perception of stress and in the strategies adopted to cope with stress.

Several authors have postulated a diabetic personality as a global factor which can be identified and which is thought to be a characteristic of individuals with the disorder. One assumption is that the vigorous demands made on the person by the management of the disorder may shape his or her whole attitude to life, and this may override normal variations in temperament. The diabetic population may thus be thought to be more homogeneous than the non-diabetic population. Attempts to define the diabetic personality, largely from retrospective studies, have been inconclusive. Baker and Bercai (1970), for example, in their review of work in this area, have stated that the literature still contains many conflicting and contradictory reports and that there is little agreement. Some authors (for example, Kubany et al., 1956) have even doubted the existence of a typical diabetic personality. Despite this it is clear that certain personality types may be better suited than others to deal with the problems inherent in the management of diabetes. Observations made in the course of the authors' studies have led to the following suggestions. Introverted diabetics tend to be more careful in balancing food intake to match insulin administration, and are more careful in maintaining sterile precautions. Furthermore, they appear more able to regulate their general life style according to the requirements of the disorder. Extroverted diabetics, on the other hand, tend to hold more easy-going attitudes towards the disorder, and tend, partly as a result, to underrate the importance of careful dieting and to be less concerned about the accuracy and timing of their insulin injections. The life style of a highly social person is to an extent incompatible with the routine necessary for the control of diabetes. These suggestions have found some support in the results of the authors' experimental studies. A significant positive correlation ($r = 0.51$, $P = 0.01$) was found to exist between average blood glucose level and the diabetic's extroversion score on the Maudsley Personality Inventory. Such a correlation could be explained by the extrovert's incautious attitude to the regulation of his blood glucose, resulting in a high, average blood-glucose level.

4.4.4 *Experimental Studies on the Role of Stress in the Control of Diabetes*

Some diabetics experience frequent episodes of keto-acidosis and coma despite a persistently conscientious regime. A study by Nabarro in 1965 reviewed 72 such cases and found that 15 per cent of these people developed the ketosis following an emotional disturbance. However, he concluded that it was impossible to discover whether they had omitted their insulin injections or whether, more interestingly, psychological factors had produced an intense resistance to insulin action.

A number of experimental studies have been carried out on this problem of ketosis being triggered by stress. Among the earliest are those of Hinckle and his colleagues (1950, 1952) who, with small groups of diabetic subjects, claimed to have shown variation in the regulation of blood glucose levels with the experience of emotion. However, these studies have been criticised for the poor control exercised over the conditions, and because no easily discernable patterns of change in blood glucose regulation were demonstrated.

More recent studies have been published by Vandenbergh and Sussman (1967) and Vandenbergh and colleagues (1967). In these studies, using hypnotically induced emotion and the experience and anticipation of electric shocks as sources of stress, they report finding in diabetics decreases in blood glucose levels without increases in urinary glucose excretion, and slight increases in blood free fatty acid content. Later Vandenbergh and Sussman (1967) looked at blood glucose levels under conditions of naturally occurring examination stress in university students with insulin-dependent diabetes mellitus. Here again, there were significant decreases in blood glucose levels during the pre-exam and exam weeks compared with a control week. In five of the six students, the decreases in blood glucose levels correlated positively with ratings showing simultaneously increased anxiety levels.

These experiments suggest that, under stressful conditions, diabetics are able to utilise more of their blood glucose than under non-stressful conditions. It is argued that these findings are compatible with results obtained by Simpson, Cox and Rothschild (1974), already discussed in chapter 3. They found that the impairment of psychomotor performance produced by loud noise could be attenuated by preloading with a small amount of glucose. The elevated blood glucose levels produced by preloading were significantly reduced during the period of task performance, the reduction being increased in the presence of noise.

A series of laboratory experiments along similar lines has been carried out and reported by Bradley (1975). The experiments were designed to test the hypothesis that a fall in blood glucose levels would be observed in diabetic subjects under stress and that the performance of these subjects under stress would be better than that of healthy subjects.

The results were more complicated than originally anticipated. Insulin-dependent diabetic males were studied, and it was immediately apparent that this section of the diabetic population could be further subdivided into two functionally distinct groups. The blood glucose changes that occurred under noise stress were dependent on the diabetics' initial blood glucose levels. The diabetic subjects could be divided into those with blood glucose levels greater than 180 mg% (the approximate normal renal threshold) and those with blood glucose levels below 180 mg%. The diabetic subject with low blood glucose who performed the psychomotor task in noisy conditions showed a fall in blood glucose level similar to that observed in Vandenbergh's diabetics, and in the healthy subjects in the Simpson, Cox and Rothschild experiment. Interestingly, performance of the task was slightly better under noise than in the quiet control condition. Diabetics with high blood-glucose levels behaved quite differently. When working in noise their blood glucose levels increased significantly. Their performance of the task was slightly worse in this condition than in the quiet. Overall there were no significant differences in performance between the various diabetic and the healthy subjects studied, despite the existence of some difference in blood glucose response. Whatever mechanism exists to link the performance and biochemical responses in healthy subjects (see chapters 3 and 5) it is affected by diabetes.

The different blood-glucose responses within the two groups of diabetics might be related to the amount of circulating insulin and glucagon.

4.4.5 The Insulin–Glucagon Hypothesis

Lefebvre and Unger (1972) and Unger (1976) have reviewed the evidence that relative, and at times absolute, hyperglucagonaemia might be present in persons with juvenile diabetes mellitus, thereby exaggerating the metabolic consequences of their insulin lack. They have also suggested that many of the unexplained manifestations of the diabetic state could well be the consequences of changes in glucagon levels in such persons.

There is some evidence to suggest that glucagon release accompanies the startle response to noise (Bloom *et al.*, 1973). In non-diabetic subjects the hyperglycaemia produced by glucagon secretion in response to stress would in turn stimulate insulin secretion, which would enable utilisation of blood glucose mobilised by glucagon. In Bradley's high blood-glucose diabetics, it would seem that there is not enough insulin to cope with the original level of glucose. Consequently, if glucagon is released in response to noise, sufficient insulin would not be available to utilise the additional glucose. The low blood-glucose diabetics might have enough endogenous insulin available to utilise the influx of glucagon-released glucose, or to inhibit glucagon release itself. The author's experiments were carried out some time after the diabetic subject's last insulin injection. Unger (1972) suggested that the glucagon-producing α cell was an insulin-requiring cell which in the absence of insulin was incapable of sensing or responding appropriately to the high glucose levels outside the cell. Thus if insulin was not available, which was likely to be the case with high blood-glucose diabetics, the release of glucagon under stress would merely exaggerate the present state of hyperglycaemia, the negative feedback control of this process being damaged. Levine (1976) cites studies which suggest that hyperglucagonaemia only caused significant hyperglycaemia in insulin-dependent diabetics who were deprived of insulin. He concludes that glucagon exerts a diabetogenic action only when there is an insulin deficiency. The low-glucose diabetic patients in Bradley's study may be presumed to have sufficient effective insulin to prevent a hyperglycaemic response to glucagon.

4.4.6   Stressful Life Events and Diabetes

In 1967, Holmes and Rahe devised a Schedule of Recent Life Experiences (SRE), consisting of 43 possible life events and their corresponding 'weights' which were meant to reflect their relative impact on life and the degree of readjustment involved in coping with them. This work was the first systematic attempt to quantify the degree of stress experienced in life events, and to demonstrate the effects of those events.

Grant *et al.* (1974) used the SRE with diabetic patients, and their findings suggested a relationship between the occurrence of life change and the aggravation of the diabetic state, with 'undesirable' events being mainly responsible for this relationship. However, no differences in the influences of life events on the diabetics' physical condition were found between juvenile- and maturity-onset types.

In an unpublished study by Bradley, Cox and Minto (1976), a questionnaire, designed by Lundberg and his colleagues (1975 for an investigation of life-change events in myocardial infarction patients, was used to study diabetic and control populations of medical and surgical outpatients. Subjects were asked to rate life events either for the amount of upset that these events would cause, or for the amount of adjustment that they felt would be required in coping. In addition, the subjects were asked to mark any events that they had experienced during the past year.

It was found that measurements reflecting the course of the diabetes did correlate with the rating of life-change events, but that both the size and direction of that correlation depended on the type of diabetes under study (insulin- or tablet-treated), and on the sex of the patient.

In the control population it was found that women rated events that they had experienced very much higher than men, for both degree of upset caused and amount of adjustment required. This sex difference in reporting stress experienced had been noted in other studies (Ekehammar, 1972). Interestingly, the control group as a whole reported significantly more events than either the tablet- or the insulin-treated diabetics, and also rated those events as being more upsetting and requiring more adjustment. It may be that diabetics use their disorder and its control as a standard by which to judge other life events and, that standard being a difficult one to surpass, few other events are perceived as significant. Sex differences in both the diabetic groups (insulin- or tablet-treated) studied were considerably smaller than those found in the control group. Possibly using the demanding nature of the disorder as a standard by which to judge other events obliterates any inherent sex differences, cultural or hormonal. The diabetic population may in this respect appear more homogeneous (see section 4.4.3).

Diabetics may measure the amount of upset experienced with life events and the degree of adjustment required in coping against the management of their disorder. They may also judge events in terms of their impact on the management of their condition and may ignore any wider implications that these events might have. An alternative hypothesis is that the elevated blood-glucose levels of the diabetic in some way act as a buffer to the perception of stressful events, in the same way that glucose preloading protected the performance of non-diabetic subjects from the detrimental effects of noise (Simpson *et al.*, 1974*a*). However, there was no way of choosing between these hypotheses from the data of the present study (Bradley *et al.*, 1976, unpublished data).

4.4.7 Comments

In conclusion, it is apparent that the diabetic's physiological reaction to and psychological perception of stress are different from the non-diabetic's. The way in which the diabetic responds to stress may depend to some extent on the degree of disruption of blood glucose regulation caused by the disorder. However, despite such differences there is no evidence that the diabetic individual is any less capable of coping with stressful events. On the contrary, as stated earlier, diabetics report that they experience fewer events and they rated those events as being less upsetting and requiring less adjustment than their non-diabetic counterparts. This attitude towards life events that could be stressful might well be an adaptive way of coping with circumstances which might otherwise cause further physiological disruption. In occupational terms it is worth repeating the established view that diabetics are good employment risks if their disorder is under control and if they are under sensible medical supervision. However, since diabetics tend to heal slowly and have a tendency to develop complications following injury, it is advisable for them to avoid work involving special physical hazards.

It is now clear that clinical management of the disorder requires knowledge of the individual diabetic's personality and capabilities. Assumptions of a single personality type common to all diabetics can only lead to misunderstandings about an individual patient's problems, and further research into the possible individual responses towards the management of diabetes may be useful in treatment. In future research it may also be useful to pay more attention to the role of glucagon in the diabetic's response to stress, and to consider not only the importance of insulin action but also the need to control glucagon secretion under stressful conditions.

5

The Management and Alleviation
of Stress

Psychology and medicine and their allied professions have long had many varied means of helping individuals cope with their problems. However, a framework which brings together all of the different techniques that are used has not evolved, and their common ground has not yet been made obvious. As a result the logical development of new techniques of helping has been retarded. In the previous chapters of this book the nature of stress was discussed, and a model developed to account for our current knowledge. This *transactional* model is now examined to see how it may be used in producing the necessary framework for a single classification and a new understanding of the different ways of helping in current use. It is hoped that this chapter will offer a new insight into the management and alleviation of stress.

The rationale behind the present prescription for dealing with stress is that the chain of events which lead up to its pathology is broken. The necessary break can be made in several different ways. First, the elements which contribute to the cognitive appraisal of demand and capability and of the consequences of coping can be altered. This may be achieved by restructuring the external environment, by changing the person's level of mental, physical and social skill, by supporting him in the use of those skills, or by altering his perceptual and cognitive processes. Second, if the occurrence and experience of stress cannot be avoided then its psychological and physiological effects may be modified, as may be the actual and perceived consequences of those effects. These prescriptions can be elaborated on by considering the specific points in the transactional model where an entry can be made to break the critical progression to pathology. These entries which form the different types of helping may be made by the person himself and/or by another person or group of people. For example, Meichenbaum (1974) has developed a self-instructional approach to stress management. Usually, however, it is the role of the therapist to produce the entry, and carry the process through to conclusion.

5.1 ALTERATION OF ACTUAL DEMAND

The occurrence and experience of stress may be reduced by an attenuation of the real demands made on the person. This is essentially an environmental and an engineering solution. Demands may arise from the person's physical environment or from the person's psychosocial environment. Examples of both are easy to generate.

5.1.1 The Physical Environment and Demand

Demands originating in the structure of the physical environment may be manifest in extremes of stimulation, *inter alia*, noise, temperature, humidity and illumination. Each may be dealt with through a programme of physical engineering geared to the reduction or increase in the level of the offending factor. The identification of these offending factors is, at a superficial level, relatively easy, and recommendations for improvement straighforward. However, the execution of the necessary change may for a variety of economic, political and practical reasons be far less easy.

Certain press-shops in the British engineering industry stand out as less than shining examples of good work environments. In particular, older shops tend to be too noisy and too dirty, too hot and too dangerous, and offer little facility for the worker to escape from the demands of the job. They tend to be overcrowded, often with old machinery which may be difficult to make safe. Such shops have come into existence largely as a result of inadequate and ill-advised investment in industry, and of inappropriate attitudes held by workers and managements. The solution is obvious: the replacement of old plant with quieter, cleaner and safer hardware, the installation of sound baffles, and air conditioning, the improvement of general decor and of ancillary facilities such as changing rooms, showers and lounges, and the promotion of health and safety awareness, including cleanliness and tidiness. Such a programme would transform offending press-shops, but would be immensely costly, and possibly only occur in an economically healthy industry.

Low cost, high-density housing may provide a disturbing example of a poor home environment. Such housing developments seem to be characterised at the level of the individual units by small space allowances, in room size and number, by poor quality finishing, and by a restricted range of built-in facilities. At the community level the facilities tend to be less than desired or needed, and the aesthetic qualities of the developments tend to be severely constrained by building costs. Recommendations for improvements are again easy to make but costly and difficult to carry through. Indeed, once again, they are only likely to be carried out in an economically healthy and enlightened society.

If changes in the physical structure of the person's environment are not possible, then the provision of personal protection devices is a possible alternative. For example, ear defenders can substantially reduce noise levels, while reflective clothing can reduce temperature. The major problem associated with personal protection devices is, however, to persuade people to use them when they are necessary, and when they are provided. It is, unfortunately, a common experience to observe workers in press-shops, for example, where the noise level is near to intolerable, refusing to wear ear defenders. The reasons given vary from them being uncomfortable through to unmanly. Persuading the work force to make full use of the safety facilities made available to them is a priority in every industry, and this is recognised in the current health and safety legislation in both the United States and Europe.

5.1.2 The Psychosocial Environment and Demand

Demand may arise as a result of social pressure, and here the solutions offered are necessarily those of social engineering: reorganising and restructuring the human aspects of the environment. Some attempt at social engineering is seen, for example, in the treatment of mental disorder in a family rather than an individual context. This is a comparatively new version of group therapy, and attempts to deal with the family members as the group, usually husband and wife and children (see Bell, 1975). The belief is that the problems of each individual family member are intimately tied up

114

with those of the other members. This has been explicitly argued for many years by child psychotherapists, who see the treatment of the child as practically useless unless the parents on whom it is dependent are involved. The goal of family group therapy is to help the members of the family group relate to each other more effectively and thus reduce the psychosocial demands made on any one of them. Each member stands to gain a more meaningful and satisfactory (less stressful) set of relationships with his or her family.

Demand may also arise from the requirements and constraints placed on the pattern and flow of that person's behaviour by his job or home life. Demand may arise internally as a reflection of the person's needs. For example, continual exposure to repetitive and boring work may create more problems than varied and stimulating work, and a harmonious and supportive home will pose fewer problems than one which is fragmented and turbulent. One of the possible keys to interpreting the effects of work and of home life is Maslow's theory of human nature (Maslow, 1943, 1954, 1968, 1973). This is discussed again in chapter 7. He postulated that the person has five types of basic need: first, a physiological need for food, water and the other prerequisites of life; second, a safety need for security and avoidance of physical harm; third, a social need for affection and friendship; fourth, a need for esteem and self-respect; fifth and last, a need for 'self-actualisation'. Self-actualisation is a difficult concept to describe. It relates to the opportunity for personal growth and development, to the feeling of worthwhile accomplishment, the liberation of creative talents, and to the feeling for self-fulfilment as a person (Maslow, 1954). These five types of need form a hierarchy: the lower needs, the physiological and safety needs, are prepotent, and the higher needs are only important when these lower ones are fulfilled. The fulfilment of all the needs is Maslow's prescription for psychological well-being. Jobs and home lives which do not allow for such fulfilment are thus a threat to well-being. The question must then be, can we redesign and restyle those jobs and home lives so that they engage the person's higher level needs?

Social engineering may take simple but extreme forms, such as moving house to escape belligerent neighbours, leaving an uncaring husband or wife, or resigning a difficult job. Such coping behaviour is usually less than completely satisfactory as its extreme nature tends to create new problems as it solves existing ones. The final judgement on what is essentially problem substitution must be in terms of which of the problems, old or new, can the person cope with most effectively.

5.2 ALTERATION OF ACTUAL ABILITY TO COPE

In response to the experience of stress, behaviour changes and attempts are made to cope with the source of that stress. Coping may or may not dominate the subsequent pattern of behaviour. Ability to cope with stress can change with a number of positive factors, such as

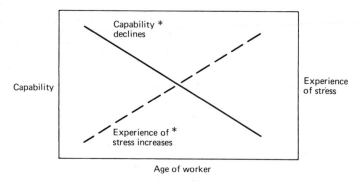

* It is assumed that the demands on the worker remain constant

Figure 5.1: Effects of Age on the Experience of Occupational Stress

education and training, and with a number of negative factors, such as ageing, drug effects, and illness and injury. Education and training must be thought of in the widest possible sense, and must be seen to embrace everything from training in basic social skills through to the training of workers in particular industrial skills. The need to acquire new skills, and yet to maintain established ones, is essential for our efficient functioning in society. Thus research in training methods is an integral part of stress research.

The interaction between the demands of work and the ability to work is a simple one, according to the transactional model. Consider ageing. If the demands of a particular job are not modified as the worker ages and becomes less able to cope, then his experience of stress will increase (see figure 5.1). This situation can be dealt with in two ways. First, the ageing worker can have his job load (work demand) reduced, or second, he can be periodically retrained.

Training is a possible solution to problems created by ageing, drugs and illness. It also stands as a companion to selection in the management of industry. Selection is never perfect, and the selecting organisation employs people who are not completely fitted for their jobs. Training may reduce or even remove the mismatch problem. Selection is essentially a matter of fitting men into jobs as a method of avoiding future stress as a result of a man–job mismatch. Research into selection techniques and their validity and usefulness can be another important area of stress research. This is most obvious if the characteristics being selected for are those relevant to high stress resistance.

5.3 SUPPORTING EXISTING ABILITY TO COPE

It may not be possible to develop a person's ability to cope. It may be possible, however, to help him cope more effectively by supporting his existing ability to cope, that is by doing a part of what is required for him. A case study may serve as an example:

> Two consultant psychologists, S and A, had worked in partnership for some time, and had grown close as friends as well as valued colleagues. However, one of the partners, S, developed marital problems; he found it difficult to maintain his previous level and quality of work, and have time and energy to deal with his marital problems. A could not help except by taking on not only his own work but also a part of S's. This reduced the demands of S's work to a level at which he could cope with them and with his other problems.

This type of help is available in many different forms. It is an integral part of parents' role in bringing up their children, it is implicit in the social contract of friendship, and it is the expressed aim of many formal and informal 'helping' organisations.

5.4 ALTERATION OF COGNITIVE APPRAISAL

As the occurrence of stress relates to a *perceptual* imbalance between demand and capability, alteration of the perceptual mechanisms is a very powerful stress management technique. The perception of each of the three aspects of cognitive appraisal, demand, capability, and the importance of coping, may be altered. The necessary modification can be brought about through the use of drugs such as nicotine, alcohol, minor tranquillisers, and other body-centred forms of palliation, through counselling and the various psychotherapeutic processes, and through meditation and religion. The psychological techniques appear to develop more realistic appraisals of the problem situation, build or rebuild self-confidence, suggest and practise possible coping strategies (say, through the use of imagery or dramatic techniques) and change attitudes and priorities. Such a list is obviously not comprehensive, and each technique cannot be appropriate in every problem situation. Indeed, some may, for particular problems, be countereffective. For example, a more realistic appraisal of a difficult situation may place the person under greater stress if he had *underestimated* the extent of his troubles. Furthermore, attitude changes resulting in the person no longer believing that failing to cope is important, may cause the precipitation of more severe problems if failing to cope *is* important.

5.4.1 The Use of Drugs

The use of drugs is a powerful way of producing an alteration of cognitive appraisal. However, it is important to note that drug effects may not only alter cognitive appraisal but also actual capability, often reducing it. This disadvantage may outweigh the advantages in the long term. Furthermore, the reward of feeling better after taking the drug, the very reason for taking it, may lead to psychological dependence, and that in some cases to physical dependence. The use of drugs in producing an alteration of cognitive appraisal can thus only be recommended with caution. Where drugs are used to relieve the experience of and effects of stress, some attempt must also be made to deal with the source of the stress. If such a strategy is not employed and successfully then the problem of psychological dependency is increased. A much longer account of the use of drugs in relation to stress is presented later, in chapter 6.

5.4.2 Counselling and Psychotherapy: Rogers

Counselling, and psychotherapy in general, have already attracted some comment in chapter 3. The essence of psychotherapy is that the therapist and his client come together in some form of discussion and relationship in the mutual hope that the therapist's ability and experience in understanding people and situations can be used to help the client find a solution to his problems. Psychotherapists will have been trained within a particular school, and different psychotherapists might offer different explanations and solutions to the same problem. Many psychotherapists are psychoanalytical in orientation, and owe much to the work of Freud and his later advocates. Others have developed along separate but somewhat parallel, and in that sense, similar, lines.

Of possible interest is Rogers' client-centred therapy. Rogers developed his therapy first (1951) and from that his theory of personality. The neurotic individual, it is suggested by Rogers, is in a constant state of tension and vulnerability because he is denying awareness of significant areas of his experience. Reinterpreting this position, the expression of neuroticism is a result of a particular way of coping with stress. The person simply denies part of his experience, and thus reduces the imbalance between perceived demand and perceived ability to cope. In order to maintain this denial the person has to live out a life style that makes it possible to overlook, minimise or distort parts of his on-going experience. The denial of experience can come about in the following way. In Rogers' view each person is constantly trying to maintain and develop a total self. This striving reflects an innate drive to actualise the self (a definition of self-actualisation has already been offered in discussing Maslow's work). Complications often occur in this process because other people are required for self-fulfilment and enhancement. As a result of a need for love and a positive regard for other people, their subjective values tend to be assumed as one's own. The neurotic is burdened with two sets of values which may contradict and conflict: the first are those intrinsic to his self-actualisation, the second are derived from others but mistakenly experienced as his own. The situation leads to an unrealistic self-concept which is maintained by denial of experience. The unrealistic self-concept is the strategy for coping with the contradiction and conflict. Therapy consists of the therapist acting as a mirror to the client's feelings in the belief that they flow from his true self. The therapist attempts to express and capitalise on those feelings so that the client may develop a greater awareness of that true self and no longer need to deny experience.

Client-centred therapy thus seeks to alter the person's cognitive appraisal of himself and of his situation.

5.4.3 Religion

Religions are very similar to certain form of psychotherapy in the way they offer to alter cognitive appraisal. In Rogers' terms they provide sets of personal and social values and methods of self-actualisation which are consistent with one another. Thus the person may, if 'successful' in his involvement in religion, be able to develop his self, and hold a true self-concept, and be free from any denial of experience. Indeed, this may be the expressed personal goal of a religion. In terms of the transactional model, religions offer relief from stress by altering the perception of demand, of capability and of the importance of coping. For example, toil and drudgery may be seen to be praiseworthy forms of worship, faith brings renewed physical and psychological strength, and admittance to a heaven is more important than success or even survival in the world. Religion actively offers distortions of perception as 'acceptable' ways of dealing with problems, and in many ways the comments made about the use of drugs in altering cognitive appraisal are appropriate here. Although emotional gains obviously accrue from being religious, there is a distinct possibility that the psychological defence strategies recommended by the religion may impair realistic behaviour, and may only be maintained at a cost to physical and psychological health. Moreover, the effectiveness of being religious in producing more-or-less immediate improvements in feeling may lead to psychological dependence. However, for many millions of people the practice of religion appears to be effective in enhancing their ability to cope with life, and thus on this evidence alone its effects must be judged to be important both by the individual and his society.

5.5 ALTERATION OF ACTUAL IMPORTANCE OF COPING

This approach to the management and alteration of stress is essentially another type of social engineering solution, and could be grouped with those already discussed.

It is often difficult, if not impossible, to alter what is important in terms of coping at the level of the individual without affecting his social reference group. Because the individual by and large conforms to social norms, changing the importance and consequences of his behaviour means changing the structure and function of his social milieu. This in part is the goal of political science and the practice of politics. Marx, for example, in laying down his aspirations for communism, was prescribing a relief for the burdens of the working man.

Erich Fromm (1941, 1947, 1955) has discussed, from an essentially psychoanalytical position, the role of society in facilitating or undermining healthy personality development. The impact of society is undoubtedly partly due to its determination of the consequences of men's actions. Unlike most orthodox psychoanalysts, Fromm has concentrated on the development of the person's social character as a product of the culture in which he lives. He believes that there is a fundamental conflict within the individual. It is between a need for personal growth and development as an individual on the one hand, and a need to belong and feel secure in the social environment and to avoid the consequences of individual action, on the other. There is no doubt that Fromm and Rogers have written about the same sort of personal conflict (see section 5.4.2). The freedom to express individuality can bring with it feelings of isolation and helplessness and the person may resolve this by a submission to social authority. Fromm believes that this is what happened in Nazi Germany, that the German people subjected themselves to totalitarianism as an escape from the loneliness and anxiety of relative freedom. Presumably the anxiety of freedom is exaggerated when the 'free' society is in a disordered socioeconomic state, as was Germany after the Great War, and as are Britain and Italy now. If Fromm was correct in his analysis it is possible that the populations of these latter countries will also seek to escape from the anxiety of freedom by accepting extremes of social authority. In his latter writing Fromm developed these ideas, identifying a number of other social needs in addition to belonging and identity. He discussed, for example, a need to transcend one's animal nature through creative expression, and a need for a stable frame of reference through which the person might understand his world. Fromm saw the failure of adjustment as largely a result of the failure of society to meet these basic human needs. This failure might be the failure of society's dealings with individual action. He believed that a more successful society can be created in which people can be brought together in bonds of fellow feeling and yet able to transcend nature by achieving self-identity. Fromm thus sees a solution to individual problems of well-being through changing the nature of society and by altering the effects on failure to cope with the social world. However, there is every reason to expect that general solutions to the individual's problems by way of 'brave new worlds' will not necessarily abolish those problems but simply alter their nature.

5.6 ALTERATION OF THE BEHAVIOURAL RESPONSE TO STRESS

Altering the behavioural response to stress is somewhat different to altering the person's attempts to cope with the source of that stress. It reflects a much wider concern with the ways in which the person's overall pattern of behaviour changes with the experience of stress. The ways in which this occurs have already been discussed in chapter 3. Two important occurrences warrant further consideration. First, with severe or continual experience of stress behaviour tends to become disorganised, and second, the 'reasoning' tends to switch from a logical to an emotional basis, perhaps reflecting a general regression to an 'earlier' form of behaviour. These changes will not only affect those aspects of the person's behaviour which are direct attempts to cope with the source of stress, but will also have a more general effect. For example, a deterioration in the general quality or effectiveness of his life style may serve to exaggerate the person's experience of stress. A vicious circle can thus be quickly and disastrously established. This circle could be prevented from being established, or may be broken if established, in two ways. First, by improving the person's ability to cope with the source of stress, and second, by supporting the other aspects of the person's behaviour and preventing their deterioration. These in turn can be achieved in various ways, but most effectively by enforcing an organised pattern of behaviour based on logical reasoning. Although such a mechanical and routine life style may not have the warmth of a more flexible and stimulating way of life, it will undoubtedly be more effective in sustaining the person during periods of stress. The more mechanical and routine the general pattern of activity the less conscious investment there need be in its control. As a result more cognitive capacity can be devoted to coping with the problems that the person faces. For many people a very routine way of life may represent a naturally occurring protective response to the continual experience of stress. It is also possible that routines, if sufficiently mechanical and repetitive, may actually reduce the sensitivity of the person's cognitive appraisal, and make them less aware of the demands on them and of their feelings (see section 7.2.4).

5.7 ALTERATION OF THE PHYSIOLOGICAL RESPONSE TO STRESS

Altering the physiological response to stress can achieve two things: it can enhance behavioural coping especially when coping requires much physical effort, and it can prevent pathological conditions from arising. Unfortunately there is the possibility that one precludes the other. The argument developed in the earlier chapters of the book is that the physiological response to stress prepares for and facilitates active behavioural coping, but that its repeated elicitation causes an increased rate of wear and tear on the body. Thus, increasing the behavioural effectiveness of the physiological response may further increase the rate of wear and tear, while the ways of decreasing that rate may also decrease behavioural effectiveness. The rate of wear and tear on the body may be further increased if the physiological response to stress is not utilised in active behavioural coping. The best possible combination of treatments may therefore be to enhance the physiological response to stress when active behavioural coping is required, but to reduce it when more passive coping is appropriate. Thus the response to stress arising through competition should be enhanced if the competition is through, say, active sport, but it should be reduced if the competition is through, say, written examination. What is being proposed is an interaction between, on the one hand, the task to be addressed in coping with stress and its behavioural requirements and, on the other, the type of alteration of the physiological response that is to be recommended. This approach is similar to that recommended by Lazarus (1966, 1976).

5.7.1 The Manipulation of Blood Glucose Levels

Research on blood glucose regulation and the performance of different tasks under stress provides one example of enhancing the behavioural response to stress by altering the accompanying physiological response. As already recounted in chapters 3 and 4, the author and his colleagues have shown that preloading subjects with small amounts of glucose could attenuate the detrimental effects of noise on psychomotor performance. Extra glucose, as administered in that experiment, improved performance under noise stress. The simple and naïve rationale behind the experiment was that a rise in blood glucose levels which has been observed to occur under stress might be behaviourally adaptive and that enhancing it by adding extra glucose into the blood system might improve the associated behavioural response. A series of experiments confirmed the predicted result if not the mechanism. An interesting interaction emerged from those experiments between the amount of glucose required to improve performance and the degree of noise stress. In an early experiment it was shown that 18 g of glucose (after that used by Murrell in 1971) was sufficient to improve tracking performance at 80 dBA but not at 95 dBA. Later experiments showed that 30 g of glucose tended to bring about an improvement at 95 dBA. This interaction was made more interesting by the demonstration that 18 g and 30 g of glucose *impaired* performance at 50 dBA; 30 g of glucose brought about a greater impairment at 50 dBA than did 18 g of glucose. It was possible that these effects were psychological rather than physiological in nature. However, an experiment in which different subjects were correctly, incorrectly, or not informed about the nature of the pre-experiment administration, suggested that the effects were part psychological but also part physiological in nature. In all the experiments carried out the changes in blood glucose levels which occurred in response to the various experimental factors although consistent in themselves showed a complex correlation with the changes in performance. A model (Bradley *et al.*, 1977) to account for the relationship between the blood glucose response and performance is shown in figure 5.2.

The key intervening process in this model is the role of the vagal–insulin system in maintaining an optimum signal-to-noise ratio in the neural events of information processing. It is suggested that by reducing cardiac and respiratory activity, and the neural noise associated with that activity, the vagal–insulin system can function to compensate for increases in externally generated neural noise. The increased vagal–insulin activity reduces blood glucose levels, and maintains performance. However, to respond to moderate levels of external noise, the vagal–insulin system needs to be primed (preloading). In quiet conditions this priming can cause the vagal–insulin system to disrupt the signal-to-noise ratio. Priming increases blood glucose levels. Disruption of the signal-to-noise ratio can cause an impairment of performance. Such a model is consistent with the transactional model of stress and with the account of physiological response to stress.

The administration of the extra glucose was shown to modify both the behavioural and biochemical response to noise stress, within the confines of the experimental situation. These results can be

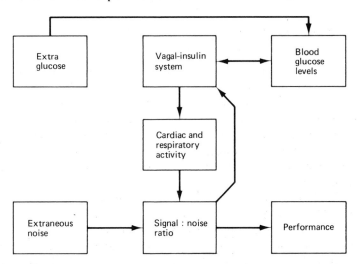

Figure 5.2: Glucose, Noise, Blood Glucose Levels and Performance

generalised, however. Brooke and his colleagues (1973*a* and *b*), for example, have demonstrated that high accident rates in an iron foundry in South Lancashire could be associated with low carbohydrate intake, and low accident rates with high carbohydrate intake. Presumably high carbohydrate intake produced a relative elevation of blood glucose levels and afforded some protection from the effects of stress, if accidents are seen to be one possible associate of the experience of stress. In the same vein, it has been observed that the blood glucose levels of motorway crash victims are surprisingly low. This could, of course, be a *result* rather than a *cause* of crashes. However, it could be argued that the classical response to the severe stress of a crash would be an *elevation* of blood glucose levels. Perhaps, however, for such a severe stress, if the glycogen stores are low, then hypoglycaemia may occur. The hypoglycaemia may be sufficiently severe to contribute to the victim's death. An alternative suggestion is that because of long journeys and insufficient food intake, probably involving missed meals, blood sugar levels drop low enough to cause an impairment of driving performance, hence the crash. This may then exaggerate the hypoglycaemia. This sequence may be prevented by the ingestion of glucose during the drive, perhaps at regular intervals and in relatively small amounts.

5.7.2 Drugs and the Physiological Response to Stress

Research by Levi and his colleagues (see Froberg et al., 1971; Carlsson et al., 1972) has shown that part of the pattern of physiological response to stress, the elevation of the blood level of free fatty acids (see chapter 4), can be blocked by the prior administration of nicotinic acid. Free fatty acid mobilisation occurs in part due to increased activity in the sympathetic–adrenomedullary system. It has even been suggested that free fatty acids may stimulate certain pancreatic cells to release glucagon and thus raise blood glucose levels.

In Levi's experiments the free fatty acid levels rose in subjects who were subjected to psychosocial stressors, but this rise was blocked in other subjects who had previously been given six administrations of 0.5 g of nicotinic acid spread over two-hour periods. The evidence obtained suggested that the blockage occurred locally in the adipose tissue. This interference with part of the overall physiological response might be capable of providing some protection against, in the first instance, hyperlipoproteinaemia (raised blood lipoprotein levels) and possibly against cardiovascular pathology (see chapter 4).

Another example is provided by the effects of the β-adrenergic receptor blocking agents, such as d-propranolol. This drug, acting directly, slows the heart rate. It also appears to reduce the experience of anxiety (Granville–Grossman and Turner, 1966; Wheatly, 1969; Suzman, 1971). Undoubtedly part of this anxiolytic action is central, but part must also be peripherally mediated, since practolol, another blocking agent, has a similar but less potent effect and yet does not affect the central nervous system (Bonn et al., 1972). Practolol cannot penetrate the blood–brain barrier. It can be argued that both propranolol and practolol effect cardiogenic anxiety, that is the experience of anxiety associated with the awareness of tachycardia (increased heart rate) (Korol and Brown, 1967). Presumably cardiogenic anxiety is established by the repeated association of anxiety feelings and tachycardia, so the latter is eventually capable of eliciting the former. Reducing tachycardia by the use of β-adrenergic receptor blocking agents, reduces the experience of anxiety and thus alters the behaviour which is contingent upon it. Reducing tachycardia may also protect the heart itself against damage.

5.8 COMMENTS

This chapter reviews the different points in the transactional model at which the experience of stress may be relieved and managed. Different management techniques are appropriate at several of these points of attack. There is not a simple one-to-one relationship. Forms of counselling, for example, are appropriate in altering the person's perception of demand, of his own capabilities and of the consequences of his action. By further example, social changes are necessary to change actual demand, and again to alter the consequences of coping.

Within the limits of this book it is not possible to develop the present discussion in depth, but what has been presented ought to establish the framework for that deeper discussion.

6

Psychopharmacology and Stress

Psychopharmacology is a rather recently developed interdiscipline, which is concerned with two types of effect: first, the effects of drugs on psychological processes, and second, the effect of psychological factors in determining the response to drugs. Drugs which can be shown to have psychological effects have been variously labelled, psychoactive and psychotropic being among the terms most commonly used.

The present chapter presents a brief review of psychopharmacology in the context of the experience and effects of stress. Such a presentation is not as narrow as it at first appears, for there are numerous areas in which the study of drugs and the study of stress overlap. Three will be examined here. First, most psychoactive drugs have been developed for their clinical properties, for their ability to ease personal distress and make overt behaviour more socially acceptable. To the extent that abnormal psychological stages reflect or involve an inability to meet life's demands, then the use of drugs in their treatment is an example of the alleviation of stress. However, some drugs have the effect of reducing the experience of stress, but at the same time of also reducing the person's ability to cope with reality. This is the second area of overlap, and includes not only the study of specific drugs such as the antianxiety agents and alcohol, but the whole process of drug dependence. Third, but not least, there is the question of the impact of drug usage on society, and the problems it poses and the solution it offers. Both drugs and stress have been quoted as characteristic, if not typical, of contemporary Western society. Their relationship at this level must therefore be examined. The present chapter follows the format suggested by the three areas mentioned above, introducing them together with necessary information about the actual drugs under discussion.

No two psychoactive drugs are identical, but many share qualitatively similar actions across a number of psychological (and physiological) processes. In the processes of their classification, psychoactive drugs have been variously ordered along many different lines, according to their chemical structure, their dominant mode of action, their pharmacological properties, or their clinical application. Since the overt purpose of classification is to produce economic frameworks around which to organise our thinking, then the particular classification constructed in any situation will reflect the interests and needs of the user population. Many important user populations exist for classifications of psychoactive drugs; for example,

    (a) *Drug abusers:*   what subjective effects do the drugs have?
                              what sort of escape from reality do they offer?

    (b) *Lawyers:*   what is the legal status of the drugs?
                              how is their illegal use defined and punished?

    (c) *Clinicians:*   what effects do the drugs have on normal and abnormal behaviour?
                              what 'conditions' are they useful in treating?

Many other user populations could be defined, and undoubtedly the interests of many would overlap. However, in practice very few classifications agree on detail, although there do appear to be at least three recognised groups of psychoactive drugs (the terms in parentheses are those suggested by Crossland (1970)).

    I. Drugs which bring about inhibition or depression of psychological processes (*psycholeptic* drugs); for example, the tranquillisers and sedatives.

    II. Drugs which excite or stimulate psychological processes (*thymoleptic* drugs); for example, the stimulants and antidepressants.

    III. Drugs which distort psychological processes (*psychomimetic* or *hallucinogenic* drugs); for example, lysergic acid diethylamide and mescaline.

Each of these three categories can be further subdivided to give the drug groupings which are commonly referred to and recognised (table 6.1). Such a classification could be further developed in different ways. For example, the *antidepressants* have been grouped according to their pharmacological properties and structure. However, Keilholz (1975) has argued that antidepressants can be more usefully

Table 6.1   Classification of Psychoactive Drugs

I. PSYCHOLEPTICS
   (a) major tranquillisers or antipsychotics
   e.g. (i) phenothiazines (chlorpromazine)
        (ii) reserpine and derivatives (reserpine and tetrabenazine)
        (iii) butyrophenones (haloperidol and trifluperidol)

   (b) minor tranquillisers
   e.g. (i) benzodiazepines (chlordiazepoxide and diazepam)
        (ii) substituted diols (meprobamate)
        (iii) diphenylmethane derivatives (benactyzine)

   (c) sedatives
   e.g. (i) barbiturates (amylobarbitone and phenylbarbitone)
        (ii) alcohol (ethanol)

II. THYMOLEPTICS
   (a) antidepressants
   e.g. (i) monoamine oxidase inhibitors (iproniazid and pargyline)
        (ii) tricyclic compounds (imipramine and amitriptyline)
        (iii) viloxazine

   (b) stimulants
   e.g. (i) agents related to neurohumoral substances (amphetamine and
           atropine)
        (ii) xanthines (caffeine and theobromine)

III. PSYCHOMIMETICS (or HALLUCINOGENS)
   e.g. (i) agents containing an indole nucleus (LSD and psilocybin)
        (ii) agents related to noradrenaline (mescaline)
        (iii) others (phencyclidine and tetrahydrocannabinol)

---

classified in terms of their effects on three different types of symptoms: inhibited drive, basic feelings of sadness, and anxiety. For example, clinical and experimental studies suggest that the effects of monoamine oxidase inhibitors (MAOIs)—iproniazid and pargyline—are dominated by increased drive and by mood enhancement, the former being the greater effect. The tricyclic compound, imipramine, has relatively little effect on drive, but has a powerful effect on mood. Neither of these two drugs produces much relief of anxiety; this can be achieved through the use of trimeprimine or chlorprothixene. Keilholz argues that the success of treating depression with psychoative drugs depends on the prescription of the drug with the appropriate spectrum of action for the particular case under consideration. Furthermore, the prescription of the wrong drug can have disastrous effects. In depressive states involving anxiety, the use of a drug which increases drive may aggravate the anxiety and by releasing inhibition may increase the risk of suicide.

Whatever classification is adopted, its value is one of economy and, not only should the properties of the drugs encompassed by that classification be investigated, but the scheme itself should be continually evaluated and modified. For example, it has been apparent for some time that terms like stimulant and depression, as applied to amphetamine-like and barbiturate-like drugs respectively, do not refer to any intrinsic properties of those drugs but to an interaction between the drug response and test situation. For example, Clark and Steele (1966) showed that the effects of amphetamine on the bar-pressing behaviour of rats was dependent on the on-going rate of bar pressing. They trained hungry rats to press a bar for food reward. Each rat was 'shaped', according to standard operant conditioning procedures, to press the lever on a three-component multiple schedule of reinforcement. A schedule of reinforcement determines when and how often, in this example, the rat is rewarded for bar pressing. The three different components of Clark and Steele's multiple schedule produced different rates of bar pressing: (a) extinction, low rate (mean: 0.01 presses per second); (b) fixed interval, medium rate (mean: 0.18 presses per second); and (c) fixed ratio, very high rate (mean: 0.84 presses per second). Increasing doses of the drug (0.5 to 4.0 mg/kg) *increased* the rate of bar pressing in the low and medium components, but *decreased* it in the high rate component.

6.2 THE USE OF DRUGS AND PSYCHOLOGICAL DISORDER

Several of the drugs mentioned in the preceding section have found use in the treatment of psychological disorder. Laurence (1973) has suggested that, in general, these drugs are less necessary in treating neuroses than in treating psychotic states. He rests his argument on the relative contributions of environmental factors to the two types of disorder. Possibly there are even fewer effective alternatives to drug therapy for the treatment of psychoses.

In treating psychoses (manic depressive illness and schizophrenia), the major tranquillisers, in particular the phenothiazines, and the tricyclic antidepressants have been shown to be of value. The phenothiazines have a remarkable ability to control hyperactive and hypomanic states without seriously impairing consciousness, and they modify abnormal behaviour in schizophrenic states. They are ineffective against depression, unless it is accompanied by agitation, and indeed may make it worse. The tricyclic antidepressants are structurally related to the phenothiazines, and may be effective in relieving both endogenous and reactive depressions.

In treating the different types of neurosis, the minor tranquillisers, in particular the benzodiazepines, and both tricyclic and monoamine oxidase inhibiting antidepressants are used. Alcohol (see later) is also highly effective; it has the advantage of not requiring medical prescription, but the great disadvantage of being very addictive. The benzodiazepines have a marked taming effect in vicious animals. They also have a muscle-relaxant effect. Perhaps their major clinical effect is due to their relatively selective action on the limbic system; they are effective in the control of emotion (see chapter 2) and are used extensively in combating anxiety and tension. Of the antidepressants, the tricyclic compounds appear to have fewer major side-effects than the MAOIs, and are therefore the drugs of first choice. They do not suit all patients though, and MAOI's may then be used. These are more effective in reactive than in endogenous depression.

The use of drugs in the treatment of psychoses may be a matter of controlling the patient's behaviour to make it more socially acceptable, and more manageable. It is hoped that the patient will benefit, either directly or indirectly, from the drug-induced changes in his behaviour. Undoubtedly patients often do. However, in some cases it could be argued that their abnormal behaviour is their way of coping with their life stress. It is obviously not completely effective and involves distress. Despite this it is a form of coping and may prevent complete collapse. Preventing or modifying his behaviour does not remove the life stress, just the patient's attempts at coping. Distress may actually increase as a result of drug therapy, although behaviour appears more normal.

The use of drugs in the treatment of neuroses is usually as a short-term crutch to allow the patients to deal more effectively with the demands on them. The anxiety experienced by a person as a result of stressful demands may exaggerate the problem by reducing capability. Without benzodiazepine treatment the patient may not cope; with the drugs he might cope effectively. Drugs used in the treatment of neuroses should be backed up by other forms of support and therapy. Unfortunately, they rarely are. The problem then arises that the short-term crutch becomes the subject of a more permanent dependence (see section 6.3). This problem may be made more severe because some drugs not only reduce the experience of anxiety (stress) but also reduce capability.

6.3 DRUGS, PLACEBOS AND SUGGESTIBILITY

The classification(s) discussed in section 6.1 makes reference to the effects of different drugs exerted through their pharmacological activity. However, psychoactive drugs may have another sort of effect, and one that is no less potent. They may have an effect which is largely psychological in origin based on the person's expectations and beliefs, and on his suggestibility. This effect has been termed the placebo effect. The eighteenth-century royal physician Peter Shaw wrote in 1750: 'And it is doubtless as well for the Patient to be cured by the working of his Imagination, or a Reliance upon the Promise of his Doctor, as by repeated doses of Physic'.

Few people, if any, can take a drug with complete indifference to and in complete ignorance of its possible effects. If we take an analgesic we do so with the expectation that it will reduce the pain of, for example, tooth- or headache. If we are prescribed a sedative, we take it with the expectation that it will bring a better night's sleep. These expectations can be self-fulfilling, and determine to a large extent the drug response. There are two approaches in considering this type of psychological effect:

(a) as a part of the overall effects of psychoactive drugs, and
(b) as the effects of pharmacologically inert placebos.

Fisher (1970) has outlined three general principles which relate to the operation of these non-pharmacological effects. These he has discussed in the clinical context. First, the more a response system involves central (brain) processes, the greater will be the role of non-pharmacological factors in determining the drug response. Second, many of these factors may be eventually explained in terms of physiological and pharmacological processes. Third, the more potent a drug is, the less sensitive it will be to such factors. It is possible that the person's expectations of the drug's effects can be contrary to its pharmacological activity. In such a situation it is more than possible that the non-pharmacological effects will dominate.

Placebos, with no known pharmacological activity, administered in a thoroughly convincing way, have repeatedly proved effective in the treatment of many types of illness. They have proved effective not only in the context of mental disorder, but also in the treatment of a large number of more physical conditions; Claridge (1972) lists severe asthma, persistent cough, diabetes, angina, seasickness, rheumatoid arthritis, and the common cold. It is interesting and important that most if not all of these 'more physical' conditions have at some time been discussed in terms of psychological (stress) factors contributing to their aetiology and prognosis. It is possibly through this mechanism that the placebo has its effects. What is being discussed here is the role of drug taking in producing a cognitive reappraisal of the individual's condition, with a subsequent relief from the experience of being ill. In turn, the relief of that stress may attenuate the physiological stress response which might be an (non-specific) exacerbating factor for the specific complaint.

The occurrence of side-effects has been noted to be associated with the use of placebos, as it has with the use of active drugs. This was observed in a study by Claridge in 1961, in which he was looking at the effects of the tranquilliser meprobamate on the performance of a choice–reaction time task. His subjects were soldiers. One half of his subject group received tablets of meprobamate, the other half received placebo tablets which were identical in appearance and taste. All his subjects were ignorant of the nature of the substance they were given. A surprisingly high number of placebo subjects reported unpleasant side-effects, usually drowsiness and nausea. In a more recent study, the author (Cox, 1975b) observed that student subjects given sugar, but believing it was a metabolic stimulant, tended to report feelings of dizziness and faintness, and of sweating and of having stomach pains. In both situations the side-effects reported were 'real' to the subjects. Knowles and Lucas (1960) noted that the introduction of the experience of stress into their experiment on personality factors and the subjective assessment of placebo effects *increased* the number of side-effects reported.

Placebos have received considerable attention in experimental situations, perhaps in their own right as much as a control for the non-pharmacological effects of a particular drug. In Claridge's (1961) experiment, the tranquilliser meprobamate impaired subjects' performance of the choice–reaction time task, but so did the placebo. Both drug and placebo groups were much worse than an 'untreated' group. The conclusion must be that simply taking 'pills' was sufficient to disrupt performance, and that whatever pharmacological action meprobamate had in this respect had no further effect. Frankenhaeuser and her colleagues (1964) deliberately manipulated the placebo effect, and measured the outcome against a battery of subjective and physiological indices, and against performance on a reaction time task. Each subject was tested twice, once after being given a gelatine capsule and told that it contained a stimulant, and once after being given the capsule and told it contained a depressant. The two types of placebo had strong and opposite effects. All the changes which occurred were in a predictable direction. For example, the 'depressant' reduced pulse rate, blood pressure, level of performance, and feelings of alertness. It enhanced feelings of sleepiness and depression.

One individual factor which is important in determining a person's placebo response is his suggestibility. It is almost self-evident that the more suggestible a person is the more strongly he will respond to placebos. An experiment by Steinbock and his colleagues (1965) attempts to demonstrate this. Steinbock was interested in whether the improvement in psychiatric outpatients treated with placebos could be predicted from their scores on the Press test of suggestibility. In the Press test, the subject is seated holding a rubber bulb attached to a manometer. The subject is told that his grip is getting tighter and tighter. His actual grip is measured under this suggestion and the pressure score obtained is taken as a measure of suggestibility. Steinbock reported a significant positive correlation between suggestibility measured in this way and positive reaction to the placebo.

One common attitude to the use of placebos is that because their effects are psychological and not pharmacological they are trivial. This is certainly not so. It could be argued that if similar effects can be brought about by a drug and placebo it is safer, in all respects, to use the latter. That similar effects can be brought about by these two types of agent cannot now be doubted. Perhaps part of the effect of a placebo or part of the non-pharmacological effects of any drug is a reflection of the doctor–patient relationship. The doctor is a status figure, and one on which the patient is very dependent. He is a figure to be respected and believed in, and possibly pleased. If the doctor says, 'this pill should make you better', he is generally believed and the patient adopts that expectation. Indeed, he may actually feel better immediately. The enthusiasm of the doctor for any particular drug therapy will be communicated to the patient; the more the doctor believes in the pill, the more the patient will. Apparently there is an old saying in psychiatry that a new technique will work miracles until the enthusiasm for it wears off. This must be particularly so for placebo effects.

6.4 COPING AND DRUGS

Drugs have long been used to alleviate the experience of stress, either as adjuncts to other types of therapy or as a therapy in themselves. The use of drugs in the management of stress has already been very briefly discussed in chapter 5.

Drugs do provide a powerful way of changing cognitive appraisal, and may do so by distorting a number of important perceptions: perception of demand, of capability, and of the consequences of attempts at coping. As a result of an altered appraisal of his situation the person may feel differently about it, and respond differently to it. A dramatic example is provided by Bruyn (1970), who reported the case of a twenty-one-year old student who was an experienced user of lysergic acid diethylamide (LSD) but who on her thirty-second trip declared she was a swan and dived to her death from a fifth-floor window. Obviously drug-induced changes in cognitive appraisal can produce particular problems such as that just described. In addition to these, two more general difficulties exist with this form of therapy. First, although a particular drug may reduce the immediate experience of stress, it may also reduce the person's ability to cope both cognitively and behaviourally. Thus, the drugs may have the seemingly paradoxical effect of both reducing and enhancing the person's difficulties. Second, because the drug reduces the experience of stress, taking it is a reward process, and this may form the basis for the development of psychological, and then possibly physical, dependence.

The first problem is highlighted in the use of alcohol to produce a relief from stress. Drinking in response to the occurrence of stressful demand is common.

Myers (1961, 1967) and Veale and Myers (1969) have studied the effects of stress on the alcohol intake of laboratory rats. When the animals were exposed to daily unavoidable electric shocks, their alcohol intake did not change. However, when they were able to work to avoid the shocks by pressing a lever, they increased their consumption. Crowding also produced increases in alcohol intake. As more and more rats were added to a constant living space, alcohol consumption progressively increased. (In 1963, Smart reported that alcoholics tended to come from large families.)

Under the effects of alcohol the person is free of feelings of anxiety, depression and incompetence. As Samuel Johnson wrote, 'in the bottle, discontent seeks for comfort, cowardice for courage, shyness for confidence'. It would appear that many use alcohol to relieve a sense of personal inadequacy, and it has been suggested that this relief may result from a release from the inhibitory control normally exerted over behaviour by the higher centres of the brain (see Crossland, 1970). It is argued that alcohol causes an irregular descending depression of the central nervous system, first affecting cortical function. Its actions at this level seem to remove restraint, and social inhibitions disappear, behaviour becoming more childlike. However, Laurence (1973) believes this view to be naïve. He sees ordinary doses of alcohol acting chiefly on the arousal mechanism of the brainstem reticular formation. Direct cortical depression then only occurs with high doses.

When alcohol is taken in relatively small amounts its effects can have obvious social value; the shy introvert becomes more talkative, the puritan sheds his prejudices, and the saint forgets the miseries of the world. All this may make for better, more jovial company—'alcohol lubricating the mechanism of social intercourse'. Perhaps the degree to which a person's social behaviour changes under the influence of alcohol provides a measure of the self-control he normally exercises. In this respect 'sobriety disguises a man'.

However, even moderate amounts of alcohol can cause significant changes in the accuracy of judgement and in the speed of reactions. Larger doses bring about more obvious and more gross changes in behaviour. Such effects increase the risk to the alcohol user and to others that interact with him. The gross effects of alcohol are summarised in table 6.2. These effects refer to the moderate drinker. They

Table 6.2   The Gross Effects of Alcohol

Amount of alcohol	Blood alcohol level	GROSS EFFECTS
Pints of beer (1 litre = 1.76 pints) 3.8% alcohol	mg/100 ml blood	
	up to 50	Feelings of satisfaction and comfort
1.5	50	Loss of social inhibition, garrulous, reckless
3	100	Lack of coordination, slurred speech
6	200	Obviously drunk but mobile
9	300	Drunk and stuporous
12	400	Dead drunk, anaesthetised, comatose
	above 400	Dead

are modified by a large number of factors. For example, the abstainer or the infrequent drinker may be dramatically and badly affected by very small amounts of alcohol, while the regular heavy drinker may appear relatively resistant to these gross effects. Tolerance, in fact, does appear to be the most important determinant of the behavioural response. However, there are other factors to consider, such as the person's sex, the time of day at which the alcohol is taken, the nature of the drink, and the amount of food in the person's stomach. Furthermore, the response to the drug is potentiated by certain tranquillisers and antihistamines. In such circumstances, very small amounts of alcohol can again have quite dramatic effects.

The balance between the satisfying effects offered by the drug and the impairment of behaviour that it causes is exemplified by the manager who in response to a difficult morning drinks at lunchtime and is thus unable to work efficiently during the afternoon. In this way he may ensure a difficult morning the following day, and in response to that will drink the following lunchtime. A vicious circle could be established, the drug both relieving and causing the experience of stress. Another example is provided by the popularly reported effects of alcohol on sex. These were neatly summarised by

138

the porter in Macbeth: 'it provokes the desire, but takes away the performance'. Without doubt this is cause for the experience of much stress.

The area which has attracted much discussion is that of the effects of alcohol on safety, and in particular on road accidents. It has already been noted that alcohol impairs judgement and changes speed of reaction. It thus poses a dangerous problem for the road user, both driver and pedestrian.

In 1969, the Automobile Association estimated, on the basis of a driver survey, that in Britain at that time about two million people were driving daily under the influence of drugs (alcohol *and* others) that could impair their driving skill. Earlier, Borkenstein and his colleagues (1964) had shown that as a person's blood alcohol level rises, as a result of increased consumption, he has progressively more chance of being involved in a road accident. Working from their results it would appear that the moderate drinker is eight times as likely to be involved in an accident after three pints of British beer as he is after a pint and a half. After about four and a half pints he is twenty times as likely to have an accident.

A study by Burn (1956) examined the effects of alcohol on experienced professional truck drivers in the United States. All the subjects of that study were well accustomed to drink. The drivers were required to perform a series of tasks which involved the precise judgement of distance and the negotiation of a number of hazards. After consuming enough alcohol to raise their blood alcohol levels by no more than 50 mg per 100 ml blood (about one and a half pints of beer) some of the drivers showed an impairment of judgement and an increase in reaction time.

In a study of Manchester bus drivers, all of whom were recipients of awards for safe driving, Cohen and his colleagues (1958) found that, even with such experienced drivers, there was no safe blood alcohol level below which it was certain that no impairment of judgement would occur. The drivers were invited to estimate through what gaps they thought they could drive their bus, and were then given a driving test to determine the smallest gap through which they would actually attempt to drive. Finally they were told to drive through gaps regardless of their opinions. The main conclusions were that after alcohol the drivers' performance deteriorated, that they were involved in greater hazards, and that they displayed a false confidence in their driving ability. Many other laboratory and field studies have been carried out on the effects of alcohol on driving and driving skills. There can be no doubt that it impairs the person's capacity to drive with the maximum skill and care of which he is capable. Statistical accident data support this. What is true for drivers is also true for users of other complex machinery, and it is obviously unwise for any person in charge of potentially dangerous equipment to take alcohol before operating it. There is also evidence that there is danger after alcohol has left the blood, during the hangover period, perhaps due to irritability and fatigue.

6.6 DRUG DEPENDENCE

The second problem with the use of drugs is that dependence on them may easily be established.

Until quite recently a discussion of the present kind would have centred around two particular terms: addiction and habituation. These were formally defined in 1957 by the World Health Organization (WHO). Addiction was seen as a state of periodic chronic intoxication produced by repeated consumption of a drug. Its characteristics included an overpowering need (compulsion) to continue taking the drug, the willingness to obtain it by any means, and a tendency to increase the dose. It was noted that addiction had a detrimental effect on both the individual and society. Habituation, on the other hand, did not necessarily involve intoxication, and involved a desire but not a compulsion to take the drug, and lacked an associated withdrawal syndrome. Its detrimental effects were obviously primarily at the individual level, and the drug was taken for the sense of improved well-being which it engendered.

Careful examination of the definitions proposed in that year reveals their weaknesses. Many of the differences are tenuous; for example, compulsion against desire. Many are too generalised; for example, the presence or absence of detrimental effects on society. Perhaps more important than these weaknesses is the explicit suggestion of two separate processes, and that one is less dangerous than the other. By 1964 it was clear that these definitions were no longer tenable, and in that year the WHO suggested that the term 'drug dependence' be used to include the conditions previously known as addiction and habituation. It was argued that, where it was necessary to be more specific about the nature of the phenomenon, that could be specified by reference to a known drug. For example, a new

140

analgesic drug might be shown to produce a dependence of a morphine- or an alcohol-type. Despite this move towards a single concept of dependence it has still been proved useful to distinguish two types: psychological and physical. This distinction had to be made because some drugs do not produce withdrawal syndromes but do produce a very strong dependence. The idea of a psychological state of dependence was developed to describe the effects of these drugs.

6.6.1 Psychological Dependence

Of these two types of dependence, psychological dependence is perhaps the more difficult to define. According to the WHO argument it involves the feeling of satisfaction; continuous administration of the drug produces this desired effect (or, at least, avoids discomfort). Central to understanding this concept is the idea that taking the drug is a rewarding experience; psychological dependence may thus be a form of learning. It has long been accepted that acts which produce a satisfying or pleasant state tend to be repeated. Their effects increase the probability of their occurrence. In the case of drugs there is the formation of a true drug habit. This may be very strong in the case of, say, cocaine, less so with nicotine, and less still with caffeine.

If psychological dependence is a matter of learning, the question is that of the nature of the reinforcement. The first, most obvious, satisfying aspect of drug taking lies in the pharmacological effects of the drug. It may produce elation, reduce anxiety, heighten the senses; the drug may make the person's world less worrying or more exciting. Through its direct effects it offers a form of escapism, or facilitates social interaction. The *act* of taking the drug may also be rewarding in *social* terms. It may afford membership of a desired group or subculture or identification with a person or group of people. The member of a sports club may not be accepted as 'one of the boys' if he does not drink. Taking cannabis may identify a person with a particular anti-establishment subculture. Smoking a particular brand of cigarette is advertised as a jet-set activity. Examples of the social rewards associated with drug taking abound, partly, perhaps, because our Western industrialised society is a system which cultivates the social rewards of drug taking.

Leavitt (1974) discusses the role, and *personal* rewards, of drug taking in dealing with life problems (stress). He suggests that drugs may be taken to avoid problems and thus the need to make decisions on them. This may be especially so during adolescence, and represents an escape from reality. Avoiding or postponing difficult decisions unfortunately does not always remove the need to make them, although it may make the decisions easier by reducing the number of alternatives possible. For example, the question of whether or not to accept a new job may be postponed until the job offer expires. The person may then find it easier to decide to remain with his present job. The vehicle for not taking the important decision in time may have been heavy drug usage.

The person may become psychologically dependent on things other than drugs. The Canadian Government Commission of Inquiry on the *Non-medical Use of Drugs* (1970) listed, *inter alia*, television, music, books, foods, hobbies, sport, money and sex. It concluded that psychological dependence may be an important part of the normal psychological condition.

Withdrawal from a drug of psychological dependence does not produce any physical disorder (withdrawal syndrome), but may produce feelings of severe discomfort. It is possible that the drug habit may be maintained simply to avoid those feelings.

6.6.2 *Physical Dependence*

The use of a drug may lead to the development of tolerance and physical dependence. Tolerance is characterised by a diminished response to a drug with repeated usage. As the drug is repeatedly administered it becomes progressively less effective. Larger and larger doses are required to produce the effect to the same degree. Tolerance can be associated with an increased rate of drug metabolism, drug breakdown, inactivation and excretion. This can be seen as an adaptive response of the person to his drug taking: his body changes to function most normally in the presence of the drug, and, by implication, somewhat less normally without it. Tolerance occurs for most but not all drugs, and for some drug effects and not others. For example, the effects of morphine on the central nervous system, analgesia, respiratory depression, sedation and euphoria, all wane with the development of tolerance. However, the peripheral effects of the drug, such as its action on the gastrointestinal tract, do not change. Tolerance is often linked to physical dependence. The latter cannot occur without the development of tolerance, but tolerance does not necessarily produce dependence. In the majority of instances in which tolerance to a drug has developed the adaptive changes which take place have no untoward consequences when administration of the drug ceases.

Physical dependence occurs when body function, including that of the central nervous system, adapts to the extent that it is only efficient in the presence of the drug, and is disrupted when the drug is withdrawn. The disruption is caused by the development of hyperactivity in the aspects of function depressed by the drug. This withdrawal (or abstinence) syndrome is often referred to as a rebound phenomenon; sedatives, for example, cause increased arousal. The withdrawal syndrome can be very severe, even fatal, and can only be prevented or relieved by taking the drug.

A term which could be used in the description of physical dependence is the 'dependence balance account'. The drug user on becoming tolerant requires more and more drug for it to maintain its effects. The quantity of drug taken becomes a threat in itself. As dependence develops, the person takes the drug not only to maintain its effects, but to prevent the withdrawal syndrome from occurring. It will occur not only if the drug is withdrawn but also if the increase in dose is not maintained. For the drug user the balance of the account is between the initial, desired drug effects and the dependence problems which taking the drug causes, and which may ensue on its withdrawal. Consider morphine: the drug is usually taken for the feelings of elevation it produces. It causes a top-of-the-world, boss, sensation. This, however, is very short-lived. While taking the drug, the morphine user tends to be introverted, has pin-pointed pupils and is constipated. On having the drug withdrawn, the user becomes restless, experiences coldness, has increased nasal secretion, and irregular respiration. This progresses into abdominal cramp, vomiting, diarrhoea, profuse sweating, muscle pain and muscle twitching. The person may then become violent, and then suffer cardiovascular collapse. The syndrome may reach a peak after three days, but may persist up to several weeks. Alcohol has a similarly bad account. Its immediate effects are common enough. On the drug being withdrawn, the person experiences tremor, nausea, vomiting, and profuse perspiration. The tremor increases and the person has visual hallucinations. These hallucinations take on a terrifying aspect, the person becomes violently agitated and suffers delusions of persecution. Hallucinations become auditory as well as visual. Fever and convulsions occur, and then cardiovascular collapse. Again the syndrome reaches its peak after three days.

6.6.3   Escalation

Closely associated with the concepts and actual problem of dependence are those of escalation. Escalation refers to progress from use of one drug to another which is more obviously dangerous. The common argument holds that the person may begin taking a relatively innocuous agent such as cannabis. He may then graduate to a more powerful drug like heroin to regain the experience lost as he grows tolerant of the cannabis. He may also do so because, having found cannabis innocuous, he is less concerned about the dangers of taking heavy drugs. He may find the graduation easy because he is already mixing with people who can readily supply the illegal heroin. However, the evidence to support this view, much researched in British and Canadian Government reports, is very equivocal and elusive. Indeed, Schofield (1971) has pointed out that heroin is not simply a more powerful form of cannabis to which people turn when the cease to get satisfying effects. It is a drug of a quite different nature and meets totally different psychological needs. However, the escalation theory should not be dismissed because it is difficult to demonstrate a progress from, say, cannabis to heroin. Perhaps availability is the key to the situation. Where subcultures discriminate between the use of soft and heavy drugs, and the availability of the latter is restricted, escalation may not occur. However, if the subculture does not make that distinction, and both soft and heavy drugs are freely available, then escalation may occur.

6.7   DRUGS AND SOCIETY

Both the legal and illegal use of all drugs has increased in Western industrialised societies, partly as a reflection of more liberal attitudes, partly with the development of national health services, and undoubtedly as a function of increased availability and marketing. Engström (1975) has pointed out that drug sales in Sweden increased from 380 million Swedish kronor in 1960 to 1484 million Swedish kronor in 1972. This pattern of increase is by no means atypical. World drug sales in 1970 (excluding the communist countries) amounted to £7200 million, about one-third of this being spent in North America, and another third in the European Community countries. It is very obvious that the major drug consumers are the developed countries; the developing countries with four-fifths of the world's population consume only one-fifth of the world's drugs.

The increase in drug consumption is maintained and promoted by organised and highly efficient marketing machines. Drug advertising occurs in most if not all developed countries. It is aimed either at the general public (or members of particular subcultures) or at the medical and paramedical professions. In many cases the nature of the advertising is very similar. Two particular themes may be discerned. The first has already been mentioned in terms of what is satisfying about drug taking. Advertising suggests that one may gain membership of a group, or identify with individuals or groups, by using particular drugs. The examples are legion; most make reference to power or status, political, socioeconomic or sexual. The other theme used in advertising is that a particular type of drug is a necessity, say antibiotics or analgesics, and that the drug in question is better than all others. It has more specific effects, is more powerful, quicker acting, is not habit-forming, and has fewer side-effects. How many new drugs have had these standard claims made for them?

It is possible that even without the help given by marketing techniques, drug sales would continue to grow, reflecting increasing need. Engström (1975) has argued that a number of social projections can be made with some certainty:

(1) the world population will increase

(2) the age distribution of that population will shift: there will be an increase in the fraction over 65 years of age

(3) the majority of that population will live in urban areas

(4) there will be an abundance of socioeconomic and political changes.

These four factors will impose an extra life stress on people, by requiring greater adaptation; this will be particularly so for those over 65. Engström's fifth projection is that there will be an increase in health problems. This will be made more likely by the changes in the physical environment, largely due to pollution and the energy shortage, and by dietary changes. As a result of this somewhat pessimistic trend greater demands will be made on drugs to provide relief from stress.

145

The Canadian Government Commission of Inquiry into the *Non-medical Use of Drugs* (1970) discussed the causes of drug use in modern society. One cause that was highlighted was *alienation*. This term was used to refer to the estrangement of many young people and adults from the institutions, processes and dominant values of society. It involved a failure to be able to think of a meaningful life and a sense of inability to influence the course of society. Alienation was seen as a result of current life stresses, and a cause of non-medical drug usage. The Commission also saw drugs as a way of filling the gap between unrealistic aspiration and capacity, as a response to anonymity, and to a loss of faith in reason and a new emphasis on emotion. They concluded that much contemporary drug use simply serves the purpose of relieving the stress and tension experienced in modern living. In their view overstimulation may lead people to resort to drugs to produce relaxation or 'instant rest', while boredom may lead to the use of stimulant and hallucinogenic drugs.

Undoubtedly the question for society is whether it should permit this increase in drug use, or whether it should curtail it. The problems with drug therapy for the experience of stress have already been discussed and cannot be ignored. Are they sufficiently severe to warrant a more conservative approach to the use of drugs? The answer must be that they are. Man needs to adapt psychophysiologically to the stresses he faces, perhaps aided by drugs. However, he should not be allowed to become dependent on them for that adaptation.

7

Stress at Work

Colin Mackay and Tom Cox

For most people at some time during their lives the work that they do acts as a source of stress. Often the experience of work stress is short-lived, and is successfully dealt with without long-lasting physical or psychological effects. Unfortunately, however, it can represent a continuous burden, and a serious hazard to comfort and health. Traditionally occupational hazards were regarded simply in terms of biological, chemical or physical agents which might more-or-less directly physically 'damage' the person. Relatively little attention, by contrast, was paid by the occupational health professions to psychosocial factors as a source of stress, or to effects on psychological health. As a result the question of occupational mental health is a comparatively new one, especially in Britain. Unfortunately this country has lagged behind in this respect, largely because much of management and many unions have been peculiarly impermeable to the importance of considering occupational mental health. They have only very recently started to participate in that discussion. By contrast, more progressive policies on the part of government, and the two industrial 'groups' in the United States and Northern Europe has meant that both legislation and the practice of health and safety at work are far more advanced in those countries than in Britain. It is to be hoped that this difference will be reduced in the next decade or so.

7.1 THE SIZE OF THE MENTAL HEALTH PROBLEM

The prevalence of poor mental health partly or directly related to work is difficult to assess in Britain due to the paucity of statistical data. The data that do exist come from varied and indirect sources.

In a review of the available evidence, Taylor (1974) notes that at first sight occupational stress as reflected in a lack of job satisfaction might not be a problem. In 1971, for example, the General Household Survey reported that a mere 2 per cent of the people interviewed were 'very dissatisfied' with their work, while only 4 per cent reported being 'rather dissatisfied'. Similar proportions occurred in a subsequent survey in 1972 (Office of Population and Censuses and Surveys, 1975). Despite this, it has been estimated that on average 37 million working days are lost per year through psychological (neurotic) disorder, through nervous debility, through headaches, and so on. This figure exceeds the 23 million days lost through accidents at work noted by Lord Robens as head of the British Government committee which studied the question of health and safety at work. Even so it is a probable underestimation as it fails to take account of absence diagnosed in terms of physical disorders which may be signs of man under stress, for example dyspepsia, skin complaints and coronary heart disease (see chapter 4). As the Office of Health Economics has pointed out, 'it is increasingly recognised that conditions like 'bronchitis', 'slipped disc', and so on, are simply used as conventional diagnostic labels for episodes of absence which owe more to social and economic factors than a simple inability to work for medical reasons'. Mental health problems are among the fastest growing sources of days lost from work. The 1970 sickness-absence figures represent an increase of 22 per cent over the preceding 15 years. However, in the same period, the number of days lost due to psychosis and neurosis rose by 152 per cent in men and 302 per cent in women.

To place too much trust in statistics such as these would be unwise. Three factors are often mentioned to caution their interpretation. First, views on the social acceptability of absence from work due to mental ill-health have changed. Second, there have been associated changes in diagnostic practice; and third, there may have been changes in propensity to stay away from work. All three could combine to produce larger changes in mental health problems than in physical health problems. However, it is unlikely that a contrast of such size could be without some real foundation.

7.2   PHYSICAL HEALTH AND STRESS AT WORK

Poor mental health is only part of the cost of stressful work. In chapter 4 the effects of stress in relation to physical health were discussed. It was concluded that there was evidence that stress did play a significant role in the aetiology and prognosis of many physical disorders. Three were specifically discussed: coronary heart disease, bronchial asthma and diabetes mellitus. Many others were mentioned. A number of the studies which were cited as evidence in that chapter examined the health effects of occupational stress. On the basis of that evidence and more that is presented in this chapter, it has to be accepted that poor physical health can result from stressful work, even where the stress and the work itself have no direct physical impact on the person.

The problem of occupational health is real, and demands study and the development of solutions to it. It is in this context that the present chapter discusses the specific nature of occupational stress. It uses the framework offered by the transactional model developed in the earlier chapters of this book; it considers some of the factors thought to be important in determining the occurrence and experience of occupational stress.

7.3 THE NATURE OF OCCUPATIONAL STRESS

Research into occupational stress is, like research in all other areas of stress, complicated by the use of many different approaches and models. Several authors, for example Kearns (1973), Warr and Wall (1975) and Cooper and Marshall (1976), use response-based approaches similar in structure to the more physiological model of Kagan and Levi (1975). Other authors have used stimulus-based approaches (Kahn et al., 1964; Parrot, 1971; French and Caplan, 1973; Kahn, 1974), or interactional ones (McGrath, 1976). Further to this variety of approaches there is a confusion between certain concepts, for example between fatigue and stress. A large amount of effort has been devoted to the study of fatigue using the same independent and dependent variables as have been used in the study of stress (for example, Dukes-Dubos, 1971). To resolve this particular problem, Cameron (1973) has attempted to reconcile the two concepts by suggesting that fatigue should be viewed as a generalised response to stress (see chapter 1). However, the difficulty with the concept of fatigue in this context is that it can equally be viewed as a source of stress.

As already pointed out in chapter 1, there are inadequacies in both

149

stimulus- and response-based approaches to stress, and an alternative to these is the interactionalist approach. One such approach is the present authors' transactional model for occupational stress (Cox, 1975a; Mackay and Cox, 1976; Cox and Mackay, 1976). The transactional model says that the experience of stress results from an imbalance between demand, both external and internal, and capability in meeting demand, when coping is important.

7.3.1 Internal Demands: Needs, Values and Satisfaction

Internal demands are a reflection of the person's needs and values. According to writers such as Locke (1976), fulfilment of the person's needs in a way which does not offend his values leads to feelings of satisfaction. However, failure to fulfil those needs or the violation of the person's values leads to feelings of dissatisfaction, which contribute to the experience of stress.

Two major theories have dominated the literature on satisfaction and dissatisfaction at work. One is Maslow's (1954) postulation of a 'need hierarchy', and the other is Herzberg's (1966) 'motivation–hygiene' theory. Maslow's ideas have already been introduced in chapter 5, but will be developed in a little more detail here. He asserts that man has five different classes of need, and that these are arranged in a hierarchy of prepotency. The less potent do not come to govern behaviour until the more potent are fulfilled. The five classes of need are physiological needs, safety needs, needs related to belonging, friendship and love, esteem needs, related first to a need for achievement, and second to a need for recognition and appraisal, and finally the need for self-actualisation. Maslow's theory has been received with approval by many psychologists, especially those operating within business and organisational studies. Acceptance of the theory is largely an act of faith, however, as very little research has been carried out to verify it. This is partly due to the difficulty in translating Maslow's higher need concepts into a form which can be tested out. Perhaps the concept of self-actualisation is the most difficult in this respect. Admittedly, there have been a number of studies which can and have been interpreted in terms of Maslow's theory. Blackler and Williams (1971) have rightly pointed out, however, that interpretation is much different from testing. The problem of verification aside, Maslow's basic postulation of a hierarchy of needs has also attracted criticism. Many would accept

150

the nature of each of Maslow's classes, but not the idea of differential prepotency and of their hierarchical structure. According to Maslow no man would starve in order to satisfy a higher need, or sacrifice his safety for the sake of self-esteem. Everyday experience suggests that Maslow is wrong. An analogy may be made with the effects of intracranial self-stimulation in rats. A rat with electrodes implanted in its median forebrain bundle (part of the midbrain) will press a lever incessantly to obtain electrical stimulation of that area. Indeed the rat will keep pressing the lever for stimulation of this 'pleasure' system, and neglect food and water to the point of exhaustion and collapse. Perhaps, similarly, a man may find his work so rewarding in terms of gaining respect, and in terms of self-achievement and self-actualisation, that he may forgo a proper diet, risk his safety and lose his friends. It is possible that most of the problems with Maslow's theory of motivation are like those with Freud's theories, a product of the nature of the theory, and that it was conceived in relation to a particular limited population sample. Maslow has been criticised by Blackler and Williams (1971) on those grounds, that it may apply to one sector of American society but not to anybody else.

The second major theory is that of Herzberg (Herzberg *et al.*, 1959; Herzberg 1966). It has been variously described as his 'motivation–hygiene' or 'two-factor theory'. He has argued that job satisfaction depends on motivator factors. Dissatisfaction, on the other hand, relates to hygiene factors in that good hygiene factors prevent dissatisfaction but do not promote positive satisfaction. Motivator factors are those which relate to the job itself, such as achievement, recognition, work itself, responsibility and advancement. Hygiene factors, in contrast, relate to the job context, in terms of pay, working conditions, security and interpersonal relations. According to Herzberg, improving hygiene factors will only reduce the level of dissatisfaction and will not promote satisfaction and increase motivation to greater productivity. Better working conditions, greater security and, surprisingly, more pay, should not bring about positive changes in the experience of work, but job enlargement and job enrichment should do. Herzberg based his theory on a study of 200 engineers and accountants in Pittsburgh using a critical incident technique administered through semi-structured interviews. Many studies employing similar methodologies have given the same results across a variety of occupational groups. However, studies using different methods have given different findings, and have generally

151

his results maybe
reflect his method
more than findings

failed to support Herzberg's theory. His results are obviously a reflection of the critical incident technique which forces individuals to think in terms of dichotomies, and of that aspect of human nature which allows people to involve themselves in descriptions of satisfying events but to blame others and external factors as sources of dissatisfaction.

In an attempt to reconcile the salient aspects of these and the other available theories, Locke (1976) has suggested that job satisfaction results from an appraisal of one's job in terms of one's needs and values. He suggests that the critical appraisal is made in terms of the possibilities for the attainment of one's basic needs. Those needs Locke sees as of two distinct but interacting types: bodily and physical needs, on the one hand, and psychological needs on the other. A particularly important psychological need is that of personal growth. Growth is made possible mainly by the nature of the work itself. The most important factors relating to job satisfaction are as follows:

(1) mentally challenging work, which the individual can cope with successfully,

(2) personal interest in the work itself,

(3) rewards for performance which are consistent with the individual's aspirations,

(4) working conditions which allow the job to be completed satisfactorily and which are not physically demanding,

(5) high-self-esteem on the part of the individual, and

(6) basic values which are not violated by the above.

If some or all of these criteria are not met then dissatisfaction with the job may result, the consequences of dissatisfaction being ill-effects of physical and psychological health, poor labour relations and productivity, high labour turnover and absenteeism, and perhaps a high accident rate.

Internal demands, so represented in needs, values and job satisfaction, interact with external demands in producing the overall level of demand as perceived by the person when he appraises his work situation.

7.3.2 *External Demand and the Work Situation*

External demands may reflect different aspects of the person's work,

152

such as the tasks which go to make up that job and the way in which they are organised, the physical work environment, the psychosocial environment, and out-of-work activities. A wartime study conducted by Fraser and reported in 1947 identified a number of factors associated with an increased incidence of 'work neurosis'. In that study over 3000 workers from light and medium engineering firms were interviewed during a six-month period. The survey produced, although a wartime one, was thought to reflect, reasonably accurately, peacetime conditions. The factors identified were (from Lader, 1975)

(1) more than 75 hours of industrial work each week
(2) domestic factors, such as an inadequate diet, reduced leisure time leading to restricted social contacts, minimal recreation and interests, widowhood or separation, difficulties associated with undue responsibilities often associated with illness in the family, financial problems and those associated with housing and excessive travelling
(3) boring and disliked work
(4) work requiring skills inappropriate to the worker's level of attainment. This could be either the unskilled worker having to perform work requiring too high a level of skill, or the reverse
(5) very light or sedentary work
(6) assembly, bench, inspection or toolroom work, especially if it requires constant attention, but has little scope for initiative or responsibility
(7) work programmes which offer little variety
(8) tasks for which the lighting is unsatisfactory.

A much more recent study by Theorell (1974) further develops this list and the previous one. He looked at the relationship between the occurrence of life events (see chapter 4) and the occurrence of myocardial infarction (form of coronary heart disease). A life event was defined as a single incident in the recent life of a person which may have been associated with the experience of stress. Theorell found that life events relating to work were more frequently reported in his myocardial infarction group than in his matched controls. Eight work items were considered:

(1) change to a different line of work
(2) retirement from work

(3) major change in work schedule
(4) increased responsibility
(5) decreased responsibility
(6) trouble with boss
(7) trouble with colleagues, and
(8) unemployment for more than one month.

When the number of subjects who reported any of these eight work items was compared across the two groups, it was found that 41 per cent of the myocardial infarction group reported such changes at work during the year preceding onset of the disease, while in the same period only 17 per cent of the matched controls reported such changes. These eight factors, and the others mentioned, can all represent sources of 'external' demand.

7.3.3 Physical Environmental Factors

Temperature and humidity, noise and vibration, and illumination are usually considered under the common heading of environmental factors (see, for example, Murrell, 1965; McCormick, 1970). In assessing the external environment as a source of demand, standardised measures of these five factors are normally taken, and it is assumed that their intensity as measured reflects their level of demand. Perhaps the relative ease with which these measurements can be made is the reason why such environmental factors have attracted so much attention. Many studies have concentrated solely on the relationship between the measured intensity of the factor, and its observable effects. While this strategy has been partially successful in relating extremes of stimulation to behavioural and physiological change, it has been able to say little about the effects of more moderate stimulation. However, as pointed out in chapter 1 (and in other chapters), it is not actual demand that is important for the occurrence of stress but *perceived* demand. Ignoring the perceptual element which intervenes between stimulus and response makes it unlikely that the relationship between those two variables will be easily uncovered.

There is not space in the present book to consider all five of the environmental factors mentioned; only one, noise, will be discussed in any detail. Much research has concerned the effects of noise on performance and well-being. It is certainly a common and potent source

154

of discomfort and demand, and it is a sad fact that with a few exceptions the advance of industrial engineering and technology has caused an increase in noise levels. An important question for modern man is, therefore, what are the effects of noise? The available evidence suggests that it effects the person in two distinct ways. First, it can damage hearing. This may result in deafness, and occur from instantaneous damage to the ear, either the middle or inner ear, or to the auditory nerves. Severely reduced sensitivity to certain sound frequencies may also occur over a period of time, and so also may numbing for a limited period of time (temporary deafness). Continuous and extensive exposure to noise levels above 80 dBA is generally considered capable of bringing about hearing loss. However, impact noise, such as that from drop forges or heavy presses, and impulsive noise, from gun or rock blasts, generally bring about an impairment of hearing more quickly than exposure to continuous noise. The loss of hearing produced may be temporary, but with increasing or repeated exposure, there is less and less recovery and more permanent loss. Second, noise can have what might be termed a stress effect. It may produce changes in mood, intellectual and motor performance, general behaviour and general bodily state, all indicative of impaired psychological and physical well-being. Many of these effects referred to here have been reviewed either by Davies (1968) or Taylor (1975).

A number of studies have claimed to show that noise can have detrimental effects on health. Epidemiological studies have shown an increased incidence of hypertension in workers exposed to high noise levels (see Carlestam *et al.*, 1973). Apparently this increase in morbidity makes itself obvious after eight or more years of continued exposure. Jansen (1959) reported a study of more than 1000 foundry workers in various parts of Germany which suggested that workers exposed to high noise levels suffered more emotional tension, both at home and at work, than did workers exposed to lower noise levels. However, this study has been much criticised on methodological grounds (see Davies and Shackleton, 1975). A more carefully controlled survey of personnel involved in aircraft launching operations aboard U.S. Navy Aircraft Carriers showed that men most exposed to aircraft noise appeared to experience more anxiety than less-exposed groups (Davis, 1958). An increased incidence of psychological complaints has also been reported in several other studies although, after reviewing studies on noise and psychological disorder, Lader (1971) concluded that noise exposure does not generally increase psychological morbidity, but might be of aetiological significance in anxious people.

The short-term effects of noise in the laboratory have been extensively studied, and are well documented. In brief, it has been concluded that loud noise is potentially annoying (Atherley et al., 1972), interferes with communication (Bell, 1966), may be over-arousing (Broadbent, 1971; Davies, 1968; Hockey, 1970), interfere with information processing and affect attention, and may mask auditory feedback and inner speech (Poulton, 1976).

Kryter (1970) used the term 'perceived noisiness' as synonymous with noise being unwanted, unacceptable, annoying, objectionable, and disturbing. The characteristics of noises which make them be perceived in this way are high intensity and frequency, intermittency and reverberation. Certainly people can adapt to these annoying features, but the adaptation is never complete. Not surprisingly, noise interferes with speech communication. The greatest distance across which two people can talk depends on the ambient noise level and the loudness of their voices. For example, with a noise level of 70 dB, the people would need to be no more than 6 inches apart to talk normally and be understood. Telephone communication is more easily disrupted by noise, and at 70 dB would be impossible. In noisy surroundings, workers tend to develop coughs, hoarseness, throat lesions and pains trying to talk through the noise (Brewer and Briess, 1960).

Noise, it has often been suggested, increases arousal. This suggestion is usually associated with another, that task performance is an inverted U-shaped function of arousal (see chapter 2), poor performance being associated with both a high and a low level of arousal. This hypothesis has been variously used to explain the effects of noise on human performance (see Broadbent, 1971). It is often suggested in this context that loss of sleep reduces arousal, and the effects of noise and loss of sleep have been compared and their interaction studied. Both sources of stress can cause an impairment of task performance, but noise produces errors of commission (incorrect response to presented information), while loss of sleep produces errors of omission (failure to respond). Incentives may improve performance in a person suffering sleep loss, but they tend to cause a further deterioration in noise conditions. It is possible that noise only impairs performance in highly motivated individuals; it may

156

even improve the performance of those that are bored, as it does for those suffering sleep loss.

Despite being able on different occasions and with different tasks to demonstrate that noise can have the above effects, there is no evidence that it can bring about a general degradation of task performance. What is clear is that the effects that it has are dependent not only on the nature of the noise and its duration and intensity, but also on the nature of the task performance affected. McCormick (1970) has concluded that the tasks which are most susceptible to noise effects are those requiring both skill and speed, and those that demand a high level of perceptual capacity. The effects of noise are also subject to great individual variation. For example, a survey in central London revealed marked variations in susceptibility to noise (McKennell and Hunt, 1966). The authors suggested that the major portion of this variation may be related to some factor of personality. Lader (1971) suggests that those most at risk with respect to noise are those who habituate more slowly than normal. Such people are often characterised by anxiety.

Most, if not all, of the effects of noise demonstrated in the laboratory can be seen to operate in industrial situations (see, for example, Broadbent and Little, 1960). In such situations it not only constitutes a threat to performance and long-term well-being, but also can be important in the aetiology of accidents (see Broadbent, 1971).

As noted above noise and task effects interact, and tasks themselves are an important source of demand.

7.3.4 Task-inherent Demand

In discussions of task-inherent demand attention has often focused on two of its aspects, workload and the repetitiveness of work.

In most tasks it is possible to distinguish between an 'energy' and an 'information' component. This distinction has allowed the development of the concept of *load* in relation to both the physical and psychological aspects of tasks. The problems of handling heavy physical loads have been extensively studied (see Passmore and Durnin, 1955; Brouha, 1960) and need not be discussed here. Suffice to say that the physical requirements of the job interact with the information handling requirements in producing the experience of stress.

Welford (1973) has proposed that man evolved in such a way as to function best under conditions of moderate (psychological) load. This proposal was introduced and briefly discussed in chapter 1. He further proposed that man's function is less than maximal under conditions of underload and overload. This impairment of function is associated with the experience of stress. Frankenhaeuser and her colleagues (1971) have demonstrated that both extremes of load produce physiological stress reactions. These experiments were discussed in some detail in chapter 3. Using a factor analytical approach, French and his colleagues (1965) produced a distinction between two aspects of overload: quantitative overload, having too much to do, and qualitative overload, being faced with too difficult a job. Both aspects related to job tension and in a more complex way to measures of self-esteem. Several studies have highlighted a relationship between the extent and duration of work (quantitative load) and various types of ill-health. For example, Breslow and Buell (1960) observed that, from a sample of workers in light industry under the age of 45, those who worked more than 48 hours a week were twice as likely to develop coronary heart disease than those who worked 40 hours a week or less. Similarly, Russek and Zohman (1958) found that of 100 young coronary patients 25 per cent had been working at two jobs, and an additional 45 per cent had jobs which required at least 60 hours work a week. These studies have already been discussed in chapter 4.

Although the concept of load is important in understanding the nature and effects of task-inherent demand, other factors can also be demonstrated to be important in determining that demand. One important factor is repetitiveness. Repetitive jobs have resulted from the practice of work simplification and from the increasing automation of work. Both may be justified on economic grounds, personal, organisational and national, but there is much evidence to suggest that the repetition they produce is detrimental to health.

People's descriptions of their jobs often focus on their feelings towards the repetitive nature of their work, and this is amply illustrated in quotes reported by Benyon and Blackburn (1972), and by Warr and Wall (1975). Two others are reported here from the present authors' studies on repetitive work in the East Midlands of Britain. These examples are taken from accounts by employees in a light engineering company.

158

I sit by these machines and wait for one to go wrong, then I turn it off, and go and get the supervisor. They don't go wrong very much. Sometimes I think I'd like them to keep going wrong, just to have something to do. I do nothing. I sit and look at this machine, then that one, and that one, and then that one over there. Then I start all over again. I listen too. It's bloody monotonous.

I make these washers on this press. If I work fast I can take home good money. It's the same thing over and over again though. Put the blank on, drop the guard, that presses out the washer. I put it in that box and get the next blank. It's the same all day, over and over again. Sometimes it gets on top of you.

The effects of repetitiveness as a source of demand have been illustrated by Benyon and Blackburn (1972). They studied workers in the food manufacturing industry, mostly carrying out repetitive work such as packing on a line system. The workers were paid on a piecerate basis. Between 50 and 60 per cent (depending on the shift) found their work dull and monotonous. About 80 per cent complained that their work gave them no sense of achievement. The authors reported many references to tension resulting from boredom. One example is given below.

My nerves are terrible since I came here. I've lost three stone altogether. I needed to I suppose, but it's gone beyond a joke now. I'm getting very jumpy and irritable too. Especially when I'm at home, especially with my little brother. It gets everyone though. A girl on one of the belts near me went screaming around the department last week. It's doing the same thing day after day that does it.

Walker and Guest (1952) investigated the relationship between repetitiveness in assembly-line work and job attitudes in American car workers. The authors measured repetitiveness in terms of the number of operations carried out by the individual. Of those performing more than five operations, 69 per cent found their jobs interesting, of those performing two to five operations only 44 per cent described their jobs as interesting, and for those involved in single operation jobs, only 33 per cent felt their work to be interesting.

In his book *Working for Ford*, Benyon (1973) describes people's reactions to repetitive production line work. What emerges from his description is that most view such work as completely dull and monotonous, tedious, and without any intrinsic interest. People talked of enduring it for the money, and of being paid to put up with the boredom: 'If you work on the line, let your mind go blank and look forward to pay day and the weekend'. It appears that a common strategy for coping with this type of work is to 'turn off' one's intellectual processes. In a recent study of changes in self-reported arousal and stress brought about by exposure to repetitive production-line work (loading, sorting and packing) the author and his colleagues found that, after even short exposures to such work, people found it very difficult to introspect and report their own feelings. Before exposure to the work the same people had no difficulty in introspecting. This effect is obviously consistent with the turning-off hypothesis to describe some of the effects of repetitive work.

In a study of car assembly workers in Detroit during the mid-1950s, Kornhauser (1965) found that many of those he interviewed (about 40 per cent) had an unsatisfactory adjustment to life and poorer mental health than white-collar workers. These differences could not be accounted for in terms of differences in educational level or other job prerequisites. The poor well-being of his assembly workers seemed to be related not so much to their pay and conditions of work as to job content factors such as interest. Kornhauser's study was meticulously carried out and clearly pointed out the cost of repetitive assembly-line work. Unfortunately, according to O'Toole (1973), it is now generally regarded as underestimating the mental health problems of assembly-line workers. A recent study of sawmill workers by Johansson (1975) has supported this unfortunate picture. People who carried out very repetitive work in this situation (work cycles of less than one minute) were compared with others on less-restricting regimes (work cycles of 3 to 30 minutes). Those in the former group were found to suffer more frequently from depression, gastrointestinal disorders and disturbed sleep patterns than those in the latter. Undoubtedly there is a high personal cost of exposure to repetitive work.

Baldamus (1961) has commented on the surprising absence of severe distress in those engaged in repetitive work given that it is as costly as is thought. He suggests that it must have concurrent satisfactions which overlie or postpone any very acute negative feelings which might arise. He further suggests that the strongest and most frequent of these relative satisfactions is traction, the feeling of being pulled along by the inertia inherent in a particular activity. This experience is perhaps pleasant, and a relief to the tedium of repetitive work. It would be predicted on this basis that jobs with a high natural rhythm would be experienced as more pleasant than those with little rhythm. The authors and their colleagues have been developing a job-description adjective checklist (JDCL) based on the adjectives used by shop-floor workers when talking about their jobs. The responses of over 500 workers were factor analysed. None of the factors which emerged was related to traction. It may be sensible to look for the satisfactions of repetitive work outside the nature of the work. For example, for any individual worker, the work may offer, *inter alia*, financial security and independence, opportunity to meet people, and escape from a more demanding home environment. These factors may overlay or postpone the negative feelings which might arise as part of the cost of this work.

In many industrial situations repetitive work is machine paced. The space requirements and noise levels associated with those machines often cause the workers to be isolated from one another. These two factors tend to increase the cost of this work. Many attempts have been made to reduce the cost using job rotation and job enlargement schemes, and many attempts have been made to replace repetitive line work with autonomous work groups. Job rotation involves workers periodically changing to a different task, either on an obligatory or on a voluntary basis. Each worker is usually assigned a series of tasks requiring equal levels of skill, and rotates his job with that of another worker at periodic intervals. Although job rotation is claimed to increase job satisfaction, this benefit may be far outweighed by the disruption of social relationships it causes, the organisation it requires, and the effects that continual readjustment to new tasks may have on the worker's wage. Job enlargement involves combining two or more jobs into a single job. The enlarged job is one which is, perhaps, more interesting, more variable, and permits the worker more control over, and responsibility for, his actions. A distinction is sometimes made between horizontal and vertical job enlargement; the former involves extending a job across tasks at the same level, while the latter involves extending the workers' tasks and responsibilities into levels formally held by a superior. The effects of job enlargement are claimed to improve job satisfaction and all that is attendant on that. Autonomous work groups are an attempt to enlarge the workers' jobs to the logical conclusion of giving groups of them responsibility for producing or assembling the completed product. For example, instead of assembling cars on a line basis, groups of six to eight workers are given the responsibility of putting together entire cars. This strategy obviously increases each person's involvement in the work, and satisfaction through carrying the job through to completion. However, autonomous work groups tend to be less economic than lines both in terms of cost and time, to have a different set and level of training requirements, and to give more individual responsibility. Their presence in an industrial setting forces a new structuring of social relationships, and produces a new class of group leaders. Differential status also arises between groups as well as within groups. In short, autonomous work groups create a situation very different from that created by repetitive line work: one which has its own structure and difficulties. An experience of establishing autonomous work groups has been reported by Blake and Ross (1976).

Demand may arise not only from the physical environment or from factors inherent in work itself, but also from the psychosocial environment. Psychosocial demands are often related to the concept of roles, and discussed in terms of three factors: role conflict, role ambiguity and responsibility. These are discussed in the next section.

7.3.5 Role-related Demand

According to Warr and Wall (1975), 'the word *role* is borrowed directly from theatrical usage and refers to behaviour which is attached to certain positions rather than to the individuals who hold those positions'. Roles are prescribed actions and words rather than people. Roles are norms that apply to categories of people. Thus different roles have different sets of demands associated with them. As one man can attempt to fulfil more than one role, role conflict can arise when the requirements of two or more roles are incompatible. Role conflict can also occur within a role. Attempting to fulfil a role which is ill-defined or ambiguous is also very demanding, as is meeting the responsibility associated with certain roles.

Kahn *et al.* (1964) and Kahn and French (1970) have defined role conflict as 'the simultaneous occurrence of two or more sets of pressures such that compliance with one would make more difficult or render impossible compliance with the other'. They have distinguished at least four types of conflict. First, conflict may arise from the instruction to carry out a particular action when the person knows that such an action is at variance with previous instructions. Second, conflict may result from the incompatibility of information from different members of an organisation. Third, conflict can arise between different roles, as mentioned above, which may be within or outside the person's work. Last, conflict can arise because personal values and needs are violated by certain job or task requirements. In summarising a number of studies carried over a 10-year period, Kahn (1974) notes that the emotional cost of role conflict is reflected in increased job tension, lower job satisfaction, and reduced confidence in the employing organisation. Conflict also seems to be associated with poor interpersonal relations, and less trust in, respect and liking for, close colleagues. The experience of conflict can also be related to physiological change. Caplan (1971), for example found that over a 2-hour work period, scientists, engineers and administrators at the Goddard Space Flight Center had mean heart rates which correlated substantially with their subjective reports of role conflict.

Role ambiguity exists when an individual has inadequate information about his role at work. This may reflect a lack of clarity about work objectives, about colleagues' expectations, about the scope and responsibilities of the job, and about the job requirements (Kahn, 1974; Warr and Wall, 1975; Cooper and Marshall, 1976). In an extensive national survey of attitudes to ambiguity and conflict in the United States, Kahn and his colleagues (1964) found that 35 per cent of their 1500 respondents were unclear as to their job responsibilities. A similar proportion expressed feelings of uncertainty and a lack of clarity about what was expected of them by their coworkers, and about their prospects for promotion. Kahn and his colleagues reported that ambiguity was correlated with job tension, with a lack of job satisfaction, with a sense of futility and with reduced self-confidence. As with studies on role conflict, it was shown that low trust in, and liking for, colleagues was also associated with job ambiguity. The Goddard Space Flight Center study (Caplan, 1971), mentioned above, also considered the prevalence and effects of role ambiguity. In this study a surprisingly high percentage of the people involved (60 per cent) reported some experience of role ambiguity. Caplan found that ambiguity related to a lack of job satisfaction, and to feelings of job-related threat to both psychological and physical well-being. A further study by Caplan (French and Caplan, 1973) at the Kennedy Space Flight Center showed that, in addition to being related to these factors, role ambiguity could also be related to anxiety and depression.

The third major source of role-related demand is that of responsibility. According to Cobb (1974) there are substantial costs to health associated with heavy responsibility. Two different sorts of responsibility seem to exist: first, responsibility for people, for their work, welfare and promotion, and second, responsibility for things, for buildings, machinery, money. Responsibility for things often implies a responsibility for people; for example, the supervisor who is responsible for a company's cranes is also to a degree responsible for the cranes' drivers. It is responsibility for people which appears to carry the greatest risk to health (Wardwell *et al.*, 1964; Cobb, 1974). A study reported by Doll and Jones (1951) showed, for example, that foremen and executives as a combined group had more duodenal ulcers than the expected frequency, while various non-supervisory skilled and unskilled workers had ulcer rates as expected. Similar findings have been reported by Vertin (1954), Pflanz *et al.* (1956) and Gosling (1958). However, Hinkle and his colleagues (1968) carried out a study of the incidence of coronary heart disease in managers and workers at the Bell System Operating Companies in the United States, and concluded that men having high levels of responsibility had no increased risk of heart disease. An occupational group with considerable responsibility and a high work load are air-traffic controllers. Not only must the controller exercise almost continuous attention, but he must be able to work with low quality information very rapidly without making any mistakes. Cobb and Rose (1973) compared the incidence of various illnesses among a group of air-traffic controllers and among a group of 'second class' airmen. Data were obtained from compulsory medical examinations taken to renew their appropriate licences. Hypertension was found to be four times as prevalent among the controllers as among the airmen, after adjustment for age effects. The incidence of diabetes (see chapter 4) and peptic ulcers was about twice as high. Despite the conclusions of the Bell study (Hinkle *et al.*, 1968) the evidence of most studies in this area points to a marked cost of heavy responsibility.

7.4 COMMENTS

The present discussion of external demand has moved from environmental factors through task-inherent factors to role-related factors. Perhaps in doing so the discussion has also moved from talking about the major sources of demand for shop-floor jobs to those for clerical and managerial jobs. It might be argued that very poor working environments are more common in factories than offices, that repetition is a problem of unskilled line work more than of skilled or professional work, but that role-related problems are greater for those groups. If this argument can be carried through, and it is simply that different jobs have different types of demand associated with them, then a job–demand matrix may be a possible exercise.

The problems faced by managers are currently under much scrutiny, and management stress is a very popular area of study. Many factors have been described as contributing to the experience of stress by managers (Kearns, 1973; Cooper and Marshall, 1975) and some have already been discussed here. One particular factor, redundancy or the threat of redundancy, is now dealt with in more detail.

7.5 REDUNDANCY AND STRESS IN THE MANAGEMENT OF INDUSTRY

It is often argued that the current depressing economic situation is without question increasing the degree of stress experienced by management in British industry. If this is so, one inevitable effect might be the decreasing effectiveness of the managerial system, with only the most adaptive and robust parts surviving over the longer term without significant disruption. Many organisations may founder, not as a direct result of the economic pressures they face, but as a result of their growing inefficiency due to the pressures on their managers. One can predict that a general increased *inefficiency* rather than increased *efficiency* will therefore by symptomatic of a harsh economic climate. This is most certainly detrimental to industry in the short term but one may conjecture that over longer periods of time it leads to the evolution of better forms of management. However, there is little evidence that this biological analogy holds true.

Perhaps the most important threat to the managerial system is through *redundancy*. This, unfortunately, now constitutes a very real threat to individual managers. For example, the Professional and Executive Recruitment service (PER) has recently reported a 40 to 45 per cent increase in registrations, but a 30 per cent decrease in management vacancies. The effects of being made redundant are greatly enhanced because managers tend to see it as a negative judgement of their job competence. Not only does redundancy cause a necessary reorganisation of a person's social role by imposing severe economic difficulties, but also brings about a loss of self-esteem and self-confidence. The redundant manager is in many ways rejected. This rejection may carry through to the family situation, which instead of providing support may become critical and hostile. Managers' wives faced with a drastic change in their own life styles may attack their redundant husbands as the immediate cause of their demise. An early and satisfactory escape from the situation by finding suitable employment is becoming less and less likely. In 1970 it was said that it took a man of over 45 years of age one month for every £1000 of salary he expected to find a new job. Several years on, the situation is bound to be much worse.

Redundancies in an organisation bring other problems. The managers who remain are threatened. They may respond by increasing their own work load to prove their value to their organisation: they may voluntarily go into a state of work overload. However, increased work loads may be forced on remaining managers as a result of having to share out the work previously carried out by their now redundant colleagues. As work loads increase to personally intolerable levels, managers begin to fail to cope and the quality of their work becomes progressively worse. In American terminology men subject to work overload show a 'graceful degradation' of performance.

Reduction in numbers of staff is usually accompanied by other economies such as freezing the existing hierarchy and freezing pay structures. Promotion prospects are therefore reduced and managers' long-term prospects are damaged. The reduction in the number of promotions may lead to fierce competition for those that do become available, and this in itself can severely damage personal relations within organisations. This situation traps the manager in his present job; no longer can he hope for relatively easy promotion, and there is little opportunity for changing organisations. The longer the situation lasts, and the older the manager, the greater his problem.

Redundancy measures are frequently accompanied by reorganisation: new sharing of responsibilities and reallocation of function. If this is not carefully planned, and generally it is not when brought about as an emergency measure, it can cause job ambiguity. It is very necessary for managers to know the requirements of their jobs, and their position in their organisation's hierarchy. They need to know to whom they are responsible and for what, and for whom. Ill-defined work objectives and open-ended responsibilities place enormous demands on managers. They experience uncertainty about their jobs, they are unsure of their relationships with other managers, and they are afraid of neglecting their duties. The indeterminate and anxious behaviour which tends to result is often judged by colleagues to reflect inadequacy in the job. This adds to their fears of being judged incompetent and of being made redundant themselves.

The responsibility for others becomes problematic when careers and jobs are threatened. Personal relationships deteriorate rapidly, and perhaps one of the most distasteful of managerial assignments is that of hatchet man. A manager occupying that particular role is unavoidably faced with a moral crisis. Redundancy not only imposes these direct and personal problems, but also sours industrial relations. As a consequence of the fear of redundancy and as a response to the pressures that it brings, relationships within organisations break down. Poor communication and a lack of consultation result. The corporate spirit of the organisation is lost, along with any psychological security offered by a sense of belonging. Trust is lost. Both managers and workers develop stereotyped and inflexible approaches to industrial problems. Each becomes more concerned with short-term victories than with long-term solutions. Gouldner's description of 'punishment-centred' bureaucratic behaviour is perhaps relevant here. Such behaviour arises in situations where either management or workers attempt to coerce the other party, perhaps because of their intransigence. One tactic variously employed by both sides is the implementation of rigid redundancy procedures. That and this general pattern of organisational behaviour can only add to the conflict and tension experienced.

As a result of the threat of redundancy the efficiency of managers' work declines. This decline in their standards is not deliberate although they may be and usually are conscious of it. Attempts to pull oneself together, and to compensate for the loss usually serve only to increase the problem. The problem's solution is obvious although difficult. A declining economic situation causes organisations to 'cut back', which eventually involves, or at least threatens, redundancy. The fear of redundancy causes the decline of the organisation's managerial system and perhaps its collapse. The solution is to prevent redundancies occurring, or to so plan and handle them as to alleviate the fear and the after effects. To do this requires action not at an individual or even an organisational level, but at the national level.

7.6 MAN–JOB FIT

The previous sections of this chapter have discussed possible sources of demand at work. The effects of demand and the possible experience of stress, it has been repeatedly argued, are determined by the person's appraisal of his situation, which takes into account his ability to cope. Ability to cope with work can be manipulated in two ways: one through selection, the other training. Selection and training are, in Rodger and Cavanagh's (1962) terminology, ways of fitting the man to the job (see figure 7.1).

The importance of achieving a good man–job fit is most easily assessed in terms of the effects of a bad fit. The previous sections of this chapter have discussed the personal and organisational effects of a lack of job satisfaction and the experience of stress. These seem to result at an organisational level in poor productivity and poor industrial relations, in high absenteeism and high labour turnover, and in high accident and sickness rates. At the personal level there is a high cost for psychological and physical health.

A number of authors (French et al., 1974) have described a theory of person–environment (man–job) fit in which two kinds of fit are emphasised. The first is the extent to which the person's abilities and skills match the demands and requirements of the job and the job environment. The second kind of fit is concerned with the extent to which the person's internal needs and values are being maintained, and with whether the desire to use his particular abilities and skills is being fulfilled. The basic prediction embodied in this theory is that whenever poor fit of either kind occurs this may result in increases in anxiety, depression and low job satisfaction, and in the physiological stress response. Van Harrison (1976) has suggested two ways in which this theory may be applied to stress management and reduction programmes. First, measures of man–job fit could be used to identify individuals who are at risk. These individuals could then be the focus

168

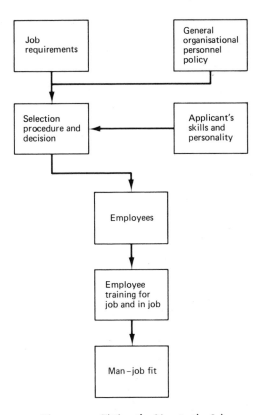

Figure 7.1: Fitting the Man to the Job

of special in-depth management programmes. He thus believes that stress is best treated at an individual rather than a group level. This point was made by the present author in the first chapter. Van Harrison's second way of applying the theory would be to place the onus of responsibility for maintaining good man–job fit on the individual employee himself. This has several important implications. The individual must, in this situation, be given scope to modify the demands of his job to suit his particular abilities, skills and needs. His possible actions must obviously fit into the overall structure and goals of the organisation in which he is employed. It would also seem to suggest that worker organisations, such as unions, ought to play an important role in developing better man–job fits. Developing better fits cannot necessarily be achieved by general group schemes such as current job rotation and enlargement programmes. Better fits are to be achieved at the individual level, and that is why responsibility for achieving them can be given to the individual.

The man–job fit approach can be applied at a population level, and this is best represented in a Venn diagram form (see figure 7.2).

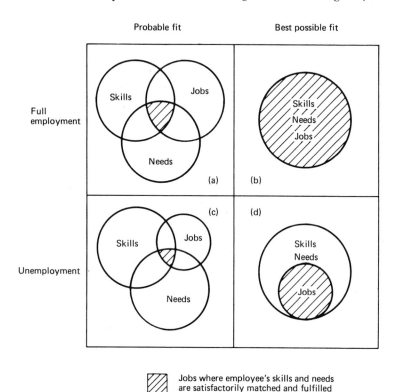

Figure 7.2: Man–Job Fit at the Population Level

The Venn diagrams shown in figure 7.2 can be interpreted in the following way. In times of full employment there are roughly equal numbers of jobs and people wanting to work. Probably not all the jobs will use the skills or fulfil the needs of the workers (a). The best possible fit, unlikely to be achieved but a goal in itself, would match these three factors (b). In times of unemployment this situation cannot be achieved, and the best match will still leave skills and needs unused and unfulfilled (d). However, in such times the situation is likely to be much worse (c).

Man–job fit is an approach to occupational stress which is an interactional one, and which is consistent with the transactional model. Indeed it follows from it in many ways.

Selection of personnel for jobs is one way of increasing the likelihood of achieving a good man–job fit. To select for any job, it is essential to know what skills and personal qualities that job requires. This information may be obtained through job analysis. This is a methodology of data collection which ought to allow the identification of aspects of the job which are relevant to what Rodger (1965) calls the difficulties and distastes of a job. The job requirements uncovered by such an analysis can be used in the choice of suitable psychometric tests to determine or at least aid the final selection decision, or as a guide in some form of interview or other subjective assessment. In many work situations job analyses have not or cannot be done, but selection is still carried out. In these situations it is still possible to develop the selection procedures systematically if psychometric tests, or at least subjective rating scales, are used. By following several years' appointees through their careers within the organisation it may be possible to distinguish between the above average and the below average. By going back to the available selection (predictor) data it may be possible to determine which tests, parts of tests, or scales most precisely make the above/below average discrimination. These 'good' tests can be retained and developed; the 'bad' tests can be rejected. Such a selection improvement programme is essentially selection validation. This is an attempt to answer the question, 'how well is the selection procedure used fitting the man to the job?' The basic problem in selection validation is the question of criterion variables, the measures used to assess how well a person is carrying out his job, how well he fits it. There are two different approaches to this assessment; one, from the person's viewpoint, asks questions to do with job satisfaction, the other, from the organisation's viewpoint, makes appraisals of job performance, job tenure, position in the hierarchy, and so on. Some criterion variables such as salary can be argued to reflect both viewpoints. Whatever variables are chosen for study validation is an essential part of the total selection procedure.

After being selected for a job, the person usually receives some form of training. This varies in many different ways. First, it may be possible to distinguish between training *for* a job, and training *in* a job. The former takes place before the person begins working and attempts to prepare him for that work. The latter takes place while the person is working, and not necessarily during the first months or even years of the job. Training in a job attempts to develop particular skills that the person is using. Unfortunately this sort of training tends in practice to be less well thought out than training *for* the job. It is usually organised around existing and offered training courses than around actual job needs. A manager may be sent on a particular course because it is there, rather than because he or the job needs to take advantage of it. As with selection, an essential part of the total training procedure is the question of 'how well is the training procedure used fitting the man to the job?' Again the basic problem is that of the choice of criterion variables.

A survey carried out by the author and his colleagues (1975–77) has shown that selection and training 'for' scores for appointees in a number of large organisations showed substantial correlations, but neither predicted actual job performance very well. Within these selection procedures psychometric tests and interviews were equally powerful predictors (Cox, 1977).

Selection and training are linked in other ways in many organisations. In educational systems poor selection may increase the amount of training needed to achieve a required standard. What was essentially a selection validation study in one British university department provides a good example of this interrelationship. The selection of applicants for the undergraduate course had been made on the basis of application forms, psychometric tests and interviews. The study, which followed several years' undergraduates from their selection to graduation, compared the effects of two selection procedures. The first, which acted as a control, was the existing procedure; the second, the experimental procedure, was based on the application forms alone. The study used achieved degree class as the criterion measure. It showed that there was no difference between the distribution of degree classes achieved under the two procedures. However, it was felt that the amount of teaching and general support required by those selected under the second procedure was greater than that required under the first procedure. The system in many ways ensured the product; the experimental manipulation simply traded the effort expended in selection for that expended in training. While the problems of selection may represent an acute demand,

172

those of training, in this situation, represent a chronic demand. The important question is, 'which demand is more severe?'

7.7 COMMENTS

The present chapter has attempted to bring together some of the literature relevant to a discussion of occupational stress, by looking at sources of demand at work, and by briefly examining the concept of man–job fit in relation to selection and training. The discussion of occupational stress extends beyond these aspects. It has been given a recent impetus by the health and safety legislation which has been passed in most Western industrialised countries. Undoubtedly it is a 'growth' area and a priority for industrial research. The goal of all concerned with industry, it is now widely agreed, is the improvement in the quality of working life. Occupational stress is *the* threat to work.

8

Concluding Remarks

It is perhaps interesting to consider that, while the discussion about stress is relatively new, much of our knowledge about it is not. This is because the concept of stress brings together fragments of information and relatively isolated ideas from a variety of different areas of concern. Much of the information and many of the ideas have been with us for a long time, albeit rather neglected. Their relationship and importance only emerged with the development of the stress concept. This owes very much to the pioneering writing of Hans Selye.

The concept of stress is not entirely successful in bringing together all the available information and ideas. This is shown in chapter 1. The difference between the three basic approaches to the definition and study of stress indicates that the lack of success is largely due to problems with the concept itself. While many still debate what we mean by the word stress, and argue over semantics, there is agreement over the possible causes of stress and over its probable effects. Possible causes are referred to in four chapters (1, 3, 5 and 7), while the effects of stress are dealt with in some detail in chapters 3 and 4. Stress causes changes in physiological state which may be well within the range of normal responses. However, some of the changes may be excessive, and some may be damaging. Stress thus effects health. This is the cost of stress. The available evidence suggests that the cost can be high. Stress can and does kill.

While our knowledge about stress is considerable, it is only useful if we can use it to deal with the problem of stress. The management and alleviation of stress is discussed in chapter 5. Much emphasis is placed on altering the person's perception of his situation, and how that might be accomplished through psychological techniques. However, alleviating stress once it occurs is only half of the problem of dealing with it. In many ways it is the less effective half. While treatment may reduce the experience of stress that has occurred it does not necessarily prevent it from recurring. Prevention *is* better than cure. With our present knowledge we should be able to prevent much of the stress we suffer from occurring. There are many reasons why we do not. Most of the reasons are economic, but some are not and are in many ways peculiar. For example, a steel worker was interviewed some time ago after expensive new safety equipment had been introduced into his workplace, greatly reducing the hazards he faced and discomfort he suffered. When asked why this seemed to make him unhappy with his work, he replied that 'it was no longer a *man*'s job'. This particular steel worker took a pride in risking his life at work; he did it when others would not. Reducing the risk he faced reduced his status as he saw it.

Programmes for the prevention and treatment of stress will need to be tailored to the individual, and if they are we might demonstrate some large individual differences based say, on age, sex or education, or on the nature of the parent society. Societal differences were briefly discussed in the preface. One priority for research on stress is to investigate these differences, especially those relating to societal differences. It would be a meaningful gesture of goodwill to extend our concern about the effects of stress to those living in societies other than our own. Nearly all the research that exists has been carried out within developed industrialised societies. It is now time to begin to investigate stress in the developing countries. For example, coronary heart disease is increasing in Middle East oil-producing countries, possibly due to their importing a Western way of life. Is this so, and what are the other factors which must contribute to this increased incidence? The people of the Middle East, of Africa and the Far East, and of South America all experience stress. What do we know of their experience and of its effects? Can we help them treat and prevent their stresses?

The use of drugs is one way of treating stress. This is discussed in chapter 6. In that chapter two negative aspects of drug treatment were underlined. First, that although some drugs, such as alcohol, may reduce the unpleasant experience of stress, they also reduce the ability to deal with stress. In that sense they represent an additional stress. Where no obvious stress is present they may introduce it through their general effects on behaviour; for example, the effects of alcohol on driving ability cause a problem for the driver who has been drinking and still has to drive. The second negative aspect of drug usage is dependence. Both physical and psychological dependence are discussed in chapter 6. A drug that is effective in reducing the unpleasant experience of stress may easily become the subject of psychological (learnt) dependence. This may lead in some cases to physical dependence. What was recommended in that chapter and in chapter 5, was that drugs be used where possible as a short-term aid, and in conjunction with some other form of treatment. This may not always be possible, and the use of the major tranquillisers, the phenothiazines, in managing schizophrenia provides a good example of long-term drug administration, and of one which may not be supported by any other form of treatment.

Treatment of stress is at present carried out by many different agencies and individuals. In the front line are members of the family, close friends, the general practitioner and the social worker. These people are not specifically trained to deal with individual problems relating to stress; some are not trained at all. Without doubt they all make some contribution to keeping those with problems functioning within society. However, an argument could be put forward that the time has come to examine how support systems could be set up to deal specifically with problems of stress. Such arguments have been advanced, and so far most have related to occupational stress. The teaching profession in some parts of Britain seems particularly aware for the need for such a system. Its design is less obvious, however, than its need. This, therefore, is another priority for research.

We have thus identified in these concluding remarks several priorities for research: individual and societal differences, prevention and treatment, and occupational support systems. If this book has sparked an interest in these areas then it has achieved something important.

References

Anand, B. K. and Brobeck, J. R. (1952). Food intake and spontaneous activity of rats with lesions in the amygdaloid nuclei. *J. Neurophysiol.*, **15**, 421

Anand, B. K. and Dua, S. (1956). Electrical stimulation of the limbic system of brain ('visceral brain') in the waking animal. *Indian J. med. Res.*, **44**, 107

Appley, M. H. and Trumbell, R. (1967). *Psychological Stress.* Appleton–Century–Crofts, New York

Ashbel, Z. Z. (1965). The effect of ultrasound and high frequency noise upon blood sugar level. *Bull. Hygiene.*, **40**, 587 (abstr)

Atherley, G. R. C., Gibbons, S. L. and Powell, J. A. (1970). Moderate acoustic stimuli: the interrelation of subjective importance and certain physiological changes. *Ergonomics,* **13**, 536

Azrin, N. H., Hutchinson, R. R. and Hake, D. F. (1967). Attack, avoidance and escape reactions to aversive shock. *J. exp. anal. Behav.*, **10**, 131

Baker, L. and Bercai, A. (1970). Psychosomatic aspects of diabetes mellitus. In *Modern Trends in Psychosomatic Medicine*, vol. 2 (ed. O. W. Hall), Butterworths, London

Baldamus, W. (1961). *Efficiency and Effort.* Tavistock Publications, London

Bard, P. (1928). A diencephalic mechanism for the expression of rage with special reference to the sympathetic nervous system. *Am. J. Physiol.*, **84**, 490

Bell, A. (1966). Noise: an occupational hazard and public nuisance. *Public Health Papers,* No. 30, World Health Organization, Geneva

Bell, J. E. (1975). *Family Therapy.* Jason Aronson, New York

Berman, M. L. and Pettitt, J. A. (1961). Urinary excretion of 3-methoxy-4-hydroxymandelic acid after several stress situations. *J.*

lab. clin. Med., **57**, 126

Benyon, H. (1973). *Working for Ford.* Penguin Books, Harmondsworth, Middlesex

Benyon, H. and Blackburn, R. M. (1972). *Perceptions of Work: Variations Within a Factory.* Cambridge University Press, Cambridge

Blackler, F. and Williams, R. (1971). People's motives at work. In *Psychology at Work* (ed. P. B. Warr), Penguin Books, Harmondsworth, Middlesex

Blake, J. and Ross, S. (1976). Some experiences with autonomic work groups. In *Job Satisfaction* (ed. M. Weir), Fontana/Collins, Glasgow

Blanchard, R. J. and Blanchard, D. C. (1969). Passive and active reactions to fear eliciting stimuli. *J. comp. physiol. Psychol.*, **68**, 129

Blanchard, R. J. and Blanchard, D. C. (1971). Defensive reactions in the albino rat. *Learning and Motivation*, **2**, 351

Bliss, E. L., Migeon, C. J., Branch, C. H. H. and Samuels, L. T. (1956). Reaction of the adrenal cortex to emotional stress. *Psychosom. Med.*, **18**, 56

Bloom, A. (1976). Learning to live with insulin. *Guardian* Special Report, July 23rd

Bloom, S. R., Daniel, P. M., Johnston, D. I., Ogawa, O. and Pratt, O. E. (1973). Release of glucagon induced by stress. *Q. Jl exp. Physiol.*, **58**, 99

Bogdonoff, M., Harlan, W., Estes, E. and Kirshner, N. (1959). Changes in urinary catecholamine excretion accompanying carbohydrate and lipid responses to oral examination. *Circulation*, **20**, 674

Bogdonoff, M., Estes, H., Harlan, W., Trout, D. L. and Kirshner, N. (1960). Metabolic and cardiovascular changes during a state of acute central nervous system arousal. *J. clin. Endocr.*, **20**, No. 10

Bonn, J. A., Turner, P. and Hicks, D. C. (1972). Beta-adrenergic receptor blockade with practolol in treatment of anxiety. *Lancet*, **i**, 814

Borkenstein, R. F., Crowther, R. F., Schumate, R. P., Ziel, W. B. and Zylman, R. (1964). *The Role of the Drinking Driver in Traffic Accidents.* Department of Police Administration, Indiana University

Bradley, C. (1975). Effects of noise stress on blood glucose levels and performance in diabetics. *Q. Res. Mtg, Nottingham Postgraduate Medical Centre*, April

Bradley, C., Cox, T. and Mackay, C. J. (1975). The effects of stress on the regulation of blood glucose levels. Paper presented to Psychophysiology Group, British Psychological Society, London,

December

Bradley, C., Cox, T. and Mackay, C. J. (1977). Factors affecting the relationship between glucose, noise and psychomotor performance. Paper presented to Psychology Laboratories, University of Stockholm, Sweden, April

Bradley, C., Cox, T. and Minto, I. (1976). Adjustment to life events, personality and diabetes mellitus. Unpublished Report, University of Nottingham

Brady, J. V. (1975). Toward a behavioural biology of emotion. In *Emotions: Their Parameters and Measurement* (ed. L. Levi), Raven Press, New York

Breslow, L. and Buell, P. (1960). Mortality from coronary heart disease and physical activity of work in California. *J. chron. Dis.*, **11**, 615

Brewer, D. W. and Briess, F. B. (1960). Industrial noise: laryngeal considerations. *New York State J. Med.*, **60**, 1737

Bridges, K. M. B. (1932). Emotional development in early infancy. *Child Dev.*, **3**, 324

Broadbent, D. E. (1971). *Decision and Stress*. Academic Press, London

Broadbent, D. E. and Little, E. A. J. (1960). Effects of noise reduction in a work situation. *Occup. Psychol.*, **34**, 133

Brooke, J. D., Toogood, S., Green, L. F. and Bagley, R. (1973*a*). Dietary pattern of carbohydrate provision and accident incidence in foundry men. *Proc. nutr. Soc.*, **32**, 44 (abstr)

Brooke, J. D., Toogood, S., Green, L. F. and Bagley, R. (1973*b*). Factory accidents and carbohydrate supplements. *Proc. nutr. Soc.*, **32**, 94 (abstr)

Brouha, L. (1960). *Physiology in Industry*. Pergamon Press, Oxford

Bruhn, J. G., Thurman, A. E., Chandler, B. C. and Bruce, T. A. (1970). Patients' reactions to death in a coronary care unit. *J. psychosom. Res.*, **14**, 65

Bruyn, H. B. (1970). Drugs on the college campus. *J. school Hlth*, Feb., 99

Buell, T. and Breslow, L. (1960). Mortality from coronary heart disease in California men who work long hours. *J. chron. Dis.*, **2**, 615

Burgess, A. W. and Holmstrom, L. L. (1974). Rape trauma syndrome. *Am. J. Psychiat.*, **131**, 981

Burgess, A. W. and Holmstrom, L. L. (1976). Coping behaviour of the rape victim. *Am. J. Psychiat.*, **133**, 413

Burn, J. H. (1956). Our national drugs—alcohol and nicotine. In

Functions of Autonomic Transmission (ed. J. H. Burn), Williams and Wilkins, Baltimore

Burrows, G. C., Cox, T. and Simpson, G. C. (1977). The measurement of stress in a sales training situation. *Occup. Psychol.,* **50,** 45

Cameron, C. (1973). A theory of fatigue. In *Man Under Stress* (ed. A. T. Welford), Taylor and Francis, London

Cannon, W. B. (1927). The James–Lange theory of emotion. *Am. J. Psychol.,* **39,** 106

Cannon, W. B. (1929). *Bodily Changes in Pain, Hunger, Fear and Rage.* Branford, Boston

Cannon, W. B. (1931). *The Wisdom of the Body.* Norton, New York

Caplan, R. D. (1971). Organisational stress and individual strain: a social-psychological study of risk factors in coronary heart disease among administrators, engineers and scientists. Unpublished Doctoral Dissertation, University of Michigan

Carlestam, C. C., Karlsson, C. C. and Levi, L. (1973). Stress and disease in response to exposure to noise: a review. Reprinted from *Proceedings of the International Congress on Noise as a Public Hazard,* Dubrovnik, Yugoslavia, by U.S. Environmental Protection Agency

Carlsson, L. A., Levi, L. and Oro, L. (1972). Stressor-induced changes in plasma lipids and urinary excretion of catecholamines, and their modification by nicotinic acid. In *Stress and Distress in Response to Psychosocial Stimuli* (ed. L. Levi), Pergamon Press, Oxford

Carruthers, M. A. (1969). Aggression and atheroma. *Lancet,* **ii,** 1170

Claridge, G. S. (1961). The effects of meprobamate on the performance of a five-choice reaction time task. *J. ment. Sci.,* **107,** 590

Claridge, G. S. (1972). *Drugs and Human Behaviour.* Penguin Books, Harmondsworth, Middlesex

Clark, F. C. and Steele, B. J. (1966). Effects of d-amphetamine on performance under a multiple schedule in the rat. *Psychopharmacologia,* **9,** 157

Cobb, S. (1974). Role responsibility: the differentiation of a concept. In *Occupational Stress* (ed. A. Maclean), Charles C. Thomas, Springfield, Illinois

Cobb, S. and Rose, R. M. (1973). Hypertension, peptic ulcer, and diabetes in air traffic controllers. *J. Am. med. Ass.,* **224,** 489

Cobb, S., French, J. R. P. and Mann, F. C. (1963). An environmental approach to mental health. *Ann. N.Y. Acad. Sci.,* **107,** 596

Cofer, C. N. and Appley, M. H. (1964). *Motivation: Theory and Research.* Wiley, New York

Cohen, J., Dearnaley, E. J. and Hansel, C. E. M. (1958). The risk taken in driving under the influence of alcohol. *Br. med. J.*, **1**, 1438

Colehour, J. K. (1964). The effects of coriolis acceleration during zero gravity parabolic flight. *Aerospace Med.*, **35**, 844

Colehour, J. K. and Graybiel, A. (1964). Excretion of 17-hydroxycorticosteroids, catecholamines, and uropepsin in the urine of normal persons and deaf subjects with bilateral vestibular defects following acrobactic flight stress. *Aerospace Med.*, **35**, 370

Conn, E. E. and Stumpf, P. K. (1967). *Outlines of Biochemistry*. Wiley, New York

Cooper, C. L. and Marshall, J. (1975). Managers under stress. *New Behav.*, **2**, 86.

Cooper, C. L. and Marshall, J. (1976). Occupational sources of stress: a review of the literature relating to coronary heart disease and mental ill health. *J. occup. Psychol.*, **49**, 11

Cox, T. (1975a). The nature and management of stress. *New Behav.* **2**, 493

Cox, T. (1975b). Behavioural pharmacology. In *Psychology Today* (ed. W. E. C. Gillham), English Universities Press, London.

Cox, T. (1977). Does selection testing really work? Paper presented to Annual Conference of Institute of Personnel Management, Harrogate, October

Cox, T. and Mackay, C. J. (1976). A psychological model of occupational stress. A paper presented to Medical Research Council meeting *Mental Health in Industry*. London, November

Cox, T., Simpson, G. C. and Rothschild, D. R. (1973). Blood glucose level and skilled performance under stress. *J. int. Res. Commun.*, **1**, 30

Craven, C. W. and Smith, C. S. (1955). Steroid excretion in airmen under stress. *J. aviat. Med.*, **25**, 200

Crossland, J. (1970). *Lewis's Pharmacology*. Livingstone, London

Danowski, T. S. (1963). Emotional stress as a cause of diabetes mellitus. *Diabetes*, **12**, 183 (editorial)

Davies, D. R. (1968). Physiological and psychological effects of exposure to high intensity noise *Appl. Acoust.* **1**, 218

Davies, D. R. and Shackleton, V. J. (1975). *Psychology and Work*. Methuen, London

Davis, H. (1958). Auditory and non-auditory effects of high intensity noise. Project ANEHIN, Joint Project 1301 Subtask 1, Report No. 7, Central Institute for the Deaf, St Louis, Missouri, and U.S.

Naval School of Aviation Medicine, Pensacola, Florida

De Molina, F. A. and Hunsperger, R. W. (1959). Central representation of affective reactions in forebrain and brain stem: electrical stimulation of amygdala, stria terminalis and adjacent structures. *J. Physiol., Lond.,* **145,** 251

Dekker, E. and Groen, J. J. (1956). Reproducible psychogenic attacks of asthma. *J. psychom. Res.,* **1,** 58

Dekker, E. and Groen, J. J. (1957). Asthmatic wheezing: compression of the trachea and major bronchi as a cause. *Lancet,* **i,** 1064

Dekker, E. and Ledeboer, R. C. (1961). Compression of the trachea and major bronchi during asthmatic attacks. *Am. J. Roentgenol.,* **85,** 217

Doll, R. and Jones, A. F. (1951). Occupational factors in the aetiology of gastric and duodenal ulcers. *Medical Research Council Special Report Series,* No. 276, H.M.S.O., London

Drever, J. (1952). *A Dictionary of Psychology.* Penguin Books, Harmondsworth, Middlesex

Dukes–Dubos, F. N. (1971). Fatigue from the point of view of urinary metabolites. In *Methodology in Human Fatigue Assessment* (eds K. Hashimoto, K. Kogi and E. Grandjean), Taylor and Francis, London

Dunlap, K. (1922). *The Emotions.* Williams and Wilkins, Baltimore

Egger, M. D. and Flynn, J. P. (1963). Effect of electrical stimulation of the amygdala on hypothalamically elicited attack behaviour in cats. *J. Neurophysiol.,* **26,** 705

Ekehammar, B. (1972). Sex differences in self-reported anxiety for different situations and modes of response. *Rep. Psychol. Lab.,* University of Stockholm (363)

Elmadjian, F. (1955). Adrenocortical function of combat infantrymen in Korea. *Ciba Fdn Colloq. Endocr.,* **8,** 627

Elmadjian, F. (1963). Excretion and metabolism of epinephrine and norepinephrine in various emotional states. *Proc. Fifth Pan American Congr. Endocr.,* Lima

Engström, A. (1975). Drugs, science and people. In *Emotions: Their Parameters and Measurement* (ed. L. Levi), Raven Press, New York

Evans, E. I. and Butterfield, W. J. H. (1951). The stress response in the severely burned. *Ann. Surg.,* **134,** 4

Fecci, R., Barthelemy, R., Bourgoin, J. Mathias, A., Eberle, M., Moutel, A. and Jullien, G. (1971). L'action des infra-sons sur l'organisme. *Med. Lavora,* **62,** 130

Ferguson, D. (1973). A study of occupational stress. *Ergonomics,* **16,** 649

Finkel, A. L. and Poppen, J. R. (1948). Clinical effects of noise and mechanical vibrations of a jet engine on man. *J. appl. Psychol.,* **1,** 183

Fisher, S. (1970). Nonspecific factors as determinants of behavioural response to drugs. In *Clinical Handbook of Psychopharmacology* (eds A. D. Mascio and R. I. Shader), Science House, New York

Fonberg, E. and Delgado, J. M. R. (1961). Avoidance and alimentary reactions during amygdaloid stimulation *J. Neurophysiol.,* **24,** 651

Frankenhaeuser, M. (1975a). Experimental approaches to the study of catecholamines and emotion. In *Emotions: Their Parameters and Measurement* (ed. L. Levi), Raven Press, New York

Frankenhaeuser, M. (1975b). Sympathetic-adrenomedullary activity, behaviour and the psychosocial environment. In *Research in Psychophysiology* (eds P. H. Venables and M. J. Christie), Wiley, New York

Frankenhaeuser. M. and Anderson, K. (1974). Note on interaction between cognitive and endocrine functions. *Percept. mot. Skills,* **38,** 557

Frankenhaeuser, M. and Rissler, A. (1970a). Catecholamine output during relaxation and anticipation. *Percept. mot. Skills,* **30,** 745

Frankenhaeuser, M. and Rissler, A. (1970b). Effects of punishment on catecholamine release and efficiency of performance. *Psychopharmacologia,* **17,** 378

Frankenhaeuser, M., Sterky, K. and Jarpe, G. (1962). Psychophysiological relations in habituation to gravitational stress. *Percept. mot. Skills,* **15,** 63

Frankenhaeuser, M. Järpe, G., Svan, H. and Wrangsjoe, B. (1964). Psychophysiological reactions to two different placebo treatments. *Scand. J. Psychol.,* **4,** 245

Frankenhaeuser, M., Nordheden, B., Myrsten, A-L. and Post, B. (1971). Psychophysiological reactions to understimulation and overstimulation. *Acta Psychol.,* **35,** 298

Frankenhaeuser, M., Post, B., Nordheden, B. and Sjöberg, H. (1969). Physiological and subjective reactions to different physical work loads, *Percept. mot. Skills,* **28,** 343

Fraser, R. (1947). The incidence of neurosis among factory workers. *Industrial Health Research Board of the Medical Research Council Report,* No. 90, H.M.S.O., London

Freeman, W., Pincus, G. and Glover, E. D. (1944). The excretion of neutral urinary steroids in stress. *Endocrinology,* **35,** 215

French, J. R. P. and Caplan, R. D. (1973). Organisational stress and individual strain. In *The Failure of Success* (ed. A. J. Marrow), AMACOM, New York

French, J. R. P., Rodgers, W. and Cobb, S. (1974). Adjustment as person–environment fit. In *Coping and Adaptation* (eds G. V. Coehlo and D. A. Hamburg), Basic Books, New York

French, J. R. P., Tupper, C. J. and Mueller, E. F. (1965). Work load of university professors. *Cooperative Research Project,* No. 2171, U.S. Office of Education, University of Michigan, Ann Arbor

Freud, A. (1946). *The Ego and the Mechanisms of Defense.* International University Press, New York.

Friedman, M. and Rosenman, R. H. (1959). Association of a specific overt behaviour pattern with blood and cardiovascular findings. *J. Am. med. Ass.,* **169,** 1286

Friedman, M. and Rosenman, R. H. (1974). *Type A Behaviour and Your Heart.* Knoft, New York

Froberg, J., Karlsson, C-G., Levi, L. and Lidberg, L. (1971). Physiological and biochemical stress reactions induced by psychosocial stimuli. In *Society, Stress and Disease,* vol. 1 (ed. L. Levi), Oxford University Press, New York

Froesch, E. R. (1971). Pathogenesis and etiology of diabetes mellitus. In *Clinical Endocrinology* (ed. A. Labhart), Springer-Verlag, Berlin

Fromm, E. (1941). *Escape from Freedom.* Rinehart, New York

Fromm E. (1947). *Man for Himself.* Rinehart, New York

Fromm, E. (1955). *The Sane Society.* Holt, Rinehart and Winston, New York

Frost, J. W., Dryer, R. L. and Kohlstedt, K. G. (1951). Stress studies on auto race drivers. *J. lab. clin. Med.,* **38,** 523

Gellhorn, E. and Loofbourrow, G. N. (1963). *Emotion and Emotional Disorders: A Neuro-physiological Study.* Harper and Row, New York

Gloor, P. (1960). Amygdala. In *Handbook of Physiology,* vol. 2 (eds J. Field, H. W. Magoun and V. E. Hall), Williams and Wilkins, Baltimore

Goodall, McC. (1962). Sympathoadrenal response to gravitational stress. *J. clin. Invest.,* **41,** 197

Goodall, McC., McCally, M. and Graveline, D. E. (1964). Urinary adrenaline and noradrenaline response to simulated weightless state. *Am. J. Physiol.,* **206,** 431

Gosling, R. H. (1958). Peptic ulcer and mental disorder. *J. psychosom. Res.*, **2**, 285

Grant, I., Kyle, G. C., Teichman, A. and Mendels, J. (1974). Recent life events and diabetes in adults. *Psychosom. Med.*, **36**, 2

Granville-Grossman, K. L. and Turner, P. (1966). The effect of propranolol on anxiety. *Lancet*, **i**, 788

Gray, J. (1971). *The Psychology of Fear and Stress*. Weidenfeld and Nicolson, London.

Green, J. R., Duisberg, R. E. H. and McGrath, W. B. (1951). Focal epilepsy of psychomotor type: preliminary report of observations on effects of surgical therapy. *J. Neurosurg.*, **8**, 157

Groen, J. J. (1971). Psychosocial influences in bronchial asthma. In *Society, Stress and Disease*, vol. 1 (ed. L. Levi), Oxford University Press, London

Groen, J. J., Tijong, B. K., Willebrant, A. F. and Kamminga, C. J. (1959). Influence of nutrition, individuality and different forms of stress on blood cholesterol: results of an experiment of 9 months duration in 60 normal volunteers. *Proc. int. Cong. diet. Voeding*, **19**, 135

Hale, H. B., Kratochvil, C. H. and Ellis, J. R. (1958). Plasma corticosteroid levels in aircrewmen after long flights. *J. clin. Endocr.*, **18**, 1440

Hames, C. (1975). Most likely to succeed as a candidate for a coronary attack. In *New Horizons in Cardiovascular Practice* (ed. H. I. Russek), University Park Press, New York

Hebb, D. O. (1955). Drives and the conceptual nervous system. *Psychol. Rev.*, **62**, 243

Heider, F. (1958). *The Psychology of Interpersonal Relations*. Wiley, New York

Herzberg, F. (1966). *Work and the Nature of Man*. Staples, London

Herzberg, F., Mausner, B. and Snyderman, G. (1959). *The Motivation to Work*. Wiley, New York

Hess, W. R. (1957). *The Functional Organisation of the Diencephalon*. Grune and Stratton, New York

Hetzel, B. S., Schottstaedt, W. W., Grace, W. J. and Wolff, H. G. (1955). Changes in urinary 17-hydroxycorticosteroid excretion during stressful life experiences in man. *J. clin. Endocr.*, **15**, 1057

Hinkle, L. E. and Conger, G. B. (1952). A summary of experimental evidence relating life stress to diabetes mellitus. *J. Mt Sinai Hosp.*, **19**, 537

Hinkle, L. E., Conger, G. B. and Wolf, S. (1950). Studies in diabetes mellitus: the relation of stressful life situations to the concentration of ketone bodies in the blood of diabetic and non-diabetic humans. *J. clin. Invest.*, **29**, 754

Hinkle, L. E., Whitney, L. H., Lehman, E. W., Dunn, J., Benjamin, B., King, R., Plakun, A. and Fleshinger, B. (1968). Occupation, education and coronary heart disease. *Science*, **161**, 238

Hockey, G. R. J. (1970). Signal probability and spatial location as possible bases for increased selectivity in noise. *Q. Jl exp. Psychol.*, **22**, 37

Holmes, T. H. and Rahe, R. H. (1967). The social readjustment rating scale. *J. psychosom. Res.*, **11**, 213

Howarth, C. I. (1978). Environmental stress. In *The Uses of Psychology* (eds C. I. Howarth and W. C. Gillham), to be published by Allen and Unwin, London

James, W. (1884). What is emotion? *Mind*, **19**, 188

James, W. (1890). *The Principles of Psychology*, Henry Holt, New York

Janis, I. L. (1962). Psychological effects of warnings. In *Man and Society in Disaster* (eds G. W. Baker and D. W. Chapman), Basic Books, New York

Jansen, G. (1959). Zur Ensebelung vegetativer Funktionsstrungen durch Larmeinwurkung. *Arch. Gewerbepath. Gewerbehyg.*, **17**, 233

Jenkins, C. D., Zyzanski, S. J., Rosenman, R. H. and Cleveland, G. L. (1971). Association of coronary-prone behaviour scores with recurrence of coronary heart disease. *J. chronic Dis.*, **24**, 601

Johansson, G. (1972). Sex differences in the catecholamine output of children. *Acta physiol. scand.*, **85**, 569

Johansson, G. (1975). Psychophysiological stress reactions in the sawmill: a pilot study. In *Ergonomics in Sawmills and Woodworking Industries* (ed. B. Ager), National Board of Occupational Safety and Health, Stockholm

Johansson, G. and Post, B. (1972). Catecholamine output of males and females over a one-year period. *Rep. Psychol. Lab.*, University of Stockholm (379)

Kaada, B. R., Anderson, P. and Jansen, J. (1954). Stimulation of the amygdaloid nuclear complex in unanaesthestised cats. *Neurology*, **4**, 48

Kagan, A. (1975). Epidemiology, disease and emotion. In *Emotions: Their Parameters and Measurement* (ed. L. Levi), Raven Press, New York

Kagan, A. and Levi, L. (1971). Adaptations of the psychosocial environment to man's abilities and needs. In *Society, Stress and Disease*, vol. 1 (ed. L. Levi), Oxford University Press, London

Kagan, A. and Levi, L. (1975). Health and environment–psychosocial stimuli: a review. In *Society, Stress and Disease*, vol. 2 (ed. L. Levi), Oxford University Press, New York

Kahn, R. L. (1974). Conflict, ambiguity, and overload: three elements in job stress. In *Occupational Stress* (ed. A. Maclean), Charles C. Thomas, Springfield, Illinois

Kahn, R. L. and French, J. P. R. (1970). Status and conflict: two themes in the study of stress. In *Social and Psychological Factors in Stress* (ed. J. E. McGrath), Holt, Rinehart and Winston, New York

Kahn, R. L., Wolfe, D. M., Quinn, R. P., Snoek, J. D. and Rosenthal, R. A. (1964). *Organisational Stress: Studies in Role Conflict and Ambiguity*. Wiley, New York

Kärki, N. T. (1956). The urinary excretion of noradrenaline and adrenaline in different age groups, its diurnal variation and the effect of muscular work on it. *Acta physiol. scand.,* **39**, Suppl., 132

Kearns, J. L. (1973). *Stress in Industry*. Priory Press, London

Kielholz, P. (1975). Psychopharmacology measurement of emotion in medical practice. In *Emotions: Their Parameters and Measurement* (ed. L. Levi), Raven Press, New York

King, F. A. and Meyer, P. M. (1958). Effects of amygdaloid lesions upon septal hyperemotionality in the rat. *Science,* **128**, 655

Klepping, J., Buisson, O., Guerrin, J., Escousse, A. and Didier, J. P. (1963). Evaluation de l'élimination urinaire des catécholamines chez des pilotes d'avions à réaction. *C. r. Séanc Soc. Biol.,* **157**, 1727

Kling, A. and Hutt, P. J. (1958). Effect of hypothalamic lesions on the amygdala syndrome in the cat. *Archs Neurol. Psychiat.,* **79**, 511

Kluver, H. and Bucy, P. C. (1939). Preliminary analysis of functions of the temporal lobes of monkeys. *Archs Neurol. Psychiat.,* **42**, 979

Knowles, J. B. and Lucas, C. J. (1960). Experimental studies of the placebo response. *J. ment. Sci.,* **106**, 231

Korchin, S. J. and Herz, M. (1960). Differential effects of 'shame' and 'disintegrative' threats on emotional and adrenocortical functioning. *Archs gen. Psychiat.,* **2**, 640

Korchin, S. J. and Ruff, G. E. (1964). Personality characteristics of the Mercury astronauts. In *The Threat of Impending Disaster* (eds G. H. Grosser, H. Wechsler and M. Greenblatt), MIT Press, Cambridge, Massachusetts

Kornhauser, A. (1965). *Mental Health of the Industrial Worker*. Wiley, New York

Korol, B. and Brown, M. L. (1967). The role of the beta-adrenergic system in behaviour: antidepressant effects of propranolol. *Curr. ther. Res.*, **9**, 269

Kryter, K. D. (1970). *The Effects of Noise on Man*. Academic Press, New York

Kubany, A. J., Danowski, T. S. and Moses, C. (1956). The personality and intelligence of diabetics. *Diabetes*, **5**, 462

Lacey, J. I. (1967). Somatic response patterning and stress: some revisions of activation theory. In *Psychological Stress* (eds M. H. Appley and R. Trumbell), Appleton–Century–Crofts, New York

Lader, M. H. (1971). Responses to repetitive stimulation. In *Society, Stress and Diseae*, vol. 1 (ed. L. Levi), Oxford University Press, London

Lader, M. H. (1975). The nature of clinical anxiety in modern society. In *Stress and Anxiety*, vol. 1 (eds C. D. Spielberger and I. G. Sarason), Halstead Press, New York

Lader, M. and Tyrer, P. (1975). Vegetative system and emotions. In *Emotions: Their Parameters and Measurement* (ed. L. Levi), Raven Press, New York

Lange, C. (1885). The emotions (translated by I. A. Haupt). In *The Emotions* (ed. K. Dunlap), Williams and Wilkins, Baltimore (1922)

Lapiccirella, V., Lapiccirella, R., Abboni, F. and Liotta, S. (1962). Enquete clinique, biologique et cardiographique parmi les tribus nomades de la Somalie qui se nourrissent seulement de lait. *Bull. W.H.O.*, **27**, 681

Laurence, D. R. (1973). *Clinical Pharmacology*. Churchill Livingstone, London

Lazarus, R. S. (1966). *Psychological Stress and the Coping Process*. McGraw-Hill, New York

Lazarus, R. S. (1976). *Patterns of Adjustment*. McGraw-Hill, New York

Leavitt, F. (1974). *Drugs and Behaviour*. Saunders Co., London

Lefebvre, P. J. and Unger, R. H. (1972). *Glucagon: Molecular Physiology, Clinical and Therapeutic Implications*. Pergamon Press, Oxford

Levi, L. (1972). Stress and Distress in Response to Psychosocial Stimuli. *Acta med. scand.*, Suppl., 528

Levi, L. (1973). Humanökologie–psychosomatische Gesichtpunkte und Forschungsstrategien. *Psychosom. Med.*, **5**, 92

Levi, L. (1974). Stress, distress and psychosocial stimuli. In *Oc-*

cupational Stress (ed. A. Mclean), Charles C. Thomas, Springfield, Illinois

Levine, R. (1976). Glucagon and the regulation of blood sugar. *Lancet,* **294,** 494

Levine, S. (1967). Maternal and environmental influences on the adrenocortical response to stress in weanling rats. *Science,* **156,** 258

Levine, S. (1975). Psychosocial factors in growth and development. In *Society, Stress and Disease,* vol. 2 (ed. L. Levi), Oxford University Press, New York

Levine, S. and Scotch, N. A. (1970). *Social Stress.* Aldine Publishing Co., Chicago

Lewis, B., Chait, A., Oakley, C. M. O., Wooton, I. D. P., Krickler, D. M., Onitin, A., Sigurdsson, G. and February, A. (1974). Serum lipoprotein abnormalities in patients with ischaemic heart disease: comparisons with control population. *Br. med. J.,* **3,** 489

Lindsley, D. B. (1952). Psychological phenomena and the electroencephalogram. *Electroenceph. clin. Neurophysiol.,* **4,** 443

Locke, E. A. (1976). The nature and causes of job satisfaction. In *Handbook of Industrial and Organisational Psychology* (ed. M. D. Dunnette), Rand-McNally College Publishing Co., Chicago

Lorenz, K. Z. (1970). *On Aggression.* Methuen, London

Lowe, R. and McGrath, J. E. (1971). Stress, arousal, and performance: some findings calling for a new theory. *Project Report, AF 1161–67,* AFOSR

Lund, A. (1964). Adrenaline and noradrenaline in post-mortem blood. *Med. Sci. Law,* **4,** 194

Lundberg, U., Theorell, T. and Lind, E. (1975). Life change and myocardial infarction: individual differences in life change scaling. *J. psychosom. Res.,* **19,** 27

McCormick, E. J. (1970). *Human Engineering.* McGraw-Hill, New York

McGrath, J. E. (1970). *Social and Psychological Factors in Stress.* Holt, Rinehart and Winston, New York

McGrath, J. E. (1976). Stress and behaviour in organisations. In *Handbook of Industrial and Organisational Psychology* (ed. M. D. Dunnette), Rand-McNally College Publishing Co., Chicago

McKellar, P. (1968). *Experience and Behaviour.* Penguin Books, Harmondsworth, Middlesex

McKennell, A. C. and Hunt, E. A. (1966). Noise Annoyance in Central London. Government Social Survey, H.M.S.O., London

Mackay, C. J. and Cox, T. (1976). A transactional model of occupational stress. Paper presented to III Promstra Seminar, Department of Engineering Production, University of Birmingham, October

MacLean, P. D. (1970). The limbic system in relation to psychoses. In *Physiological Correlates of Emotion* (ed. P. Black), Academic Press, New York

MacLean, P. D. (1975). Sensory and perceptive factors in emotional functions of the triune brain. In *Emotions: Their Parameters and Measurement* (ed. L. Levi), Raven Press, New York

Macrae, D. (1954). Isolated fear: a temporal lobe aura. *Neurology*, 4, 497

Magnus, O. and Lammers, H. J. (1956). The amygdaloid complex. Part I. Electrical stimulation of the amygdala and periamygdaloid cortex in the waking cat. *Folia psychiat. neerl.*, 55, 555

Mann, G. V., Schaffer, R. D. and Rich, A. (1965). Physical fitness and immunity to heart disease in Masai. *J. Atheroscler. Res.*, 2, 1308.

Maranon, G. (1924). Contribution à l'étude de l'action émotive de l'adrenaline. *Rev. Fr. Endocr.*, 2, 301

Margetts, E. L. (1975). Stress, homeostasis, and the human ecological continuum in time—some implications for psychiatry. In *Society, Stress and Disease*, vol. 2 (ed. L. Levi), Oxford University Press, New York

Maslow, A. H. (1943). A theory of human motivation. *Psychol. Rev.*, 50, 370

Maslow, A. H. (1954). *Motivation and Personality*, 2nd edition, Harper and Row, New York

Maslow, A. H. (1968). *Toward a Psychology of Being*. Van Nostrand, New York

Maslow, A. H. (1973). *The Farther Reaches of Human Nature*. Penguin Books, Harmondsworth, Middlesex

Mason, J. W. (1959). Hormones and metabolism—psychological influences on the pituitary–adrenal cortical system. *Recent Prog. Horm. Res.*, 15, 345

Mason, J. W. (1968). Organisation of psychoendocrine mechanisms. *Psychosom Med.*, 30, No. 5, Part II

Mason, J. W. (1971). A re-evaluation of the concept of 'non-specificity' in stress theory. *J. psychiat., Res.*, 8, 323

Mason, J. W. (1975). Emotion as reflected in patterns of endocrine integration. In *Emotions: Their Parameters and Measurement* (ed. L.

Levi), Raven Press, New York

Mason, J. W., Sachar, E. J., Fishman, J. R., Hamburg, D. A. and Handlon, J. H. (1965). Corticosteroid responses to hospital admission. *Archs gen. Psychiat.*, **13**, 1

Mechanic, D. (1962). *Students under Stress.* Free Press, New York

Meichenbaum, D. (1974). *Cognitive Behaviour Modification.* General Learning Press, Morristown, New Jersey

Mendelson, J., Kubzansky, P., Leiderman, P. H., Wexler, D., Du Toit, C. and Solomon, P. (1960). Catecholamine excretion and behaviour during sensory deprivation. *Archs gen. Psychiat.*, **2**, 37

Miller, N. E. (1951). Learnable drives and rewards. In *Handbook of Experimental Psychology* (ed. S. S. Stevens) Wiley, New York

Miller, N. E. and Weiss, J. M. (1969). Effects of the somatic or visceral response to punishment. In *Punishment and Aversive Behaviour* (eds B. A. Campbell and R. M. Church), Appleton–Century–Crofts, New York

Moruzzi, G. and Magoun, H. W. (1949). Brainstem reticular formation and activation of the EEG. *Electroenceph. clin. Neurophysiol.*, **1**, 455

Murray, J. A. H., Bradley, H., Craigie, W. A. and Onions, C. T. (1933). *The Oxford English Dictionary.* Oxford University Press, London

Murrell, K. F. H. (1965). *Ergonomics.* Chapman and Hall, London

Murrell, K. F. H. (1971). Blood sugar level and performance. *Occup. Psychol.*, **45**, 273

Myers, R. and Carey, R. (1961). Preference factors in experimental alcoholism. *Science,* **134**, 469

Myers, R. and Holman, R. (1967). Failure of stress of electric shock to increase ethanol intake in rats. *Q. Jl Stud. Alcohol.*, **28**, 132

Nabarro, J. D. N. (1965). Diabetic acidosis: clinical aspects. In *On the Nature and Treatment of Diabetes* (eds B. S. Leibel and G. A. Wrenshall), Excerpta Medica Foundation, Amsterdam

Nathan, P. W. and Smith, M. C. (1950). Normal mentality associated with a mal-developed 'rhinencephalon'. *J. Neurol. Neurosurg. Psychiat.*, **13**, 191

Nelson, G. N., Masuda, M. and Holmes, T. H. (1966). Correlation of behaviour and catecholamine metabolic excretion. *Psychosom. Med.*, **28**, 216

Office of Population Censuses and Surveys (1974). *The General Household Survey: 1971.* H.M.S.O., London

Office of Population Censuses and Surveys (1975). *The General Household Survey: 1972.* H.M.S.O., London

Oken, D., Grinker, R., Heath, H., Sabshin, M. and Schwartz, N. (1960). Stress response in a group of chronic psychiatric patients. *Archs gen. Psychiat.,* **3,** 451

Ostfeld, A. M., Lebovits, B. A., Shekelle, R. B. and Paul, O. (1964). A prospective study of the relationship between personality and coronary heart disease. *J. chronic Dis.,* **17,** 265

O'Toole, J. (1973). *Work in America,* Report of a Special Task Force to Secretary of Health, Education and Welfare. MIT Press, Cambridge, Massachusetts

Papez, J. W. (1937). A proposed mechanism for emotion. *Archs Neurol. Psychol.,* **38,** 725

Parrott, J. (1971). The measurement of stress and strain. In *Measurement of Man at Work* (eds W. T. Singleton, J. G. Fox and D. Whitfield), Taylor and Francis, London

Passmore, R. and Durnin, J. V. G. A. (1955). Human energy expenditure *Physiol. Rev.,* **35,** 801

Penfield, W. (1958). *The Excitable Cortex of Conscious Man.* Liverpool University Press, Liverpool

Penfield, W. and Jasper, H. H. (1954). *Epilepsy and the Functional Anatomy of the Human Brain.* Little, Brown and Co., Boston

Persky, H., Hamburg, D. A., Dasowitz, H., Grinker, R. R., Sabshin, M. A., Korchin, S. J., Herz, M., Board, F. and Heath, H. A. (1958). Relation of emotional responses and changes in plasma hydrocortisone level after stressful interview. *Archs Neurol. Psychiat.,* **79,** 434

Pflanz, M., Rosenstein, E. and von Vexkull, T. (1956). Sociopsychological aspects of peptic ulcer. *J. psychosom. Res.,* **1,** 68

Plutchik, R. (1962). *The Emotions: Fact, Theories and a New Model.* Random House, New York

Pool, J. C. (1954). The visceral brain of man. *J. Neurophysiol.,* **11,** 45

Poulton, E. C. (1976). Continuous noise interferes with work by masking auditory feedback and inner speech. *Appl. Ergonom.,* **7,** 79

Price, D. B., Thaler, M. and Mason, J. W. (1957). Pre-operative emotional states and adrenal cortical activity. *Archs Neurol.,* **77,** 646

Price, J. (1967). The dominance heirarchy and the evolution of mental illness. *Lancet,* **ii,** 243

Raab, W. (1943). Sudden death of a young athlete with an excessive concentration of epinephrine-like substances in heart muscle. *Archs Path.,* **36,** 388

Raab, W. (1944). Sudden death with an excessive myocardial concentration of epinephrine-like substances in a case of obesity and cystic thyroid disease. *Archs Path.*, **38**, 110

Raab, W. (1971). Cardiotoxic biochemical effects of emotional–environmental stressors—fundamentals of psychocardiology. In *Society, Stress and Disease*, vol. 1 (ed. L. Levi), Oxford University Press, London

Roberts, L. (1961). Activation and interference of cortical functions. In *Electrical Stimulation of the Brain* (ed. D. E. Sheer), University of Texas Press, Austin

Rodger, A. (1965). The seven point plan. *National Institute of Industrial Psychology Paper*, No. 1

Rodger, A. and Cavanagh, P. (1962). Training of occupational psychology. *Occup. Psychol.*, **1**, 82

Rogers, C. R. (1951). *Client-Centred Therapy: Its Current Practice, Implications and Theory.* Houghton Mifflin, Boston

Rosvold, H. E., Mirsky, A. F. and Pribram, K. H. (1954). Influence of amygdalectomy on social behaviour in monkeys. *J. comp. physiol. Psychol.*, **47**, 173

Ruff, G. E. and Korchin, S. J. (1964). Psychological responses on the Mercury astronauts. In *The Threat of Impending Disaster* (eds G. H. Grosser, H. Wechsler and M. Greenblatt), MIT Press, Cambridge, Massachusetts

Russek, H. I. (1962). Emotional stress and coronary heart disease in American physicians, dentists, and lawyers. *Am. J. med. Sci.*, **243**, 716

Russek, H. I. and Zohman, B. L. (1958). Relative significance of hereditary, diet, and occupational stress in CHD of young adults. *Am. J. med. Sci.*, **235**, 266

Schachter, S. S. (1964). The interaction of cognitive and physiological determinants of emotional state. In *Advances in Experimental Social Psychology*, vol. 1 (ed. L. Berkowitz), Academic Press, New York

Schmid, E. and Meythaler, C. (1964). Untersuchungen über die sympatico-adrenale Reaktion bei Autofahrern mit Hilfe der Vanillinmandelsäurebestimmung in Harn. *Klin. Wschr.*, **42**, 139

Schofield, M. (1971). *The Strange Case of Pot.* Penguin Books, Harmondsworth, Middlesex

Schreiner, L. and Kling, A. (1953). Behavioural changes following rhinencephalic injury in cats. *J. Neurophysiol.*, **16**, 643

Schreiner, L. and Kling, A. (1956). Rhinencephalon and behaviour.

Am. J. Physiol., **184,** 486

Scott, J. P. and Fredrickson, E. (1951). The causes of fighting in mice and rats. *Physiol. Zool.,* **24,** 273

Seligman, M. F. P. (1975). *Helplessness: On Depression, Development and Death.* Freeman and Co., San Francisco

Sells, S. B. (1970). On the nature of stress. In *Social and Psychological Factors in Stress* (ed. J. E. McGrath), Holt, Rinehart and Winston, New York

Selye, H. (1950). *Stress.* Acta, Montreal

Selye, H. (1956). *The Stress of Life.* McGraw-Hill, New York

Selye, H. (1975). Confusion and controversy in the stress field. *J. hum. Stress,* **1,** 37

Serra, C., Barone, A., De Vita, C. and Laurini, F. (1964). Riposte neurohumorali alla stimolazione acustica intermittente. *Acta Neurol. (Naples),* **19,** 1018

Shand, A. F. (1914). *The Foundations of Character.* Macmillan, London

Shand, A. F. (1922). Contribution to symposium: *The Relations of Complex and Sentiment.* Reported in *Br. J. Psychol.,* **13,** 123

Shealy, C. N. and Peele, T. L. (1957). Studies on amygdaloid nucleus of cat. *J. Neurophysiol.,* **20,** 125

Sherrington, C. S. (1906). *The Integrative Action of the Nervous System.* Yale University Press, New Haven

Silverman, A. J. and Cohen, S. I. (1960). Affect and vascular correlates to catecholamines. *Psychiat. Res. Rep.,* **12,** 16

Simpson, G. C., Cox, T. and Rothschild, D. R. (1974). The effects of noise stress on blood glucose level and skilled performance. *Ergonomics,* **17,** 481

Simpson, G. C., Mackay, C. J. and Cox, T. (1974). Blood sugar levels in response to stress. *Ergonomics,* **17,** 562 (abstr)

Smart, R. (1963). Alcoholism, birth order, and family size. *J. abnorm. soc. Psychol.,* **66,** 17

Smith, P. and Bennett, A. M. H. (1958). Vanillic acid excretion during stress. *Nature,* **181,** 709

Smythies, J. R. (1970). *Brain Mechanisms and Behaviour.* Blackwell, Oxford

Snapper, L. (1941). *Chinese lessons to western medicine: a contribution to geographical medicine from the clinics of Peiping Union Medical College.* Interscience Publishers, New York

Steinbook, R. M., Jones, M. B. and Ainslie, J. D. (1965). Suggestibility and the placebo response. *J. nerve. ment. Dis.,* **140,** 87

Stout, C., Morrow, J., Brandt, E. N. and Wolf, S. (1964). Unusually low incidence of death from myocardial infarction: a study of an Italian–American community in Pennsylvania. *J. Am. med. Ass.*, **188**, 845

Suzman, M. M. (1971). The use of beta-adrenergic blockade with propranolol in anxiety states. *Postgrad. med. J.*, suppl., **47**, 104

Symonds, Sir C. P. (1947). Use and abuse of the term flying stress. In *Air Ministry, Psychological Disorders in Flying Personnel of the Royal Air Force, Investigated During the War, 1939–1945*. H.M.S.O., London

Taggart, P. and Carruthers, M. (1971). Endogenous hyperlipidaemia induced by emotional stress of racing driving. *Lancet*, **i**, 363

Talma, S. (1898). Uber asthma nervosum. *Ned. Tijdschr. Geneesk.*, **34**, 390

Taylor, R. (1974). Stress and work. *New Society*, **30**, 140

Taylor, R. (1975). *Noise*. Penguin, Harmondsworth, Middlesex

Terzian, H. and Dalle Ore, G. (1955). Syndrome of Kluver and Bucy reproduced in man by bilateral removal of the temporal lobes. *Neurology*, **5**, 373

Thayer, R. E. (1967). Measurement of activation through self-report. *Psychol., Rep.*, **20**, 663

Theorell, T. (1974). Life events before and after onset of a premature myocardial infarction. In *Stressful Life Events: Their Nature and Effects* (eds B. S. Dohrenwend and B. P. Dohrenwend), Wiley, New York

Tolson, W. W., Mason, J. W., Sachar, E. J., Hamburg, D. A., Hanlon, J. H. and Fishman, J. R. (1965). Urinary catecholamine responses associated with hospital admission in normal human subjects. *J. psychosom. Res.*, **8**, 365

Ulrich, R. E. and Azrin, N. H. (1962). Reflexive fighting in response to aversive stimulation. *J. exp. Analysis Behav.*, **5**, 511

Ulvedal, F., Smith, W. R. and Welch, B. E. (1963). Steroid and catecholamine studies on pilots during prolonged experiments in a space cabin simulator. *J. appl. Physiol.*, **18**, 1257

Unger, R. H. (1972). Pancreatic alpha-cell function. In *Glucagon* (eds P. J. Lefebvre and R. H. Unger), Pergamon Press, Oxford

Unger, R. H. (1976). Diabetes and the alpha cell. *Diabetes*, **25**, 136

Ursin, H. and Kaada, B. R. (1960). Functional localisation within the amygdaloid complex in the cat. *Electroenceph. clin. Neurophysiol.*, **12**, 1

Vandenbergh, R. L. and Sussman, K. E. (1967). Alterations of blood glucose levels with emotional stress: the effect of final examinations in university students with insulin-requiring diabetes mellitus. 27th A. Mtg Am. Diabetic Ass., Atlantic City, *Diabetes,* **16,** 537 (abstr)

Vandenbergh, R. L., Sussman, K. E. and Vaughan, G. D. (1967). Effects of combined physical-anticipatory stress on carbohydrate-lipid metabolism in patients with diabetes mellitus. *Psychosomatics,* **8,** 16

Van Harrison, R. (1976). Job stress as person–environment misfit. A symposium presented at the 84th Annual Convention of the American Psychological Association, Michigan, September

Veale, W. and Myers, R. (1969). Increased alcohol preference in rats following repeated exposures to alcohol. *Psychopharmacologia,* **15,** 361

Vertin, P. G. (1954). *Bedrijfsgeneeskundige Aspecten van het Ulcus Pepticum.* Thesis, University of Groningen and Hermes, Eindhoven

Viney, L. L. and Bazeley, P. (1977). The affective reactions of housewives to community relocation. Macquane University (unpublished communication)

Walker, C. R. and Guest, R. H. (1952). *The Man on the Assembly Line.* Harvard University Press, New York

Wardwell, W. I., Hyman, M. M. and Bahnson, C. B. (1964). Stress and coronary disease in three field studies. *J. chronic Dis.,* **17,** 73

Warr, P. and Wall, T. (1975). *Work and Well-being.* Penguin Books, Harmondsworth, Middlesex

Weil, A. A. (1956). Ictal depression and anxiety in temporal lobe disorders. *Am. J. Psychiat.,* **113,** 149

Weiskrantz, L. (1956). Behavioural changes associated with ablation of the amygdaloid complex in monkeys. *J. comp. physiol. Psychol.,* **49,** 381

Weiss, P., Schmid, E., Sicha, L., Süss, G. and Süss, E. (1965). Untersuchungen über die emotionelle. Belastung verschietlener zahnärztlicher Eingriffe an Hand der Nebennierenmarkund Nebenrindenfunktion. *Dtsch. Zahñarztl.,* **20,** 638

Weitz, J. (1970). Psychological research needs on the problems of human stress. In *Social and Psychological Factors in Stress* (ed. J. E. McGrath), Holt, Rinehart and Winston, New York

Welford, A. T. (1973). Stress and performance. *Ergonomics,* **16,** 567

Western Collaborative Group Study (Rosenman, R. H. *et al.*) (1970) Coronary heart disease in the Western Collaborative Group Study. *J. chronic Dis.,* **23,** 173

Wheatley, D. (1969). Comparative effects of propranolol and chlordiazepoxide in anxiety states. *Br. J. Psychiat.*, **115**, 1411

Williams, D. (1956). The structure of emotions reflected in epileptic experiences. *Brain*, **79**, 26

Wingate, P. (1972). *The Penguin Medical Encyclopaedia.* Penguin Books, Harmondsworth, Middlesex

Wood, C. D. (1958). Behavioural changes following discrete lesions of temporal lobe structures. *Neurology*, **8**, 215

Wolf, S. (1971). Psychosocial forces in myocardial infarction and sudden death. In *Society, Stress and Disease*, vol. 1 (ed. L. Levi), Oxford University Press, New York

Zeman, W. and King, F. A. (1958). Tumors of the septum pellucidum and adjacent structures with abnormal affective behaviour: an anterior midline structure syndrome. *J. nerv. ment. Dis.*, **127**, 490

Index

Type A   98–100

Ulcers   91, 93, 164
U-shaped functions   16, 43–4, 78, 156–7

Vagus   55, 58, 69–70, 72, 124–6
Van Harrison, R.   168–70

Wall, T.   149, 158, 162–3

Warr, P.   149, 158, 162–3
Welford, A. T.   15–17, 158
Western Collaborative Group
   Study   99–100
Withdrawal syndrome   140–3
Workload   15, 157–8, 166

Zohman, B. L.   94, 158